Dominion Undeserved

DOMINION UNDESERVED

Milton and the Perils of Creation

ERIC B. SONG

CORNELL UNIVERSITY PRESS
ITHACA AND LONDON

First published 2013 by Cornell University Press
Printed in the United States of America

Library of Congress Cataloging-in-Publication Data

Song, Eric B., 1979–
    Dominion undeserved: Milton and the perils of creation / Eric B. Song.
      p. cm.
    Includes bibliographical references and index.
    ISBN 978-0-8014-5185-0 (cloth: alk. paper)
    1. Milton, John, 1608–1674—Criticism and interpretation.   2. Milton, John,
1608–1674—Political and social views.   3. Homeland in literature.
4. Imperialism in literature.   5. Creation in literature.   I. Title.
    PR3592.H552S66   2013
    821'.4—dc23   2012032786

Cornell University Press strives to use environmentally responsible
suppliers and materials to the fullest extent possible in the publishing of
its books. Such materials include vegetable-based, low-VOC inks and
acid-free papers that are recycled, totally chlorine-free, or partly composed
of nonwood fibers. For further information, visit our website at www.
cornellpress.cornell.edu.

Cloth printing   10 9 8 7 6 5 4 3 2 1

CONTENTS

Acknowledgments

It may reflect poorly on my character that I wrote a book about the loss of happy homelands while living in a number of delightful places. I started this project at the University of Virginia under the supervision of James Nohrnberg, Gordon Braden, and Katharine Eisaman Maus. It is hard to imagine a trio of scholars more impressively learned and eclectic in their approaches and temperaments. Each of them has taught me unique lessons that continue to shape my teaching and scholarship. During the formative stages of the project, Jennifer Wicke offered her characteristically incisive advice, and she has remained a stalwart ally and mentor. I will always cherish the camaraderie and intellectual excitement I shared with my fellow graduate students at Virginia. Michael Genovese, Omaar Hena, David Sigler, and I frequently transformed the Shebeen pub in Charlottesville into a salon where we discussed one another's work. Sara Bryant arrived at UVa just as I was starting this project and bore with me patiently as I completed it. She has continued to put up with my antics as I have embarked upon life as an assistant professor. Other friends—too numerous to list here—made my time at Virginia a particularly happy one.

The English department at Queens College, CUNY, was a wonderful place to teach, to learn, and to write as an assistant professor. My fellow early modernists Richard McCoy and Carrie Hintz welcomed me graciously into the fold; I also thank Nancy Comley, Tom Frosch, Duncan Faherty, Wayne Moreland, and John Weir. Andrea Walkden and Amy Wan remain close friends who make me feel welcome every time I return to New York. During my time at CUNY, I had the good fortune to meet Joe Wittreich, and I became one of the many Miltonists who have benefited from his wisdom and generosity. I thank him even as I continue to accrue debts of gratitude to him.

During all of June 2008 I was able to work at the Rare Book and Manuscript Library at the University of Illinois at Urbana-Champaign thanks to the John "Bud" Velde Visiting Scholar Program. The library's impressive collection was matched by its superb staff. I thank Valerie Hotchkiss, Alvan Bregman, and Dennis Sears for their kind assistance. At UIUC I met Feisal G. Mohamed, who continues to inform my thinking through his scholarship and informal exchanges. I am grateful to Feisal for inviting me back to UIUC to participate in the English department's early modern workshop group in 2009.

At Swarthmore College, my current professional home, I am lucky to be part of a department that fosters productivity and collegiality in equal measure. I am grateful to the entire department, and I single out for thanks Peter Schmidt, my former chair, and Nora Johnson, my current chair and senior early modernist. Rachel Buurma and Betsy Bolton provided much-needed advice as I completed and revised my book. I also thank the various members of Swarthmore's interdisciplinary junior faculty writing group, which continues to be a source of enrichment and conviviality. Outside of Swarthmore, the Philadelphia-area Works in Progress group has provided one of the most vibrant intellectual communities I have encountered anywhere.

Milton's writings suggest that happy homelands may be metaphorical or virtual rather than real places, and my experiences have confirmed this. I benefit from exchanges with a community of scholars across the country, including Penelope Anderson, Brooke Conti, and Tobias Gregory. David Hawkes, Thomas Luxon, Shannon Miller, and Kristen Poole have been gracious enough to wade through much of my work, and I am grateful to them for their thoughtful responses. I am especially indebted to Steve Fallon, who helped guide the book to port during its final stages.

I thank Peter Potter at Cornell University Press for his interest in this project and Karen Hwa for seeing the book through to completion; Amanda Heller copyedited the manuscript patiently and meticulously. An early version of chapter 1 appeared as "Nation, Empire, and the Strange Fire of the Tartars" in *Milton Studies* 47 (2008): 118–44. A version of chapter 2 was published as "The Country Estate and the Indies (East and West): The Shifting Scene of Eden in *Paradise Lost*" in *Modern Philology* 108 (2010): 199–223, © 2010 by The University of Chicago. All rights reserved. I thank Duquesne University Press and the University of Chicago Press for their permission to reprint these materials here.

And the last shall be first: I express my gratitude to my parents, Allan Hwa Sik and Kwang Ok Song, for their unflagging support.

Abbreviations

CPW *Complete Prose Works of John Milton*
FQ The Faerie Queene
PL *Paradise Lost*
PN Richard Hakluyt, *The Principal Navigations*
PR *Paradise Regained*
SA *Samson Agonistes*

Dominion Undeserved

INTRODUCTION

After the restoration of the English monarchy in 1660, John Milton found himself estranged from his native country.[1] During these evil days, Milton was briefly imprisoned and in some danger of execution for having passionately defended the beheading of the restored king's father. Milton's dire situation occasions a dour etymological joke in his last surviving piece of correspondence, dated August 15, 1666. Milton's friend Peter Heimbach had praised him in writing for his personal and civic virtues. Milton responds by objecting, "One of those Virtues has not so pleasantly repaid to me the charity of hospitality, however, for the one you call *Policy* (and which I would prefer you call *Patriotism*), after having allured me by her lovely name, has almost *expatriated* me, as it were." Milton goes on to remark soberly, "One's *Patria* is wherever it is well with him." Heimbach had addressed his letter to "a most noble and celebrated man, John Milton, Englishman," echoing the signature that Milton had himself used often throughout his career. Milton's response, however, is tersely signed,

"London, August 15, 1666" (*CPW* 8:2–4). Proud national identification gives way to mere facts of time and place.[2]

These difficult lessons anticipate key questions in the great epic that would be published for the first time a year later. In the first book of *Paradise Lost*, Satan grapples with the trauma of exile from his heavenly home:

> Farewell happy fields
> Where joy forever dwells: hail horrors, hail
> Infernal world, and thou profoundest hell
> Receive thy new possessor: one who brings
> A mind not to be changed by place or time.
> The mind is its own place, and in itself
> Can make a heaven of hell, a hell of heaven.
> What matter where, if I be still the same.
>
> (1.249–56)[3]

In an effort to cheer his fallen troops (and, most likely, himself as well), Satan gives voice to the author's sense of expatriation and its potentially salutary consequences. This optimistic position quickly proves untenable. In book 2 the devils reject the option of reigning contentedly in Hell, and Satan assumes the role of explorer. Once Satan alights upon the newly created world, he discovers that the answer to his rhetorical question "What matter where?" remains the same only because he carries Hell within him wherever he goes. Milton's reader would note this just punishment with satisfaction but for the fact that Satan's voyage of unhappy self-discovery precipitates the loss of Eden.

Milton's late writings apply intense intellectual and artistic force to pursue a set of basic questions. What underlying causes lead to the loss of a seemingly happy homeland? What can be done to recuperate or to found a better home, literal or metaphorical? In this book I argue that these investigations confront a fundamental impasse, whereby all forms of creativity are rendered internally divided in Milton's writings. Any coherent entity—a nation, a poem, or even a new world—must be carved out of and guarded against an original unruliness. Despite being sanctioned by God, this agonistic mode of creativity proves ineffective because it continues to manifest internal rifts rather than overcoming them. To explore the question of original causes, Milton traces the problems that beset creativity to divine creation itself. His answers become necessarily divided. On the one hand, a pervasive sense of unruly origins serves as motivation to reform the self, the nation, language, and eventually the entire world. On the other hand, the atavistic knowledge that no force has ever fully succeeded in suppressing chaotic beginnings casts doubt on these forward-looking projects. Such ambivalence bears consequences for the practical question of what should be done. Milton consistently prescribes political and religious reform. Yet Milton's later writings give voice to a sobering awareness that reform assumes the preexistence of a form—nationhood, epic poetry, or a divine kingdom—that proves unstable because of its origins.

Rather than being stymied, Milton's writings derive artistic and political urgency by operating within and testing the limits of this impasse. Milton thus emerges as a great poet of multiple perspectives, of the *either/or/or* rather than of the *either/or*. His writings exhibit what Gordon Teskey has described as a rarefied form of delirium.[4] Milton's delirium, according to Teskey, results from an oscillation between divine creation (and its concomitant, human creatureliness) and human creativity, between a past that has been conferred on us and a future that we might be able to shape. *Dominion Undeserved* offers a new account of the conflicted impulses that give rise to Milton's writings. The argument traces Milton's artistic, theological, and political energies to a single, shared dilemma. My approach thus responds to readings of Milton that achieve clarity by subordinating political concerns to religious ones. In *How Milton Works*, Stanley Fish accumulates decades of scholarship to present a comprehensive view of Milton's writings. For Fish, Milton's poetry and prose constitute a unified effort to negotiate between perfect and fallen visions of the truth, and thereby to spur the reader to creaturely obedience before the Creator.[5] More recently, David Ainsworth has described Milton's writings as training the reader in a discipline of godly hermeneutics. Although Fish's and Ainsworth's readings register the occasional purposes of Milton's writings, exigent and historically situated concerns become subordinated to a general religious pattern. According to Ainsworth, for example, Milton's reader learns to prioritize "spiritual concerns and sacred truths over worldly philosophy and politics."[6] In this book I locate the unified logic of Milton's major writings and aim to show that spiritual and worldly concerns come into sharper focus through their connections. In the chapters that follow, I discuss various manifestations of Milton's divided view of creativity: allusions to the barbarism of the so-called Eastern Tartars; Milton's engagements with country house poetry and accounts of the New World; Milton's half-articulated thoughts about Anglo-Irish affairs after the Restoration; questions about how the Son of God seeks to overcome the politics of undeserved dominion. Together, however, these discussions present a totalizing—although by no means exhaustive—view of how Milton works in response to a systemic problem that besets not only sinful humanity but also an entire cosmos governed by an all-powerful deity.[7]

Tracing Milton's convictions to a basic impasse allows us to avoid inaccuracies that hinder our understanding of his writings. It has been possible to describe Milton as simply representing or even harmonizing conflicting possibilities.[8] Milton is the great poet of multiple perspectives, but coexisting perspectives are not mere equivalents.[9] I describe how the force of Milton's artistry lies in turning genuine contradictions into the grounds of focused commentary and critique. At the same time, attending to the basic dilemma that structures Milton's writings makes it unnecessary to reduce Milton's positions in an effort to elucidate them.[10] By making strategic use of theological problems that remain genuinely intractable, Milton's writings avoid both indeterminacy and simplistic one-sidedness.[11] Milton reveals the shortcomings of all projects that seek to tame chaotic forces while, at the same time, describing such power as sanctioned and exemplified by God.

Say First What Cause

Paradise Lost explores the loss and recuperation of homelands at the cosmic level of divine creation. The end of history proves clear enough: what God wants is to be "all in all." This future consummation promises a universe that cannot regress or lapse, one in which the fullness of the Father will serve as an eternal home for his perfected creatures. God suggests the implications of his projected wholeness when he declares to the Son, "Then thou thy regal sceptre shalt lay by, / For regal sceptre then no more shall need, / God shall be all in all" (*PL* 3.339–41). Divine plenitude will obviate the need for any dominion. Yet in a poem that investigates beginnings, questions emerge about why God must want and wait to be all in all. The unending border conflict between chaos and God serves as an etiological myth of the forces that unsettle both political stability and the integrity of the self. Through Milton's monism—a belief in "one first matter all" that nonetheless allows for fraught divisions—questions about the individual, the nation, and language become interconnected rather than analogous.

The force of chaos reverberates throughout Milton's systems of thought, connecting the intimately personal with the mythic and the political. When Milton describes chaos as the womb and the tomb of creation, he participates in a long-standing alignment of matter as feminine and form as masculine.[12] The gendered challenge that chaos poses for Milton's theodicy has been a familiar source of debate. Against readings of Milton's chaos as a morally neutral realm, Regina M. Schwartz argues that the opening description in Genesis of the Spirit moving upon the deep (*tehom*) both suppresses and preserves the Babylonian narrative of the god Marduk using the dismembered body of the goddess Tiamat to create the world.[13] The Hebrew Bible's assertion of a single, masculine Creator works to forget the pagan, maternal body that existed before the beginning. According to Schwartz, *Paradise Lost* transforms *tehom* into a realm that proves far more hostile and threatening to God than does Satan. Schwartz opts not to carry out her insights to their logical end, choosing instead to maintain the integrity of Milton's theodicy by turning to a *felix culpa* argument. The problem of chaos becomes the grounds for God's display of benevolent creation. Yet the *felix culpa* is a paradox precisely because it cannot answer in logical fashion why Milton's cosmos should be divided in the first place. John P. Rumrich notes that a primordial matter inclined toward destruction would render Milton's theodicy "absurd." He thus interprets chaos as an essential aspect of God's creative being, the feminine and maternal aspect of deity.[14] Such an argument leads Rumrich to deny that Milton's concern for limits, purity, and transgressions applies to the prelapsarian world; otherwise a chaos internal to God would render him impure. Divine creation begins, however, with establishing precise boundaries between chaos and God's kingdom. Edenic life, too, manifests the sacredness of boundaries, as Adam and Eve's bower is a place that "beast, bird, insect, or worm durst enter none; / Such was their awe of man" (4.704–5). Only after the Fall does Michael deny the sacredness of place (11.334–54).

The terms of this debate should be redefined by understanding Milton's chaos as abject in the sense that Julia Kristeva has theorized. Abjection precedes good and evil; its more elemental nature threatens basic divisions such as inside and outside that make moral distinctions possible. Kristeva bases her theory in a mode of thought deeply compatible with Milton's, one that links the gendered cosmology of Plato's *Timaeus*, Hebraic notions of holiness, and the body's role in language. Abjection, in other words, names ideas and sentiments deeply familiar to Milton; Kristeva and Milton share central concerns, including purity versus abominable mixtures, the maternal body, and prohibited food. Abjection registers the force of chaos in a monotheistic world as a threat to personal and cultural boundaries.

The abject is fundamentally that which "disturbs identity, system, order. What does not respect borders, positions rules. The in-between, the ambiguous, the composite."[15] Although abject objects include excrement and menstrual blood, abjection is primarily an oral phenomenon. Revulsion in the presence of unclean objects—especially food—harkens back to the infantile process of weaning from the maternal body and thereby gaining a discrete identity as a linguistic subject. Abjection maintains not only an individual body but also the boundaries of a holy nation. By following dietary prohibitions, Israel separates itself from neighboring fertility cults and prepares itself for the divine Law. Even for a reader skeptical of Kristeva's psychoanalytic thought, her reading illuminates the ordering of codes in the eleventh, twelfth, and thirteenth books of Leviticus, which rapidly transition from dietary prohibitions to laws of purity regulating childbirth to methods of dealing with unclean lesions.[16] After establishing the boundaries of the self at the mouth and from the womb, prescriptions against abjection define the contours of the healthy body within a holy nation.

The oral nature of abjection is not limited to diet but also manifests itself in language. Abjection calls into question the closure of the process that leads to a discrete, unified subject. The nonsignifying elements of speech—the rhythmic, the guttural, the euphonic—bear witness to the corporeal remainders within language. For Kristeva, the transition from Judaism to Christianity marks a drastic change in the relationship between the self and the abject. Abjection is no longer excluded from but rather located within the subject. Christ declares that food cannot defile because it merely enters and exits the belly; it is rather that "which cometh out of the man, that defileth" (Mark 7:20)[17]. Sin, writes Kristeva, is "subjectified abjection."[18] Christianity thus integrates abjection more fully within speech. Repeated acts of confession give voice to sin but transform it into the possibility of grace, and this new mode of speech—replete with bodily impulses—accommodates the beauty of Christian poetry.

Abjection conditions Milton's central problem: pointing back to the original confrontation between chaos and divine order, abjection locates mythic and cultural meaning in the quotidian experiences of food, language, and sex. Abjection thereby locates gender as an elemental fault line. Responding to the limitations of psychoanalytic readings, Rumrich has attempted to redirect our attention to Milton's relationship with his mother.[19] This is a necessary corrective, yet biographical evidence of Milton's attachment to his mother remains scant. Attending to the abject logic of Milton's writings allows us to register the more diffuse force of maternity. While abjection tests the limits even of divine creativity, the injunction to be holy as God is holy compels the Christian poet and his nation to separate themselves from chaos.

Reading Milton's cosmology as abject acknowledges his suspicion of unbridled feminized matter.[20] Chaos menaces as the eternally suffocating maternal realm endangering the integrity of the self.[21] Satan describes chaos as an "abortive gulf" that threatens anyone who enters with "utter loss of being" (*PL* 2.440–41). Kristeva provides an apt gloss on Satan's description when she calls abjection the place where "the vacillating, fascinating, threatening, and dangerous object is silhouetted as non-being—as the abjection into which the speaking being is permanently engulfed."[22] Later Satan will encounter Chaos, who allegorizes abjection's threat to the speaking subject: the anarch responds to Satan "with faltering speech and visage incomposed" (2.989). At the same time, reading chaos as abject shows how rigorously Milton calls into question the efficacy and fairness of the very patriarchal logic he sets forth. The Miltonic dilemma ensures that no simple prescriptions about gender obtain. Taming the indistinguished space of the chaotic womb remains the fundamental mode of creation, but Milton literally gives Chaos a voice to ask how this should be so.

Chaos persists to challenge the stability not just of creation but even of divine being. What ultimately needs to be justified is not God's goodness or his ways to man but his primacy as a divine Father. According to the angel Raphael, when God first commissions the Son to create, he blurs the distinction between inside and outside, the divine and the chaotic:

> ride forth, and bid the deep
> Within appointed bounds be heaven and earth,
> Boundless the deep, because I am who fill

> Infinitude, nor vacuous the space.
> Though I uncircumscribed myself retire,
> And put not forth my goodness, which is free
> To act or not, necessity and chance
> Approach not me, and what I will is fate.

> (*PL* 7.166–73)

God's logic in this passage is famously slippery. He seems to explain that the boundlessness of the deep derives from (is "because" of) his own infinite spatial extension. God renders the scope of *tehom* dependent on him, and he exercises his freedom to absent his goodness from it. As Raphael explains, matter proceeds toward divine perfection only if it is "not depraved from good" (5.471). Yet this volitional withdrawal is apparently not sufficient to hold the deep of chaos at bay. A more troubling possibility thus emerges: perhaps the Son must set bounds because *tehom* is coextensive with God's boundlessness even though he retracts his goodness from it. God must actively prove that no competing maternal realm compromises his complete and eternal autonomy.[23] God finds the ideal agent for this work in a Son who is begotten as the perfect reflection of his sole parent and serves as the Father's word, wisdom, and "effectual might" (3.170).

Yet abject dregs unsettle the grounds of creation. In *De Doctrina Christiana*, Milton argues that primordial matter was merely disordered rather than hostile to God, and that it "could only have been derived from the source of all substance" (*CPW* 6.308). Read against *Paradise Lost*, such a declaration proves more of a defensive mandate than a stable truth. According to Raphael, even after the Son uses golden compasses to demarcate the boundaries between creation and chaos, God's Spirit must downward purge "black tartareous cold infernal dregs / Adverse to life" (7.238–39). Defecation serves at once as an infantile fantasy of giving birth and as a begrudging acknowledgment of the abject traces of a maternal body.[24] Purging the dregs of chaos allows God's Spirit to assume an unrivaled agency in creation; the Spirit seeks to arrogate to itself both female and male roles by "brooding" and infusing "vital virtue" (7.235–36). God's abjection of chaos is thus an act of pre-creation, the all-important clearing of his throat that allows him to speak the newest outpost of creation into existence with his omnific word.

God actively invites Adam—and, by extension, the fallen reader—to investigate the integrity of his divine being. In book 8 of *Paradise Lost*, Adam recounts to Raphael his earliest exchange with God. When Adam requests a mate, God asks,

> What thinks thou then of me, and this my state,
> Seem I to thee sufficiently possessed
> Of happiness, or not? Who am alone
> From all eternity, for none I know
> Second to me or like, equal much less.

(8.403–7)

The enjambment at the end of line 404 leads us to believe that what is at stake is not merely God's "happiness" but his very wholeness. Before the next line adds "of happiness," God seems to be asking Adam, "Don't I seem composed and put-together to you?" God's account of his solitary condition openly contradicts other moments in the epic. In the Son, for example, God surely knows one who is both second to him and like him. The context of God's question makes it difficult to account for such inconsistencies. God later reveals that he has merely been testing Adam; God's claims may be more rhetorically motivated than precise. Or perhaps inconsistencies should be attributed to Adam's memory of his colloquy rather than to God.

At stake in this interpretive problem is the way that man's innate desire for a mate—his profound sense of "single imperfection"—conditions his interactions with and knowledge of his Creator (*PL* 8.423).[25] The diction of God's rhetorical question to Adam registers one consequence of a chaotic realm that can be neither repelled nor incorporated comfortably. As a state where "chance governs all," chaos imperils the authority of a divine will that should be wholly free of contingency (2.910). David Quint points out how "Milton emphasizes the 'hap' in happiness: the element of fortune, chance, and contingency."[26] When asked about divine happiness, Adam affirms that God must be "possessed / Of happiness." This syntactically jarring conclusion registers the contamination of divine will by chaotic chance. Thinking alongside Adam, the fallen reader acknowledges and works to deny the intolerable possibility that God is possessed by happiness as much as he is its possessor.

Paradoxically, Adam proves his godlike nature by insisting on his need for a mate, by contrasting his imperfection with his Creator's infinite unity. In return, Adam receives his wish "exactly to [his] heart's desire" (*PL* 8.451). The gender politics of God's confrontation with chaos thus finds new expression in human experience. According to Rumrich, Eve's innate nature, "constitutionally unpredictable and resistant to easy explanation," shares with the maternal realm of chaos an inclination toward fertility that leads to excess.[27] Adam is called to husband Eve, but he confesses to Raphael the difficulty of maintaining his sense of primacy over his other self, "manlike, but different sex" (8.471). Adam betrays his confused state in his rushed, inelegant speech: Eve seems "wisest, virtuousest, discreetest, best," as if she were the "one intended first" (8.550, 555). Adam's lived experience suggests to him the conjugal politics of undeserved dominion. Although his position of superiority has been fully sanctioned by God, it seems precarious and even unmerited. In response, Raphael admonishes Adam not to accuse nature, for "she hath done her part" (8.561). The angel teaches that Eve's rightful role is to be unruly; the ambiguous antecedent of "she" (which might refer either to Eve or to nature) emphasizes this message. In the context of Adam's confession, Raphael suggests that God has bequeathed to man the challenge of maintaining primacy before a preposterous female presence that refuses to conform to a derivative status.

In *Paradise Lost*, Adam's struggle to maintain his primacy as man leads to the loss of Eden. If a conjugal narrative helps to explain the loss of humanity's first happy homeland, marriage also offers possible redemption. In the final books, Adam and Eve face the same crisis of banishment from home that Satan had initially encountered. The angel Michael directs Adam to "possess / A paradise within" (12.586–87). Although Adam's resources of faith, hope, and love differ markedly from Satan's, the latter's failure to secure internal repose casts a shadow on Michael's advice. One solution lies with Eve, who expresses to her husband her readiness to leave Eden: "thou to me / Art all things under heaven, all places thou" (12.617–18). Milton's wager—on which he had already staked part of his public reputation and his private life—is that the solace of marriage grants sufficient fortitude to offset human uprootedness. What Satan could not achieve alone, Adam and Eve attempt hand in hand. Yet the poem's conclusion attempts to redeem one aspect of satanic rhetoric: attachment to place should prove irrelevant to well-being. When Adam and Eve unite, *patria* should be wherever it is well with them.

Adam and Eve's affective bond emerges as the poem's closing answer to the urgent question of what can secure a better homeland. Eve forsakes attachment to paradise by humbly accepting her metaphorical place as Adam's wife. If the etiological project of looking back to primordial origins produces confusion, Adam and Eve look to a future in which they will overcome the division of gender as one flesh, one heart, one soul. Yet the conclusion of *Paradise Lost* needs to be preternaturally beautiful to over-compensate for the simple fact that marriage will not resolve the matters that beset Milton's monist cosmos or the estrangement of postlapsarian life. This the reader knows full well. As Adam suspects even before the Fall, marriage originates in the sanctioned but undeserved dominion of a husband over a wife, and it can represent only a tenuous solution to a problem of creativity that inheres in the very foundations of the world.

Tyranny Must Be

Milton's writings invite reinterpretation because of the complexity that results when his mythic and political modes of thought converge. David Quint and David Norbrook, for example, have both influentially described Milton's republican poetics. Quint places Milton within a tradition of epic poets who follow Lucan rather than Virgil to write from the vantage point of the defeated; Norbrook shows how the skeptical attitude toward Augustan mythology displayed in *The History of Britain* informs the way *Paradise Lost* aligns itself with the republican *Pharsalia*. Yet Quint and Norbrook disagree about the political valence of the most basic confrontation in Milton's cosmology. For Quint, God's victory over the wild, chaotic uproar of primordial matter makes him the one true Caesar who can confer on the world the coherence necessary for the epic poet to narrate history. God's imperial reign is the exceptional basis of Milton's otherwise anti-Virgilian poetics.[28] Norbrook, by contrast, argues for a cosmology thoroughly consistent with Milton's republicanism. In his account, Milton's chaos (which derives in part from Ovid's *Metamorphoses*) is not evil, and its unruliness serves to affirm the link between anarchy and monarchy. Divine creativity manifests itself not as imperial conquest but as artful and virtuous labors of reform.[29] The possibility of such divergent readings arises from Milton's depiction of God's fraught relationship with chaos. God's creative authority must ground all legitimacy, yet chaos generates questions about the nature, methods, and significance of divine empire building.

The title of this book is taken from an episode in *Paradise Lost* that crystallizes the political consequences of this contradiction. In book 12 the angel Michael describes Nimrod, the "mighty hunter" mentioned briefly in Genesis, as the first political ruler.[30] Michael censures Nimrod as one who will "arrogate dominion undeserved / Over his brethren, and quite dispossess / Concord and law of nature from the earth" (12.27–29). Adam subsequently declares Nimrod an execrable son, yet the angel adds a troubling qualification: "tyranny must be, / Though to the tyrant thereby no excuse" (12.95–96). The single word "must" conveys an unhappy truth about the fallen world, in which liberty and peace necessarily succumb to conquest and usurpations of power. Michael goes on to describe tyranny as a just punishment for entire nations that "will decline so low / From virtue" (12.97–98). Such judgment falls upon Milton's post-Restoration England. Yet far from being merely a pitfall to be avoided or even a fitting punishment for wicked nations, undeserved dominion must be because it advances history. Before Nimrod, only familial and tribal rule had been established. The very form of nationhood may trace its origins to Nimrod's prideful actions, which culminate in the Tower of Babel, the division of languages, and the reemergence of factious violence in the postdiluvian world.

The story of Nimrod conveys a double bind whereby the project of nationhood is declared both necessary and intrinsically flawed. In response to claims that the modern nation emerges only after the late eighteenth century, scholars have shown how multiple, often conflicting discourses in Elizabethan and Stuart England strive to generate a sense of nationhood.[31] Richard Helgerson describes how England's "sixteenth-century national self-articulation began with a sense of national barbarism, with a recognition of the self as the despised other, and then moved to repair that damaged self-image."[32] By Milton's time, the pattern of confessing and urging the reform of national barbarism had become deeply ingrained. In *The History of Britain*, Milton imagines cultural and moral chaos at the origins of his country. He describes the ancient Britons as having lived without stable polity, "mistrustfull, and oft-times warring one with the other" (*CPW* 5:60). Moral corruption accompanies political anarchy; the Britons are described as having led "a lew'd adulterous and incestuous life." They are, in short, "progenitors not to be glori'd in" (*CPW* 5:61). The Britons cannot rescue themselves from such cultural debasement, and only external intervention can lay the groundwork for reform. Milton affirms that the Roman Empire "beate us into some civilitie" (*CPW* 5:61). Yet *The History of Britain*, as the work of a republican thinker, registers a very familiar ambivalence about Rome. Julius Caesar begins the work of beating civility into the savage Britons, yet Caesar's successes in Britain would confer the prestige he needed to betray the republic and to return Rome to a state of imperial tyranny. Norbrook writes that in the divided viewpoint of the English republican, "Caesar's landing brings at the very same time republican civility and the monarchical tendencies that will undermine it."[33] Caesar's dominion, like Nimrod's, proves unjust while generating necessary forms of polity.

The implications of the Miltonic dilemma for both nationhood and expansionism should be clarified further. Theorizing the political landscape of the twentieth century, Benedict Anderson has influentially argued for the "inner incompatibility of empire and nation."[34] Milton, writing at a juncture in history that compels him to look back to Roman *imperium* and ahead to nascent colonialism, describes nation and empire as inseparable.[35] Yet the centrifugal pull of national identity and the centripetal push of expansionism prove incompatible nonetheless. Paul Stevens has described Milton's nationalism as Janus-faced: it anticipates an ecumenical modern subject free from feudal ties, but it nonetheless reverts to parochial bonds of soil and blood.[36] Stevens borrows the concept of Janus-faced nationalism from Tom Nairn, who locates the origins of the modern nation in the emergence of Britain's "developmental priority" between 1640 and 1688—which is to say, largely during Milton's adult life. Nairn stresses that England's internal economic and political developments "were interwoven with, and in reality dependent on, external conditions"—namely, "the history of overseas exploitation."[37] England's increasingly global ambitions intensify the need for but also render difficult a coherent expression of nationhood. This tension eventually gives rise to the Janus-faced nation that retreats into insular myths in order to restrict the modern subject to national boundaries.

For Milton and his contemporaries, the English nation articulates itself against forms of barbarism at once native and foreign. This dividedness suggests a powerful series of answers to the question of why seemingly happy homelands come to be untenable. Some of the foundational texts of postcolonial criticism take as their starting point the fissures within the discursively produced nation. These works have exposed the modern nation as a polysemous construction, divided along lines that are at once ethnic and temporal, and thus susceptible to forms of contestation ranging from mimicry to violence.[38] Such insights have informed scholarship about early modern English literature and culture, but scholars have also been cautious about the possibility of anachronism in mapping a postcolonial paradigm onto earlier periods. Barbara Fuchs's call for an "*imperium* studies" for dealing with the classical through early modern periods is in many ways a sensible prescription.[39] Select moments in this book, however, adopt and adapt postcolonial paradigms. Without ignoring the epochal differences between the seventeenth century and our own day, I aim in the following chapters to contribute to the excavation of continuities between *imperium*, European colonialism, and the emergent modern nation. Milton's political commitments have struck generations of readers—including Whigs and Tories, America's founding fathers, African American slaves, and Marxist historians—as compelling, troubled, and important. *Dominion Undeserved* offers a new way to conceptualize what Nigel Smith has described as a "contradictory energy" within Milton's political thought.[40] In particular, this book joins scholarly work that situates Milton's Anglocentrism within an international matrix.[41] Milton paradoxically strives to articulate a national identity for the sake of a global vision, to work through the particular in order to reach an elusive universality.

In what follows I trace the numerous contradictions that arise from Milton's view of creativity against chaos. This book begins with divine creation and geopolitical affairs, then narrows progressively to England's ambitions abroad and close to home in the British Isles. Chapter 1 examines allusions to the Eastern Tartars in Milton's prose and poetry. In *Paradise Lost*, the repeated association of chaos with these nomadic peoples aligns divine creation with the imposition of polity on a teeming, unruly population. Milton describes these projects as necessary for civilization and yet always imperfect, thereby expressing his ambivalent and critical attitudes toward a sense of divinely sanctioned expansionism. In chapter 2 I argue that Milton's poetic account of Eden conjoins the insular perspective of rural verse and the expansionist ambitions of colonialist discourse. The narrative of Eden's fall thereby advances a critique of the related patterns of dominion at home and abroad. Chapter 3 continues this political reading of *Paradise Lost* by showing the consequences of the uneasy hierarchical relationship between Adam and Eve for Milton's evolving thoughts about Ireland. Yet the lesson that colonialist power cannot lead to gracious cooperation can only remain half-spoken because Milton would never relinquish his belief in England's divinely sanctioned position over Ireland.

Throughout these discussions the logic of abjection reveals how the forces that fracture mythic creation and political homelands are felt at the microcosmic level, upon the body. Abjection also serves to show how such concerns enter into speech, especially in the form of poetry that carries artistic, intellectual, and corporeal energy across centuries. In a brief coda to the first chapter I argue that Milton's necessarily imperfect efforts to banish rhyme from his epic perform at the level of linguistic creation the pattern of combating and internalizing cultural impurity. Chapter 4 completes this conceptual arc by attending to the politics of abjection versus incorporation in its most condensed form: in the lives of Milton's Jesus and Samson. I read Milton's 1671 poems alongside theories of the archive as mediating between bodily experience and the transmission of knowledge, between private and public discourse, and between past, present, and future. The pairing of *Paradise Regained* and *Samson Agonistes* highlights the fact that Jesus seeks a universal and all-encompassing realm while obeying the divine prescriptions given to an elect nation. Paradoxically, Jesus cannot enjoy the liberty that he justifies—retroactively, in the case of the pre-Christian hero Samson, and prospectively, in the case of the Christian poet. The same power of abjection that Jesus feels within his body governs how Milton's linguistic artistry can arise out of the perpetual crisis that binds together the past, the present, and the future.

Scholars have responded to the challenge to relate Milton's writings to freshly relevant concerns.[42] Such critical work teaches us to be mindful of our separation from and connection to the past, as well as of the exigencies that lead us to confront history anew. My outlook is primarily historicist, and I aim to understand Milton's writings in their own cultural moment. Such inquiry, however, is motivated by an unnerving recognition that we may still live in an outgrowth of the world that Milton envisioned with artistic clarity and urgency over three hundred years ago. When past and present confront a shared impasse, historicist inquiry can be a form of concern for the present. Chapter 4 reorients the discussion to meditate more explicitly on how Milton's political and theological impasse gives rise to poetic writings that address the future reader. It ends with a brief discussion pairing Milton with recent post-secular theories of messianic time and a supposedly liberated political subject. The binding of *Paradise Lost* and *Samson Agonistes* reveals that Milton's archive is established in the space and time between elect nationhood and universality. Milton's poetry leads us to confront the aporia in our own optimistic turn to the universal by making us aware that the tension between abjection and incorporation is written on our minds and bodies. This explicit turn toward present-day concerns is necessarily fleeting, but my hope is that this postscript aptly concludes the book by suggesting ways that we can continue to engage with Milton's creative dilemma. The epilogue turns to Olaudah Equiano's deployment of Milton's poetry in his abolitionist autobiography. Equiano finds in *Paradise Lost* a valuable resource for his own political, religious, and artistic project; these new aims, in turn, retroactively alter our sense of the Miltonic archive and its potential significance. Equiano is among the many writers who have been compelled to grapple with Milton's writings, which, by confronting a crisis of creativity, speak difficult lessons at once old and new.

1

THE STRANGE FIRE OF THE TARTARS

No! These people are too impossible. What do they mean by importing their
methods of Crim-Tartary here? A Turk would have more decency.
—Joseph Conrad, *The Secret Agent*

Creation begins by expelling chaos. In book 7 of *Paradise Lost* Raphael
describes how

> on the watery calm
> His brooding wings the spirit of God outspread,
> And vital virtue infused, and vital warmth
> Throughout the fluid mass, but downward purged
> The black tartareous cold infernal dregs
> Adverse to life.

(7.234–39)

John Rogers has interpreted these lines within the context of "the contemporary physiology of tartar," which names "the inassimilable elements purged
from the system in the process of digestion."[1] These dregs are fecal and
abject, and must be purged before creation can begin. But "tartareous" also
evokes in the early modern reader's mind and ear the name of the Eastern
Tartars. The connection between Tartarus and the Tartars is, in fact, quite

an old one, dating back at least to the thirteenth-century writings of Matthew Paris, whom Milton calls "the best of our Historians" (*CPW* 3:219).[2]

Tracing the figure of the Tartar in Milton's poetry and prose reveals the cultural and religious logic behind his conflicted attitudes toward expansionism. Milton's allusions rely on a body of medieval and early modern texts that often depict the Tartars as a violent menace against neighboring nations and as an abominable people against whom Christians define themselves. Yet an abject, uncivilized people are not simply an evil people. The Tartars are described not only as a hostile external threat but also as living relics of the barbarism at the heart of all nations. Parallels between Milton's two prose histories, *A Brief History of Moscovia* and *The History of Britain*, align the Tartars with the ancient Britons, who embody a native inclination toward debasement that threatens England's religious and political integrity. Allusions to the Tartars thus connect cosmological and political manifestations of the central Miltonic dilemma. Polities must civilize unruly populations in the same way that God tames chaos in order to create his kingdom. A Tartarean residue works to undermine both divine and human creations; the only readily available response—continued exertions of force—would reproduce rather than resolve the problem. In *Paradise Regained*, Jesus registers this impasse but refuses to participate in a political mode that would only perpetuate the dilemma of imperfect conquest. Even in the absence of a viable alternative, this refusal advances Milton's cultural commentary, especially in the context of contemporaneous claims that the Tartars were the Lost Tribes of Israel and that their conversion would help bring about the end times.

The logic of abjection helps us account for the way allusions to the Tartars enact theological, cultural, and political thought. Anne McClintock has provided a model for a "situated psychoanalysis" in part by focusing on "the paradox of abjection as a formative aspect of modern industrial imperialism."[3] The seemingly spontaneous experience of revulsion and fascination before forbidden elements performs complex religious and political functions. Levitical codes of purity demonstrate the relationship between divine decree and national or ethnic boundaries: Israel keeps itself holy by shunning the filth of neighboring peoples. By associating both Satan and chaos with the Tartars, *Paradise Lost* suggests how cultural impurity and political strife harken back to a primordial form of chaos that disrupts an ostensibly monist world by revealing its fissures. Far from merely reasserting Western supremacy, Milton's writings deploy the figure of the Tartar both to question the stability of kingdoms, divine and human, based on exclusion or conquest and to advance a critique of expansionist ambitions underwritten by a sense of ascendancy.

A Barbarous and Inhumane People

The category of "Tartar" wanders as widely as the nomadic peoples it designates. The geographical area termed Tartary spanned from the eastern borders of Europe (the Caspian or even the Black Sea) to the Bering Strait. "Tartars" could thus refer to a wide range of Turkic and Mongol peoples. From the earliest European writings about the Tartars, this nebulous, borderless quality is imputed to them as a characteristic trait. Yves of Narbonne's thirteenth-century epistle (recorded by Matthew Paris) describes the Tartars as "an huge nation, and a barbarous and inhumane people, whose law is lawlesse, whose wrath is furious, even the rod of Gods anger, overrunneth, and utterly wasteth infinite countreyes, cruelly abolishing all things where they come, with fire and sword."[4] The Tartars embody a violent threat on the border between East and West; Yves's occasion for writing is the Tartars' incursion into Hungary. At the First Council of Lyons (1245), Pope Innocent IV would echo Yves's sentiments in speaking against "the wicked race of the Tartars," who, "seeking to subdue, or rather utterly destroy the christian people . . . have entered Poland, Russia, Hungary and other christian countries. So savage has been their devastation that their sword spared neither sex nor age, but raged with fearful brutality upon all alike."[5]

Yet other writings express ambivalence about the Tartars. European perceptions of the Mongols (whom medieval and early modern writers consistently call Tartars) are especially telling. In the thirteenth century, these previously obscure nomads established an empire that would eventually stretch from Poland to Korea. Their military success generated the sense of terror that Yves and Innocent IV convey; yet Mongol victory could also create evangelical and political opportunities for the West. The Mongols were perceived as not having an established religion, and as more welcoming to Christians than their Muslim neighbors. Even though the Mongols would eventually convert to Islam, "Mongols did not act like the Moslem rulers whom they had replaced," Claude Cahen observes, often fostering diplomatic relationships with Europe. Thus, despite the pervasive fears about the Tartars' encroachment, medieval Europeans "quickly saw that a Mongol defeat of nearby Moslems was almost as good as a Frankish victory."[6]

A decade after Yves of Narbonne's brief report and Innocent IV's decree, the Franciscan William of Rubruck traveled as a missionary to the Tartars, eventually reaching the Mongol Mangu (or Möngke) Khan in Karakorum. When William begins to describe the Tartars, he declares memorably, "me thought I was come into a new world." He then links the Tartars' nomadic culture to their godlessness: "They have in no place any settled citie to abide in, neither knowe they of the celestiall citie to come" (*PN* 1:234). For a missionary, this lack of knowledge represents the potential for conversion. William often writes favorably about the Tartars, praising the beauty of their crafts and describing their relatively favorable treatment of Christians.

There are, however, stark limits to such attitudes. The biblical logic of abjection sanctions the traveler's shock and disgust and leads him to reinforce the cultural boundaries between West and East. William describes how the Tartars come close to practicing incest: "They keepe the first and second degrees of consanguinitie inviolable, as we do: but they have no regard of the degrees of affinity: for they wil marrie together, or by succession, two sisters." He calls this affront to civilized decorum "abominable & filthy" (*PN* 1:246). Even more revealing are the unclean dietary habits of the Tartars. "Concerning their foode and victuals," William writes to Louis IX of France, "be it knowen unto your Highnesse that they do, without al difference or exception, eat all their dead carrions" (*PN* 1:239). This is not only an affront to a European sense of decorum but also a direct violation of Levitical laws, which declare that the carcass of any animal that dies without being properly slaughtered is unclean and unfit for any physical contact.[7] It is a mark of distinction among neighboring Christian peoples that they refrain from the Tartars' diet. Their religious identity is founded on the rejection of "cosmos" (or kumis), a drink made of mare's milk, for "they accompt themselves no Christians after they have once drunke of it, & their priests reconcile them unto the Church as if they had renounced the Christian faith" (*PN* 1:252). Earlier in the account, William likens common kumis to almond milk and describes the more refined version as "marveilous sweete and holesome liquor" (*PN* 1:240–41). Once he learns, however, that drinking kumis constitutes apostasy for Christians in the region, William and his party politely refuse the drink although they are under no strict obligation to do so.

Marco Polo's *Travels* (written half a century after William's account) praises the Tartars' staple beverage as "excellent to drink" by comparing it to white wine, but nowhere does Polo suggest that kumis is taboo among neighboring Christians.[8] He rarely suggests that the Tartars practice impure or abject customs; this is unsurprising, given his claim to have served under Kublai Khan as a diplomat and even as a provincial governor. When Polo describes the Tartars' marriage customs ("They can also take the wife of their own brother, if the latter dies"), he only remarks on the sumptuousness of their weddings.[9] Polo makes strategic use of the fact that the Torah prescribes a specific form of consanguinity, *yibbum,* or levirate marriage. Although Leviticus declares marriage to a sister-in-law unclean (Lev. 20:21), Deuteronomy teaches that if a man dies without children, his brother must marry the recent widow under penalty of public opprobrium (Deut. 25:5–10). Whereas William disapprovingly mentions Tartar men marrying two or more sisters, Polo aligns the Tartars' mores with biblically sanctioned behavior.

Polo prefaces the *Travels* with an account of Kublai Khan's sincere interest in learning more about Christianity. Polo's father and uncle return from the East to Italy (where they pick up young Marco) in a failed attempt to facilitate communication between the Khan and the pope. The *Travels* repeatedly proclaims the Khan's generosity toward Christians and the potential for converting the Tartars. Yet the chief concern of the Polo family is mercantile rather than missionary. For Polo, the Tartars represent an enormous potential for trade; his narrative repeatedly emphasizes Kublai Khan's advanced system of currency.

Enormous cultural and geopolitical shifts would occur between the medieval writings of William and Marco Polo and the English ambassador Giles Fletcher's report on Russia (composed circa 1589). In the *Brief History of Moscovia*, Milton cites Fletcher as a major source, calling his writings "judicious and exact" and "best red entirely by themselves" (*CPW* 8:534–35). Yet as Richard Cogley points out, "despite his then-current reputation as an authority on the subject, Fletcher's comments about the Tartars were as crude and unsophisticated as those of English writers who had never ventured near Tartary or conversed with Russians about the region and its people."[10] Fletcher, echoing centuries-old tropes, depicts the Tartars as violent nomads who threaten political, cultural, and religious order.

Fletcher does so in part by drawing comparisons and distinctions between the Tartars and the Turks. Some Tartars are indeed "of the Turkish religion" and will thus eat no pork (*PN* 3:394). The Tartars' beliefs, however, "differ from the Turkish religion, for that they have certaine idole puppets made of silke, or like stuffe, of the fashion of a man" (*PN* 3:395). Fletcher goes on to clarify the significance of such comparisons by alluding to a theory that "the Turks took their beginning from the nation of the Crim Tartars" (*PN* 3:398). The Tartars are potentially aligned with the Turks as hostile non-Christian peoples, but they embody a level of primitivism that even the Turks have surpassed. The Tartars' barbarism makes them especially dangerous. Fletcher describes "how different the Tartar is in his desperate courage from the Russe and Turke"; whereas the Russian soldier faced with defeat will retreat, and the Turk will surrender, the Tartars will fight suicidally "and are seene when they are slain to bite the very weapon, when they are past striking or helping of themselves" (*PN* 3:393). Fletcher conveys the general impression that whereas the Turks represent a unified enemy, the primitive Tartars represent an amorphous conglomeration of smaller tribes impossible to locate with any precision. The Tartars, even though they have come to be associated with the Turks, pose a more fundamental threat to European civilization: "utterly voide of all learning, and without written Law," the Tartars resist the very notion of unity or order (*PN* 3:401).

Following William of Rubruck's precedent, Fletcher describes the Tartars's abject cultural practices, including nearly incestuous customs. A revealing new detail in Fletcher's treatise concerns one of the Tartars' purported habits: "to weare any base attire, and to patch their clothes whether there be any neede or not: that when there is neede, it be no shame to weare a patcht coate" (*PN* 3:401). Fletcher's description calls to mind Christ's comment, "No man putteth a piece of new cloth unto an old garment, for that which is put in to fill it up taketh from the garment, and the rent is made worse" (Matt. 9:16). Contrary to Christ's logic, the Tartars are in the habit of patching their clothes even when there is no need. The Tartars are completely alien, acting as "no man" ever would. Fletcher's brief commentary about the Tartars' attire is especially suggestive because of the motivation it ascribes to them. The Tartars supposedly patch their clothes even before they are torn in order to alleviate an anticipated shame; yet such a sentiment would be peculiar among a people accustomed to wearing "any base attire." This shame, which Fletcher projects onto the Tartars, alludes to a Levitical prohibition against unclean mixtures of cloth: "Ye shall keep my statutes. Thou shalt not let thy cattle gender with a diverse kind: thou shalt not sow thy field with mingled seed: neither shall a garment mingled of linen and woollen come upon thee" (Lev. 19:19).

Fletcher's report relies on an early Orientalist mode of discourse that denudes Eastern peoples of their actual histories, turning instead to a "reservoir of accredited knowledge, the codes of Orientalist orthodoxy."[11] It would be a mistake to conclude that Orientalist modes of representation remain simply static and mired in old fictions. On the contrary, Orientalist discourse adapts to changing dynamics between European and Eastern interests. Despite Fletcher's penchant for academic musings and pronouncements against the Muscovites, he played an official role in the ongoing effort to establish profitable relations between England and Russia.[12] As the long-standing enemies of England's would-be trading partner, the Tartars (more specifically the Golden Horde and, later, the Crimean Tartars) do not represent a profitable contact.[13] Cloth making was one of England's primary industries, and a people accustomed to wearing "any base attire" not only would have been unclean but also would have been unfit trading partners. Whereas, three centuries earlier, Marco Polo had suggested the possibility of lucrative dealings with the Tartars, Fletcher claims that the Tartars do not even comprehend the notion of currency (*PN* 3:397). He connects the Tartars' nomadic culture with their inability to enter a marketplace of commodities and symbolic goods.

Late in life Fletcher composed a two-part treatise (published posthumously in 1677) arguing that the Tartars were actually the Lost Tribes of Israel in a long-standing state of separation from God. Fletcher's argument anticipates a future in which these lost Israelites will convert to Christianity, return to the Holy Land, and help to usher in the end-time. Yet this text also exhibits Fletcher's sense of the Tartars' utter cultural abjection. Separated from God, the Lost Tribes of Israel have become "a savage people, without society or commerce with other Nations."[14] Theology and commercial concerns intersect once again to suggest the extent of the lost Israelites' cultural degeneration and the effort required for their eschatologically decisive conversion.

Seventeenth-century Catholic missionaries, by contrast, follow some of their medieval predecessors by describing the Tartars in a relatively favorable light and suggesting the possibility of their immediate conversion. In 1655 an English translation of the Jesuit Martino Martini's *Bellum Tartaricum, Or The Conquest of The Great and most Renowned Empire of China, By the Invasion of the Tartars* was published together with Alvarez Semedo's history of China. Martini begins by repeating the familiar claim that the Tartars are an ancient people, "the most ancient Nation . . . in *Asia*, the Parent of many Nations."[15] The Han Chinese regard the Tartars as barbarians, but Martini often writes favorably about them. He prefaces his narrative of the end of the Ming dynasty and the rise of the Manchu (whom he refers to as Tartars) by praising "the Divine Providence of God, who raised so sharp War against *China*" in response to the Han persecution of Christians.[16] The Manchu, by contrast, are more receptive to a Christian presence; later in the treatise Martini urges more missionary work because "many [Tartars] have imbraced our Religion, nor do we doubt but many more would follow their example, if we could enter *Tartary*."[17]

Yet any optimism about the Tartars' receptiveness to Christianity is always qualified by a fear of their teeming, unruly potential. Martini concludes his brief addendum to the *Bellum Tartaricum* by once again reiterating the hope that the Tartars will be converted. He describes new excursions by the Manchu, however, and likens the "boundlesse power of the *Tartars*" to "an impetuous Torrent."[18] Anxieties about the Tartars were certainly not limited to Europeans who had traveled to Asia. The Western Tartars (whom Martini describes as more barbarous than the Manchu) continued to impinge upon European borders. A news report from Vienna, dated August 14, 1624, reads: "The Tartars have done great hurt in *Polen*, and defeated many Polonians. . . . Whereby it appeareth, that it is not true that (as some reported) the Polonians should have defeated the Tartars which made the late inuasion in *Polonia*."[19] As in the thirteenth century, Western writers would label as Tartars the potent military (often mercenary) presence on the eastern fringes of Europe.

The marauding Tartars appear in the last work that Milton published in his lifetime, an English translation of the official announcement of John Sobieski's election to the throne of Poland. The *Declaration* argues that the Poles had elected the right man to the throne by describing how Sobieski had proved his merit in battle against Scythians, Turks, and Tartars.

His successful campaigns against Swedes, Muscovites, and Cossacks had been but "a *Prelude* to greatest Victories in the memory of man. Miriads of *Tartars* had overrun within this six years with their plundering Troops the coast of *Polonia.*"[20] The treatise proudly announces Sobieski's victories over the Crimean Tartars and his subsequent triumph over forty thousand Turkish soldiers. Through these defeats, Sobieski avenged the deaths of his uncles Stanislaus Zelkievius (Stanisław Żółkiewski), who had fallen victim to "the *Turkish* rage," and Stanislaus Danilovitius (Daniłowicz), who had been killed by "*Cantimiz* the Tartarian Cham, in revenge of his Son by him slain."[21] Milton would have been interested in the Polish monarchy primarily as an elected kingship, yet the treatise also bears witness to how, well into the seventeenth century, European nations continued to define themselves against Tartarian barbarism. The legitimacy of Sobieski's elected rule must be affirmed by his family's history of killing and being killed by the Tartars.

The Tartars in (and against) Milton's Histories

Milton, as we have seen, cites Fletcher as one of the sources for his *Brief History of Moscovia.* Fletcher's economic pessimism, and not Martini's evangelical optimism, proves to be a primary influence. Milton was, predictably, quite suspicious of accounts of Asia by Jesuit missionaries; Robert Markley has described Milton's "brusque dismissal" of writers such as Martini on historiographical and theological grounds.[22] Although Milton does not go out of his way to describe the Tartars as abominable or unclean, they emerge frequently as a political menace in *A Brief History.* Even after the indigenous Tartars are subsumed by Russian history, they also persist in challenging its stability. Once internalized, the Tartars remain a dangerous, mercenary presence. Yet Milton's writings are informed by the ambivalent depictions of the Tartars as hellish or redeemable, evil or morally unformed. The Tartars were not perceived merely as a distant threat on the extreme border between East and West; as we shall see, they were often described by English writers as the ancestors of other "barbarous" peoples, including the unruly Irish. In the early modern imagination, the Tartarian threat was very much present within the British Isles. The Tartars could also represent the internal possibility of ancient barbarity for the English themselves. Through suggestive echoes with *The History of Britain*, Milton's *Brief History of Moscovia* underscores a "sense of national barbarism" by forging connections between the Tartars and the lawless ancient Britons.

Milton explains in the preface to *A Brief History of Moscovia* that Russia was a suitable topic for his first historical study, it *"being the most northern region of* Europe *reputed civil; and the more northern Parts thereof, first discovered by* English *Voiages"* (*CPW* 8:475). Beyond this "most northern region" lies not only Lapland (associated with witches in *Paradise Lost*) but the *"Crim Tartar"* and the *"Nagayan Tartars"* as well (*CPW* 8:477). Russia represents the limit of civilization, and its strife with its neighbors serves as a test case between civilizing and barbarous forces. In a chapter on Russian political history Milton remarks, "The great Dukes of *Muscovy* derive their Pedigree, though without ground, from *Augustus Caesar*; whom they fable to have sent certain of his Kindred to be Governours over many remote Provinces" (*CPW* 8:511). As John Michael Archer notes, Milton's "hedging on Russia's reputation for civility is telling, and his inclusion of Russia in Europe would have seemed a novel idea in the eyes of many Western Europeans."[23] Despite Milton's frequent aspersions against the Russians, their alleged Roman pedigree aligns them with Western civilization against the forces of Eastern barbarity. If it sounds as if Milton is mocking this claimed ancestry when he points out that it is "without ground," we should keep in mind that Milton himself relies on groundless fables to explore the origins of his own country. *The History of Britain* opens with the oft-quoted admission, "The beginning of Nations, those excepted of whom sacred Books have spok'n, is to this day unknown" (*CPW* 5:1). Milton goes on to suggest that his *History* is a bricolage of facts and enabling fictions: "Nevertheless . . . I have . . . determin'd to bestow the telling over ev'n of these reputed Tales; be it for nothing else but in favour of our English Poets, and Rhetoricians, who by thir Art will know, how to use them judiciously" (*CPW* 5:3). Much of Milton's own sense of national history is as conjectural as the supposed Roman ancestry of the Russians.[24]

The connection between *The History of Britain* and *A Brief History of Moscovia* is not coincidental. Milton composed only two histories, "a history of Britain by an Englishman, and a history of a Russia first discovered by *English* voyages," writes R. D. Bedford, adding, "A patriotic edge is detectable here."[25] Yet Milton registers deep skepticism about England's overseas ambitions: in *A Brief History* he declares that the "discovery of *Russia* by the northern Ocean, made first, of any Nation that we know, by *English* men, might have seem'd an enterprise almost heroick; if any higher end than the excessive love of Gain and Traffick, had animated the design" (*CPW* 8:524). Milton proceeds ambivalently, at once captivated by the ability of trade to open up new worlds, but deeply skeptical about the motivations for and the effects of commerce.

Echoes between Milton's two histories suggest that what happens at the distant border of European civilization informs England's sense of national identity. In *A Brief History*, the Russians are the (relatively) civilized people who subjugate the barbaric Tartar tribes. At the very least, the Russians have a legible history, codified laws, and a pattern of political succession. Here we note another parallel between Milton's two histories, connecting the Russian conquest of the Tartars to the Roman conquest of the ancient Britons. The supposed Roman ancestry of the Russians emphasizes the similarities between the subjugated Britons and the Tartars. The ancient Britons were, like the Tartars, politically amorphous and culturally abject, guilty of idolatry and abominable sexual mores. Yet as a republican thinker, Milton is deeply ambivalent about the Roman Empire, which had embodied both the strength and the tenuousness of civility. Although it had been strong enough to impose order on barbarous peoples, its internal flaws brought about its demise.

Many of Milton's pre-Restoration works urge the English to resist both the internal and external forces that threaten their moral and political integrity. As we have seen, *The History of Britain* (which, though first published in 1671, was probably composed during the 1640s and 1650s) aims for coherence even as it announces its own historiographical flaws and describes the ancient Britons as shameful ancestors. Partly because the Britons are originally barbarous, Milton urges his fellow citizens to assert their political and cultural integrity against the degenerative forces of Catholicism, the monarchy, and the Irish. The Irish play a particularly prominent role in Milton's political thought because they are dangerously allied with both Catholicism and the Caroline monarchy. Through much of the 1640s and 1650s Milton officially endorsed force and subjugation as means of imposing civility on a barbarous neighboring people threatening England's stability.

If we compare English representations of the Irish to those depicting the Tartars, we see that the two bodies of discourse are vitally linked
through the imperialist logic of cultural degeneracy. In Spenser's *View of
the State of Ireland*, the informed Irenius repeatedly alludes to the Scythian
genealogy of the Irish. He ascribes, for example, an abominable Scythian
practice to the Irish: "Also the Scythians used, when they would binde any
solemne vow or combination amongst them, to drink a bowle of blood together, vowing thereby to spend their last blood in that quarrell: and even
so do the wild Scots . . . and some of the Northern Irish."[26] English writers
often designated Scythians as Tartars; Milton does so when he mentions
"Tamerlan, whom they call *Temirkutla,"* as the son of a Tartar prince (*CPW*
8:513). The alleged Tartarian roots of Irish customs were often invoked to
legitimize a colonialist agenda in the so-called Celtic fringe.[27]

Yet transplanted forms of Tartarian barbarity were not limited to the
Celtic fringe. In 1632 Thomas Morton responds to "the opinion of some
men, which shall be nameles, that the Natives of New-England may pro-
ceede from the race of the Tartars, and come from Tartaria into those par-
tes, over the frozen Sea."[28] As J. Martin Evans notes, this was among "the
most popular theories concerning the identity of the men and women of
the New World."[29] English writings often linked Irish and Native American forms of primitivism, and a supposedly shared Tartarian ancestry confirms this connection. Whether in Asia, the New World, or the British
Isles, the Tartars precede and threaten to subvert civilized order.

After the Restoration, it would have been increasingly doubtful for
Milton whether the English nation could stave off the forces of barbarism. It is thus fitting that *A Brief History of Moscovia*—a text written by a
younger Milton but not published until 1682, newly prefaced and perhaps
revised by the author in the 1670s—draws historical parallels between the
ancient Britons and the barbarous Tartars. And just as the civilizing force
of the Romans had encountered native resistance in Britain, the supposed
Roman descendants who found Russia encountered persistent opposition
from the Tartars. Milton records that in 1237 Moscovia was subdued "by
the *Tartar* prince *Bathy,"* and from "that time the *Tartarians* made such
Dukes of *Russia,* as they thought would be most pliable to their ends"
(*CPW* 8:512). The agon between the Tartars and the Russians continues
through much of Milton's chronicle. John Vasiliwich unified his rule over
all of Russia through political subterfuge and warfare, but it was only his

second wife, Sophia, who "at length by continual perswasions, and by a wile found means to ease her Husband, and his Country" from vassalage to the Tartars (*CPW* 8:514). Yet in the sixteenth century, Juan Vasiliwich (or Ivan IV, whom we know as Ivan the Terrible) was still fighting against the Tartars: "at 25 years of age he vanquished the *Tartars* of *Cazan* and *Astracan*, bringing home with him their Princes captive" (*CPW* 8:514).

Tensions between the Tartars and the Russians would subside after Ivan IV's rule. Milton records that "a great alteration in the Government follow'd, yet all quietly, and without tumult. These things reported abroad strook such awe into their neighbour Kings, that the Crim *Tartar* . . . came to visit . . . the *Russian*" (*CPW* 8:516–17). Even before this "great alteration," a marked change had been developing in the interactions between Russians and Tartars. By the time the first English explorers arrived in Russia, the Tartars had already become a familiar presence; they had been not only subjugated but also domesticated. When Sir Hugh Willoughby's party arrived in Russia, "two *Tartarians* then of the King's Stable were sent for" (*CPW* 8:525). Later, in 1557, Anthony Jenkinson observed "two thousand Tartars who came to serve the Duke in his Wars" dining in the hall of the Russian emperor (*CPW* 8:529–30). It would be a mistake, however, to assume that the Tartars' disruptive potential had been neutralized by assimilation. In 1571 the Tartars were deployed as mercenaries by Russian factions; "but some of the Nobles incited by [Ivan IV's] cruelty, call'd in the Crim *Tartar* who in the Year 1571. broke into *Russia*, burnt *Mosco* to the ground" (*CPW* 8:515).

Milton first mentions this fire in his chapter on Russian political history; he describes it in more detail in the following chapter on "*The first discovery of Russia*" by English merchants. Milton explains that when the Tartars burned Moscow down, the English also suffered: "The *English* house, and diverse *English* were smother'd in the Sellars, multitudes of the People in the City perish'd, all that were young led captive with exceeding spoil" (*CPW* 8:531). Milton's skepticism about "the excessive love of Gain and Traffick" manifests itself in a bitter irony. The English were "smother'd in the Sellars," presumably where they had stored their share of the "exceeding spoil" that would come to be plundered. In his commonplace book entry on avarice, a younger Milton records from an Italian source the story of Mango (or Möngke) Khan, who converted to Christianity and set out to conquer the holy lands in the thirteenth century. The caliph of Baldac succumbs to Möngke Khan because he has been hoarding his riches rather than hiring knights for defense. Möngke Khan's brother takes this occasion to teach the caliph a lesson about greed; he "starved [the caliph] to death by saying that it would be fitting that he should live by his treasure" (*CPW* 1:366). In *A Brief History of Moscovia*, the Tartars again act as a scourge of the greedy, but the guilty victims are English merchants rather than a Muslim caliph. A century before the English nation would succumb to its internal, metaphorically Eastern barbarism by restoring the Caroline monarchy, English merchants—driven to the fringes of Western civilization by a desire for profit—suffered the consequences of making literal contact with the Tartars.

Strange Fire

In *Paradise Lost*, allusions to the transgressive Tartars emerge at strategic points, linking infernal forces and the primordial abjection of chaos to specific forms of cultural debasement. As Satan lands on the outermost sphere of the newly created world, the border between creation and chaos, Milton describes him through an elaborate simile:

> Here walked the fiend at large in spacious field.
> As when a vulture on Imaus bred,
> Whose snowy ridge the roving Tartar bounds,
> Dislodging from a region scarce of prey
> To gorge the flesh of lambs or yeanling kids
> On hills where flocks are fed, flies toward the springs
> Of Ganges or Hydaspes, Indian streams.

(3.430–36)

Alastair Fowler's note on this passage proves instructive: "In the vehicle, the journey is from the snowy *Imaus* (which failed to bound *the roving Tartar* Genghis Khan) to rivers of India; in the tenor, from the 'frozen continent' (ii 587) of Tartarus (which did not stop Satan's roving) to Paradise with its rivers."[30] Satan is aligned with the Tartar in his breaking of limits and boundaries. Satanic transgression is a dark inverse of divine creation, which begins with the establishment of limits. Appropriately, when Milton connects Satan's journey through chaos to the boundary-breaking of the abominable Tartars, he also describes Satan as a vulture, an unclean devourer of carrion.

The simile in book 3 alludes obliquely to Genghis Khan, who serves more as a stock literary character than as a historical personage. Genghis Khan is not even named but merely called "the roving Tartar." Milton's interest in the Tartars is as much poetic as historical. In *Il Penseroso*, he invokes the half-told story of Cambuscan (lines 109–15).[31] Chaucer begins the story of this Tartar king in the unfinished *Squire's Tale*; Spenser reconstructs it in the fourth book of *The Faerie Queene*. In *Paradise Regained*, Milton refers to the Tartar king Agrican, whose tale is previously told in Boiardo's *Orlando Innamorato*. Allusions to literary Tartars thus play a small but recurring role in Milton's lifelong attempt to position himself within poetic history, both English and continental. The allusions in *Paradise Lost* to the Tartars make strategic use of the ambivalence between static fictions and historically responsive representations within early Orientalist writings about the Tartars. As both historian and poet, Milton knows "how to use them judiciously." Bridging mythic, poetic, and historical registers, the figure of the Tartar mediates between God's confrontation with chaos and the imposition of Western order upon Eastern peoples. Reading *Paradise Lost* alongside Milton's prose histories reveals a pattern: civilized empires must impose order on preexisting, chaotic realms. Although abjection is conquered, it can never be entirely banished; on the contrary, the internalized threat of barbarism eventually strikes from within.

In book 10, after Satan returns to Pandaemonium from his mission, the devils awaiting him in Hell are compared to Tartars:

> As when the Tartar from his Russian foe
> By Astracan over the snowy plains
> Retires, or Bactrian sophy from the horns
> Of Turkish crescent, leaves all waste beyond
> The realm of Aladule, in his retreat
> To Tauris or Casbeen.

(10.431–36)

The double meaning of "waste" suggests that the Tartars are indeed a tartar-like people, destructive and fecal. Allusions to the Tartars thus encompass both legs of the satanic journey that allows Sin and Death to erect a bridge between the newly created world and Hell. J. Martin Evans suggests that this icy bridge might allude to the theory that the Tartars crossed to the American continent over a frozen passage across the Bering Strait: deadly forces gain access to God's latest creation in the same way that the Tartars may have traveled to the New World.[32] Observing the contact between the world and the Tartar-like devils, God comments:

> See with what heat these dogs of hell advance
> To waste and havoc yonder world, which I
> So fair and good created, and had still
> Kept in that state, had not the folly of man
> Let in these wasteful furies.

> (10.616–20)

God's repetition of "waste" points back to the Tartar who "leaves all waste." What allows such wasteful elements to disrupt creation is not only the "folly of man" but also the satanic voyage, which Milton likens to mercantile explorations.

The young author of *A Brief History of Moscovia* had expressed reservations about international commerce even while embracing the new forms of knowledge it brought about. During the Interregnum, Milton would have further witnessed the political consequences of trade. As Latin Secretary, Milton was involved, to one degree or another, with the tense negotiations between Portugal and England that revolved largely around overseas interests; with Hermann Mylius's protracted ordeal securing an English safeguard for the County of Oldenburg; and with the conflicts leading to the first Anglo-Dutch War, which pitted two Protestant powers against each other largely over disputes about maritime commerce.[33] In *Paradise Lost*, Milton expresses wariness about and even scorn for trade as an instrument of peaceful growth. In book 2, as Satan departs for his mission to Eden, a well-known simile compares him to a spice merchant traveling to India (2.636–43). This simile, as David Quint notes, constitutes an ironic revision of Vasco da Gama's celebrated voyage in *The Lusiads*, whereby

Milton mocks Camões's attempt to downplay his hero's base mercantile motives.[34]

Milton's narrative proceeds to link satanic mercantilism to more aggressive forms of expansionism. When Satan proposes a pact with Chaos and Night, it is apparent that he is not merely a merchant or a trader:

> if I that region lost,
> All usurpation thence expelled, reduce
> To her original darkness and your sway
> (Which is my present journey) and once more
> Erect the standard there of ancient Night;
> Yours be the advantage all, mine the revenge.

(2.982–87)

Here we find the dark inverse of Gama's declaration to the ruler of Calicut in *The Lusiads*: "*His* [the Portuguese king's] shall the *glory*, *thine*, the *Gain* be found."[35] Whereas Gama disavows the Portuguese desire for profit in order to lay tenuous claim to nobler motives, Satan overtly allies himself with Chaos as a political saboteur seeking to overthrow the newest outpost of God's empire. Milton's *Brief History* denounces "excessive love of Gain and Traffick"; *Paradise Lost*'s description of Satan's mission registers a more intense skepticism about the motives and effects of expansionist ambitions.

Even before Satan ventures out of Hell, an allusion to the Tartars highlights the consequences of the alliance between satanic and chaotic forces. In book 2 Moloch recalls the effects of gunpowder to advocate another war against God:

> when to meet the noise
> Of his almighty engine he shall hear
> Infernal thunder, and for lightning see
> Black fire and horror shot with equal rage
> Among his angels; and his throne itself
> Mixed with Tartarean sulphur, and strange fire,
> His own invented torments.

(2.64–70)

Comparing Moloch's description of "Tartarean sulphur" with Raphael's description of the "tartareous cold infernal dregs" reveals how precisely Milton calibrates explicit references to the Tartars with mere hints of their name. Raphael aligns the dregs of chaos with Tartarus and with digestive tartar. Only a broader network of associations can activate the echo of "Tartars" in "tartareous." By contrast, "Tartarean" (or its variant "Tartarian") can refer directly to the Tartars.[36] Whereas tartareous dregs purged by God prove cold and lifeless, matter that retains fiery potential within the limits of creation is likened more properly to the Tartars. Moloch's speech thus helps to explain the epic similes that compare Satan and his followers to the Tartars. The devils achieve Tartarian power through their manipulation of chaotic matter in Heaven and in their alliance with Chaos. Such contact renders the devils themselves unclean, wasteful, and Tartar-like.

As a number of readers have noted, *Paradise Lost* draws damning connections between Satan, Eastern despotism, and the Caroline monarchy.[37] In book 1 Satan is called a "great sultan" (1.348). His opulence overshadows the wealth of Ormuz and India in the opening lines of book 2, and in book 10, as we have seen, his followers are likened to the forces of the Persian shah (the "Bactrian sophy") immediately after they are compared to Tartars. The long history of associating the Tartars with the Turks but also of differentiating between their relative levels of barbarism proves relevant here. The anarch Chaos personifies a nebulous threat and exercises limited agency in undermining God's kingdom. Yet Chaos can forge alliances with satanic forces. In Milton's *Brief History*, as we have seen, the subjugated Tartars become newly dangerous when enlisted as mercenaries in a struggle between Russian factions. The Tartars then burn Moscow to the ground. Similarly, the devils pursue war against God with the aid of a "strange fire" that briefly threatens to reduce Heaven itself to a state of abject confusion. The image of gunpowder connects the upheavals within *Paradise Lost* to political and sectarian strife in seventeenth-century England: "Tartarean sulphur" echoes the phrase "sulphureo curru" in Milton's first epigram on the Gunpowder Plot.[38] Just as in Milton's histories, the Tartarian threat points to political and cultural dangers closer to home.

Milton's allusions to the Tartars confirm the culturally barbarous nature of the chaotic womb. Long-standing questions about the Tartars—whether their abject status represents a dangerous menace or the possibility of conversion—inform the ambivalent representation of primordial matter in *Paradise Lost*. The Tartars transgress boundaries not only because they are impure but also because they are wildly productive. Writers such as William of Rubruck and Fletcher might describe the Tartars as having abominable sexual mores, yet Martini describes them as "the most ancient Nation . . . in *Asia*, the Parent of many Nations." The simultaneously intolerable and productive nature of chaos becomes evident in Satan's original discovery of gunpowder in Heaven. Satan's description of gunpowder partly resonates with Raphael's account of chaotic dregs: the dregs are black, tartareous, cold, and infernal, while the gunpowder lies deep underground, "dark and crude" (6.478). Satan, however, deems material residue not cold or inert but "pregnant with infernal flame" (6.483). As one already described as a global explorer, Satan expresses an attitude toward matter that accords with the optimism that Polo and Jesuit missionaries express about the Tartars' potential for trade and for conversion. For Satan, to fail to recognize crude matter as the source of "plant, fruit, flower ambrosial, gems and gold" amounts to seeing superficially with the eye and not with the mind (6.475). Satan's impure motives still lead to genuine insights, for the poem as a whole confirms the indispensable nature of the unbridled and dangerous potential of chaos.

Milton's allusions to the Tartars reveal how divine creation takes part in the historical and epic motif of conflict between East and West. As David Quint has shown, this confrontation is central to the Virgilian epic, in which the West stands for unity and reason, the East for decadence and flux. Eastern and effeminate forms of decadence converge in the figure of Cleopatra, who is sent fleeing from Actium by Roman forces.[39] In *Paradise Lost*, chaos is a simultaneously feminized and Eastern space that must be subjugated before order can prevail. The Miltonic world is neither stable nor immutable but established against an opponent marked by both sexual and cultural difference. The Tartars are generally without a voice in European texts, but if they could speak, they might echo Chaos's complaint about the encroachment on what he claims is his rightful, native domain: "I upon my frontiers here / Keep residence; if all I can will serve, / That little which is left so to defend" (2.998–1000). Chaos's critique of divine creation as unjust occupation acquires historical significance through his association with the Eastern Tartars.

When "God shall be all in all," he will have either completely purged the chaotic dregs from or converted them into the goodness of creation. The world will then enjoy a wholeness that chaos can no longer challenge. The theory of the Tartars as the Lost Tribes of Israel, whose conversion would signal the end-time, might have relevance for Milton's eschatological vision. It is unclear whether Milton was familiar with Fletcher's treatise *The Tartars Or, Ten Tribes*, which was composed circa 1610 but survived only in manuscript form until its publication in 1677. As Richard Cogley notes, however, Fletcher's argument was an English version of a hypothesis that had existed for some time in continental Europe.[40] *Paradise Lost* suggests a specific link between Tartars and biblical Israelites when Moloch associates "Tartarean sulphur" with a "strange fire" potent enough to contaminate God's throne with an unholy mixture. Tartarian violence and biblical abomination converge in this resonant phrase. "Strange fire" alludes directly to the transgressive offering of the priests Nadab and Abihu as described in Leviticus 10 and Numbers 3.

Even if Milton had been aware of the conjectural link between the Tartars and the Lost Tribes of Israel, we know that his attitudes toward Jews were ambiguous. Jeffrey Shoulson argues that Milton's role "as both insider and outsider to English politics, religion, and culture" leads to an imagined affinity with the Jewish diaspora.[41] Yet Shoulson and other critics have had to negotiate Milton's marked silence about the proposed readmission of actual Jews in the 1650s.[42] The case of the Tartars and their hypothetical status as the Lost Tribes suggests ways that Milton's Hebraic thought influences his conflicted sense of nationhood within the context of increasingly geopolitical affairs. In Milton's writings, the figure of the Israelites stands at once for national election, the impetus to spread religious reform across national boundaries, and a nation's internal potential for debasement.[43] Achsah Guibbory has traced how the alignment between the godly community and the Hebraic nation in Milton's earlier writings gives way to anti-Jewish rhetoric. Lapsing from freedom into tyrannical kingship would be akin to lapsing from Christian and Protestant truth into Israelite bondage. Guibbory concludes that even though Milton remains "the most deeply Hebraic of English literary writers," his commitment to elect and universalizing Protestant nationhood leads him to denounce Jewish backsliding—even during the years when the English were considering readmitting Jews back into their country.[44] Milton's Hebraic thought partly governs his allegiance to the nation, but Protestant internationalism frames anti-Semitic strains of Milton's thinking.

Milton would have detected the historical and theological inconsistencies of Fletcher's argument about the Tartars. Yet both his personal sense of persecuted godliness and his lasting desire for national redemption suggest reasons why Milton would have had sympathy for a narrative in which the restoration of the Israelites-turned-Tartars would advance the supreme consolidation of God's kingdom. Nevertheless, in Milton's cosmology there are some abject dregs that simply cannot be recuperated. We have seen that in book 10 the fallen angels are compared to the Tartars, who leave only "waste" in their path. Unlike fallen humans, these devils can never be redeemed: "man therefore shall find grace," God declares, "The other none" (3.131–32). Unlike Fletcher's Tartarian Israelites, and certainly unlike the Tartars as represented by missionaries like Martini, Milton's Tartarian devils pose a limit to grace. Those who are guilty of "strange fire" cannot be forgiven: Nadab and Abihu are "devoured" by "fire from the LORD" (Lev. 10:2). This devouring is a form of complete erasure, as the two priests die childless (Num. 3:4). For some writers, the link between the Tartars and the Lost Tribes makes possible a narrative of conversion and restoration. Milton's writings bear witness to the enduring politics of subjugation and eradication, whereby God confronts strange fire with a consuming fire of his own.

Agrican with All His Northern Powers

In *Paradise Regained*, Jesus prefers a politics of grace. In contrast with his youthful desire for "victorious deeds" and "heroic acts," Jesus holds it "more humane, more heavenly first / By winning words to conquer willing hearts, / And make persuasion do the work of fear" (*PR* 1.215–23).[45] Yet Jesus's gracious politics registers the necessity of forceful subjugation. Earlier in the short epic, Jesus prefers a metaphorical, inward rule over oneself to power over others. When Satan tempts him to assume the place of Tiberius Caesar, Jesus refuses but makes a revealing qualification. Jesus describes the Romans as "now vile and base, / Deservedly made vassal, who once just, / Frugal, and mild, and temperate, conquered well, / But govern ill the nations under yoke" (4.132–35). The contrast between conquering well and governing ill points to the double bind of political creation. Roman conquest may be commendable, but it proves inimical to virtuous governance of other nations and of the self. Caesar's imperial office corrupts Tiberius, and internal decadence—according to one of the most familiar historical narratives of the West—leads to the fall of the empire. In Jesus's account of his own kingdom, however, the language of conquest must persist, and not only as a metaphor for conversion. Jesus leaves subjugation open as a future possibility, should "winning words" fail to persuade (1.222). In the final book, Jesus likens his future kingdom not only to a spreading tree that provides shelter but also to "a stone that shall to pieces dash / All monarchies besides throughout the world" (4.149–50).

Satan urges Jesus to use violence sooner rather than later. When the temptations of food, wealth, and glory fail, Satan reminds Jesus, "But to a kingdom thou art born, ordained / To sit upon thy father David's throne" (*PR* 3.152–53). Appealing to Jesus's "zeal and duty" to God and to Israel, Satan offers the military powers of Parthia and Rome (3.172). David Quint argues that "the temptations of Parthia and Rome . . . are really the same temptation: Pompey wants Parthian arms in order to regain possession of Rome." Jesus's subsequent rejection constitutes "Milton's most explicit alignment of his epic poetry with the anti-Virgilian, anti-imperial epic tradition of Lucan."[46]

The temptation of Parthia and Rome is also the temptation of Tartary. After showing Jesus the "numbers numberless" of the Parthian army, Satan comments:

> Such forces met not, nor so wide a camp,
> When Agrican with all his northern powers
> Beseiged Albracca, as romances tell;
> The city of Gallaphrone, from thence to win
> The fairest of her sex Angelica
> His daughter, sought by many prowest knights,
> Both paynim, and the peers of Charlemagne.
> Such and so numerous was their chivalry.

(*PR* 3.337–44)

This reference to the Tartar king Agrican is not only suggestive within the larger context of Milton's other allusions to the Tartars but also meaningfully ambiguous in and of itself. Initially, it would seem that Satan is offering Jesus a military force strong enough to defend against the marauding Tartars. Just as the Parthians amass an enormous army "against the Scythian, whose incursions wild / Have wasted Sogdiana" (3.301–2), Gallaphrone (the king of Cathay, whose capital city is Albracca) wages war against the besieging Tartars in Boiardo's *Orlando Innamorato*. As the vision evolves, however, it becomes increasingly difficult to tell which side of the "camp" Satan is directing Jesus (and the reader) to behold. Jesus sees how quickly the Parthian forces wheeled, "and flying behind them shot / Sharp sleet of arrowy showers against the face / Of their pursuers, and overcame by flight" (3.324–26). This mode of attacking while fleeing, however, is one of the most frequently described traits of the Tartars.[47] This ambiguity is heightened in the final lines: Satan refers to "their chivalry," yet he has just explained that "prowest knights" can be either "paynim" or the "peers" of the Holy Roman Empire (3.342–44). Satan unwittingly advances a powerful case against warfare by suggesting that the battlefield tends not to distinguish but to confuse barbarous and civilized or even pagan and nominally Christian forces. Waging war against the Tartars turns into a Tartarian act that imperils coherence.

Milton's Jesus recognizes that the true threat to Israel is not subjugation from without but degeneration from within. In rejecting military force, he denounces the Israelites as a people who "wrought their own captivity" (*PR* 3.415). Originally planted in the land of Canaan by God's covenant with Abraham, the Israelites have not only succumbed to the abominations of their neighbors but also lapsed back into their innate proclivities, committing "their other worse than heathenish crimes" (3.419). Divine initiative, not military action, may redeem the Israelites:

> No, let them serve
> Their enemies, who serve idols with God.
> Yet he at length, time to himself best known,
> Rememb'ring Abraham by some wondrous call
> May bring them back repentant and sincere.

(3.431–35)

The description of God's "wondrous call" receives immediate qualification from the cautious "may." The equivocation seems to center on God's foreknowledge; even Jesus cannot know when he will restore Israel. Yet if God has mysteriously but firmly set a time to call Israel, the uncertain outcome—in Milton's Arminianist soteriology—depends on the human response. Jesus has already acknowledged that the stubborn will not heed divine persuasion. The description of Israel's potential or conditional restoration thus leaves open the possibility of inexorable recalcitrance. Perhaps even the Israelites will come to be numbered among the stubborn whom Jesus will subdue, their nation among those that he will dash. Only then can the complete fullness of the divine kingdom arrive.

Decisive acts of divine conversion or conquest will be necessary, but nothing in sacred or human history reveals how such acts may come about. In *Paradise Lost*, Milton's repeated allusions to the Tartars underscore the question of why the world should have been divided in the first place. Geopolitical history informs Milton's cosmology, perhaps at the cost of theological coherence. An ethnically marked chaos tends not to resolve but to heighten the problems with Milton's monism. Yet Milton's theodicy is thereby also a probing interrogation of the relationship between the civilized and the barbarous, the Western and the Eastern. If even God must impose order upon a barbarous chaos, exclusion or conquest proves necessary for creating any unified order. Yet the instability of the divine kingdom speaks to the internal vulnerability of any formation based on subjugation and disavowal.

Coda. Wretched Matter: Milton and Rhyme

In a letter written in 1638, Milton commends the Florentine scholar Benedetto Buonmattei for his study of the Tuscan dialect. The letter deems the benefits that linguistic study confers on a country second only to statecraft. Milton then compares the merits of the statesman and the linguist: "For if we wish to compare the usefulness of the two men, the one alone is able to effect an upright and holy society of Citizens; the other alone can make it truly noble, and splendid, and brilliant, which is the next thing to be wished." Ineloquence signals moral and political decay, and the good author works to "overcome and drive out Barbarism, that filthy civil enemy of character" (*CPW* 1:329). Decades later, Milton would cast himself in precisely this role. In writing the great English epic, Milton eschews rhyme, and a now famous note added in 1668 calls rhyme "the invention of a barbarous age, to set off wretched matter and lame meter."[48] For Dryden and Augustan poets, couplets enact at the level of poetic form social decorum that should counteract any barbarous excess. Milton, however, deems rhyme but a "jingling sound," a risibly mechanical formal device that fails to conceal the true wretchedness within the matter itself. Linguistic barbarism needs to be banished.

Milton's rejection of rhyme takes part in a long history of poetics and politics. In a chapter titled "Two Versions of Gothic," Richard Helgerson traces the opposition between the gothic and the classical—an opposition that would remain vital in English thought at least through the Victorian period. As Helgerson's title suggests, however, this is not a stable opposition, as the gothic itself has two versions: a defense of rhyme (against the ultimately unsuccessful experiments of importing classical, quantitative verse into English) and a deployment of chivalric romance. As different as these trends seem, what "unites the two is a shared resistance to the totalizing encroachment of a royal authority on which both nevertheless depend."[49] Rhyme expresses such resistance by appealing to the kind of popular English custom that challenges the cultural authority of the throne. Chivalric romance, by contrast, appeals to aristocratic values that tend to decentralize authority by focusing on the noble deeds of individuals. Milton, republican and defender of regicide, surprisingly rejects both gothic conventions. Whereas a young Milton had ambitions to write a chivalric romance, *Paradise Lost* disavows the genre and derides its conventions (9.27–31). After declaring rhyme a barbarous invention, Milton's note aligns his work instead with "that of Homer in Greek, and of Virgil in Latin." Helgerson concludes that Milton "does not . . . abandon the absolutist ambition of the neoclassical epic. He simply transfers that authority from the monarch to God and, more significantly, to the individual moral agent." Or, even more simply, "Milton himself assumes this kingly role."[50]

As illuminating as Helgerson's discussion is, his reading is incomplete. Milton's poetic craft does mirror divine creativity not only by rejecting the "wretched matter" that rhyme represents but also by failing to do so fully. Milton had good reason to denounce rhyme as "barbarous." Roger Ascham had mounted perhaps the most famous sixteenth-century attack on rhyme. In book 2 of *The Scholemaster* he declares that "to follow rather the *Gothes* in Ryming, than the Greekes in trew versifying, were euen to eate ackornes with swyne, when we may freely eate wheate breade emonges men."[51] The cultural debasement that rhyming represents takes on a biblical dimension, as the imagery of eating acorns with swine recalls the Prodigal Son's most abject moment in the New Testament parable. For Ascham, rhyming has come to be associated with the Italian threat of Catholicism and immorality. In book 1 of *The Scholemaster* he quotes from Thomas Watson's translation of the *Odyssey* and praises it for "auoidyng barbarous ryming." Ascham then exhorts the English traveler to be like Ulysses, to avoid falling "into the lappe of some wanton and dalying Dame *Calypso*. . . . Some *Siren* shall sing him a song, sweete in tune, but sownding in the ende, to his vtter destruction. . . . Some *Circes* shall make him, of a plaine English man, a right *Italian*."[52] Rhyme is certainly one of these persistent Italian temptations. Ascham later laments that shops in London are full of "lewd and rude rymes."[53]

Milton's comments on rhyme echo Ascham's conviction that rhyme is barbarous, decadent, and effeminate. By striving to expel wretched matter from his creation, the poetic maker likens himself to the divine maker, who must purge the abject dregs of primordial matter before speaking creation into existence. The absence of wretched matter would make the compensatory imposition of rhyme unnecessary. Yet as a number of readers have discussed, *Paradise Lost* does rhyme on occasion. John Diekhoff has identified seventeen rhymed couplets in the epic; J. M. Purcell rejects some of Diekhoff's couplets but suggests others to come up with his own set of seventeen.[54] Even Milton's God turns out to be a rhymer. God's first speech in the poem contains rhyme and rhyme-like components:

> And now
> Through all restraint broke loose he wings his way
> Not far off heaven, in the precincts of light,
> Directly towards the new created world,
> And man there placed, with purpose to assay.

>   (3.86–90)

Milton's God uses a rhyme between "way"—one of the epic's keywords— and "assay" to reinforce the logical connection between Satan's journey

and his future act of temptation. As God continues his speech and denies his own culpability, the repetition of sound and sense (while it might
not constitute strict rhyming) reinforces his rhetoric: "fall," "fault," "fall,"
"failed," and "fell" are used as terminal words in the span of eight lines.
Later in book 3, after the Son begins to intercede for humanity, the Father
proclaims, "O Son, in whom my soul hath chief delight, / Son of my bosom,
Son who art alone / My word, my wisdom, and effectual might" (3.168–70).
In book 6 God echoes his sentiments in another exhortation to the Son: "By
sacred unction, thy deserved right, / Go then thou mightiest in thy Father's
might" (6.709–10). God self-consciously adjusts his own rhyming patterns,
turning a tercet about the might he shares with his Son into a couplet.

    Milton's poetic career had trained him thoroughly in the ways of rhyme.
The clumsy and mechanical couplets of his paraphrase on Psalm 114 (supposedly written at the age of fifteen) give way to the lively elegance of
L'Allegro and *Il Penseroso*; the Petrarchan sonnet allows Milton to practice
rhyming both in English and in the potentially lewd Italian tongue; the
elaborate and irregular patterns of *Lycidas* reveal a young poet who surely
knows how to build a lofty rhyme; in *Samson Agonistes*, rhyme emerges
sporadically but strategically to highlight rhetorical fervor.[55] Whether
Milton deploys rhyme deliberately in *Paradise Lost* or whether rhyme
emerges accidentally in the long composition of a blind poet must remain,
to some degree, a matter of speculation. Nevertheless, a poet so sensitive
to the sound of his language must have recognized some of the rhymes
in his epic. Yet the very question of chance versus agency helps to situate
Milton's poetic project. It would be accurate to say that Milton retroactively
attempts to banish the signs of "wretched matter" that he knows to be in
his work by chance or by design. Yet "denial is always a retroactive process; a half acknowledgement of that otherness [that] has left its traumatic
mark."[56] Milton's disavowal of rhyme as well as its persistence reveal at
the level of poetic language the pattern of abjecting and internalizing barbarism that characterizes divine creativity and its human manifestations.

    In the *Poetics,* Aristotle famously declares that a degree of barbarism
proves necessary because its admixtures and strange words vitalize language. In Milton's view, wretched rhyme may function as a necessary barbarism in epic poetry. W. M. Clarke has summarized a long-debated question
about classical verse: "Is rhyme in ancient poetry intentional, or is it merely
the inevitable result of agreement in an inflected language?" Clarke argues
for the strategic and extensive use of rhyme for rhetorical embellishment in

the *Aeneid* and the *Metamorphoses*.[57] Both the great Augustan epic and the wily, exilic, and quite possibly parodic Ovidian poem generate questions about rhyme. Perhaps, as Helgerson argues, Milton's rejection of gothic for classical poetics points to his absolutist ambition as a writer. Neither divine nor poetic empires, however, can succeed in ridding themselves fully of wretched barbarism. On the contrary, if Milton arrogates to himself a kingly role, he does so by referring self-consciously to the linguistic dregs that trouble and energize the history of reading and writing epic verse.

Milton atavistically rejects the "modern bondage of rhyming" in favor of an alignment with "ancient liberty," but his note on verse anticipates the future reception of *Paradise Lost*.[58] The story of Dryden "tagging" *Paradise Lost* with Milton's permission has become a famous literary episode in its own right.[59] The impact of Milton's thoughts on rhyming has also reached much further across temporal and geographical divides. Angelica Duran reminds us that the 1812 Spanish translation of *Paradise Lost* by Canon Juan Escoiquiz omits Milton's note on verse. Duran hypothesizes that this omission takes part in the project to bowdlerize elements contrary to Catholicism; the history of associating rhyming with lewd, Roman Catholic culture serves as evidence.[60]

In twentieth-century Argentina, however, Jorge Luis Borges would champion Milton's rejection of rhyme. For Borges, the surprise that unrhymed verse offers (in contrast to the regularizing force of rhyme) fosters a spirit of liberty within readers. Against the aesthetics of fascist politics, Borges turns to the English Milton to shape the Spanish language into new forms of Argentinian national literature. As Duran points out, Borges believes in national poetry leading to "great universal poetry" that addresses a select audience drawn from "the mass of his fellow citizens of the world of diverse time periods."[61] Milton does and should continue to serve as a poet of liberty. At the same time, however, the context of his rejection of rhyme teaches us to be cautious. Even at the level of sense and sound, Milton's poetry warns that unruliness and chance imperil freedom of will from within. The impasse of creativity means that the quest for refined universality operates hand in hand with forms of dominion that can neither fully assimilate nor expel a residue deemed impure and wretched.

2

EDEN, THE COUNTRY HOUSE, AND THE INDIES (EAST AND WEST)

For the price of a woman is one hundred *castellanos*, the same as that of a farm.

—Christopher Columbus, on his third voyage

Eden should have been the happiest of homelands. In the Miltonic universe, however, Eden's origins may help to explain its rapid loss. God creates Eden in the aftermath of a war that reveals the fissures within his kingdom. In book 6 of *Paradise Lost*, Raphael narrates the height of the war in Heaven and recalls that "war seemed a civil game / To this uproar; horrid confusion heaped / Upon confusion rose: and now all heav'n / Had gone to wrack" (6.667–70). By inviting the reader to rearrange the words in the phrase "war seemed a civil game," the poet acknowledges that, writing in the tumult of seventeenth-century England, he imagines the very first civil war. Yet the battle between faithful and rebellious angels harkens back to the even more ancient strife between God and chaos. I have discussed how the warring devils excavate the dregs of chaos and transform them into incendiary material. In Raphael's account, the reintroduction of chaos momentarily reduces created order to multiple layers of ancient confusion. Without divine intervention, chaos threatens to reign eternally. Raphael's "now" registers the potency of this threat by projecting the narrated past into potentially unending turmoil.

After the Son drives the offenders out of Heaven, God works to shore up his rule. He explains that he is creating a new world in order to "repair / That detriment" that Satan has effected upon Heaven (*PL* 7.152–53). The angel Raphael goes on to describe Adam and Eve's home as "this new created world / The addition of his empire" (7.554–55). *Paradise Lost* depicts God as the "sovereign planter" of Eden; this description is the first example that J. Martin Evans gives of the "explicitly colonial terms" that Milton deploys in his epic.[1] Divine colonialism is at once Virgilian and resonant with early modern European imperialism, as God plans to re-create an old empire in a new setting. Anthony Pagden describes how the "conquerors and colonizers of America did their best to transform this 'New' world . . . into a likeness of the Old."[2] This is precisely the intended destiny of the Edenic colony: "And earth be changed to heaven, and heaven to earth, / One kingdom, joy and union without end" (7.160–61). The seamless union of Heaven and earth, imperial center and colony, is intended to advance creation toward the wholeness of "all in all." Yet this fulfillment can never take place in the meantime of history, and the Edenic project quickly collapses.

I turn now to focus on the ways in which Milton's poetry describes the earthly consequences of the predicament confronting even divine creation. Milton channels the cosmological implications of a world poised between union and fragmentation into a critical commentary on English nationhood and expansionist projects. Experimentation with genre facilitates this political commentary, as *Paradise Lost* yokes the pastoral and the epic together into unstable coexistence. I begin by putting Milton's account of Eden in dialogue with seventeenth-century country house poetry and with colonialist writings. If England's internal crises necessitate the harmonizing vision of rural verse, expansionism also demands an epic outlook. This dual perspective allows Milton to interrogate the linked concerns of rural verse and New World writings. The Jonsonian country house poem describes harmonious domestic spaces insulated from foreign entanglements. Milton rebuts such a vision by describing the happy rural seat of Eden through a global lens, shuttling the reader rapidly between the Near Eastern setting of the biblical Eden, familiar English landscapes, the New World, and the Far East. Eden contains everything that "earth all-bearing mother yields / In India east or west" (*PL* 5.338–39). After the Fall, however, Eden's all-encompassing abundance gives way to dizzying dislocation. A famous simile compares the fig tree leaves that Adam and Eve use as clothing after the Fall to the leaves of the Indian banyan tree (9.1099–1110).³ A few lines later Milton silently puns on the two meanings of "Indian": "Such of late / Columbus found the American so girt / With feathered cincture, naked else and wild" (9.1115–17).

By oscillating between domestic and global perspectives, *Paradise Lost* imagines Eden as at once homely and unhomely, familiar and distant. Both Eastern and New World imagery locates within Eden the internal problems it inherits from the divine kingdom at large. In its identifications with Eastern opulence, Hell should exist as a distinctively wicked place. Milton, however, provides numerous clues that Hell's exotic extravagance mimics Heaven's. Even though the Eastern setting of Eden is offset by its rural modesty, devilish mimicry underscores the connections among all the realms God has created. The comparison of Eden with the New World, by contrast, maintains the distance between the center and the periphery of God's kingdom. Heaven and earth are destined to grow similar over time, yet the physical space between them needs to be managed. God appoints Uriel as an overseer of the distant outpost of his empire, but the angel's inability to guard against satanic intrusion imparts a lesson about the political function of visual perspective. Milton's narrative deems ineffective the strategies of surveillance shared by plantations at home and abroad.

In the latter half of this chapter I turn to the gender politics that Eden shares with God's kingdom. At this level, too, Milton's poetry rebuts visions of domestic stability and expansionist ambitions. The Jonsonian country house poem imagines a metonymic link between the estate and the lady to celebrate her role as mother, which alone ensures proper transmission of familial property. Writings from the New World famously describe territory as a virgin body to be desired and possessed. In *Paradise Lost*, by contrast, Adam's struggle to maintain his authority manifests the Miltonic crisis at the level of both conjugal and territorial politics. Even in paradise, patriarchal authority over reproduction pointedly fails to ensure stability or to expand dominion. On the contrary, the connection between love and property helps to account for the loss of Eden. The cultural logic of Milton's poetic narrative reveals precise ways in which Adam loses the rural seat of his global empire by failing to maintain control over his wife. A house divided—or, in the case of Eden, a colony that replicates an empire divided—cannot stand. Milton's epic begins by asking why paradise is lost; its answers articulate a double-edged skepticism about domestic and expansionist politics. This simultaneously political and poetic message gains poignancy when Adam's bewildering experience of conjugal love reflects, at an intimate and personal level, the very crisis that produced his Edenic home.

Divided Empire

As Satan departs from Hell in book 2 of *Paradise Lost*, he is compared to an explorer, "Close sailing from Bengala, or the isles / Of Ternate and Tidore, whence merchants bring / Their spicy drugs" (2.638–40). Yet as the reader knows, Satan's destination lies not in the Far East but in the Near Eastern Fertile Crescent. In book 4 another simile compares the "native perfumes" of Eden to "Sabean odours from the spicy shore / Of Arabie the blest" (4.158–63). It is somewhat of a surprise, then, that Satan eventually finds himself in a recognizably English setting. As Barbara K. Lewalski has remarked: "The description of Eden as Adam's estate, his 'happy rural *seat*,' prepares us to discover the structural patterns of the country house poem within the Edenic idyl. We are led through Eden much as we are led through Penshurst or Appleton House."[4] Subsequent critics have followed Lewalski's suggestion by examining Milton's revisionary deployment of the country house genre.[5]

Many of the salient features of the country house poem are present in Milton's Eden. The Jonsonian country house poem celebrates architectural modesty ("Thou art not, Penshurst, built to envious show") and the magical fecundity of the landscape (the partridges at Penshurst are "willing to be killed" while the fish "leap on land" to be consumed).[6] Milton's Eden is, naturally, just as bountiful, even though its vegetarian inhabitants require no animal sacrifice. Adam and Eve sit down to eat "nectarine fruits which the compliant boughs / Yielded them" (*PL* 4.332–33). Milton deploys the Jonsonian design principle of usefulness to describe the Edenic bower: "it was a place / Chosen by the sovereign planter, when he framed / All things to man's delightful use" (4.690–92). Instead of opulence, hospitality is praised as the crowning achievement of the country house. In Thomas Carew's "To Saxham," "the strangers welcome, each man there / Stamp'd on his chearfull brow, doth weare."[7] Adam and Eve are hospitable hosts at their country estate; when Raphael arrives, Adam commands Eve to "bring forth and pour / Abundance, fit to honour and receive / Our heavenly stranger" (5.314–16).

Milton did not need to turn to poets like Jonson or Carew for such topoi. *Paradise Lost* and country house poetry share classical sources such as the poetry of Horace, Martial, and Virgil. Yet the country house subgenre adapts the motifs of utilitarian modesty, natural abundance, and hospitality specifically to address pressing concerns in Stuart England. The idyllic vision of "To Penshurst" negotiates between feudal and proto-bourgeois concepts of nobility and property. The subgenre brought into vogue by Jonson's poem was designed (but ultimately failed) to smooth over some of the crises that would lead to the mid-century Civil Wars: questions of landownership, class conflicts, and the rift between the urban court and the countryside.[8] Reacting to the flight of nobility from the country to London, James I endorsed the gentry's aristocratic and "natural" control of the rural landscape. Yet James's project was contradictory, for a policy of repastoralization threatened to set "the court . . . against the court," implicitly pitting aristocratic feudalism against centralized monarchical power.[9] The country house poet thus relies on what Heather DuBrow has called the "negative formula, a kind of understated compliment" to praise the hospitable estate while denying it any excessively regal grandeur that could potentially rival the monarch's.[10]

The country house poem attributes such damning opulence to the so-called prodigy house. The contrast between the proper estate and the prodigy house serves an important role in the country house subgenre's attempt to mediate the rift between urban center and the countryside.[11] Rather than competing with the court, the Jonsonian country house is hospitable without being ostentatious, and eager to receive royal visitations. D. M. Rosenberg argues that Hell is the prodigy house that serves as a foil to Eden's humble perfection.[12] Milton's rural paradise, as we have seen, is welcoming to angelic emissaries yet relatively modest in its natural abundance. Pandaemonium, by contrast, does look like a garish prodigy house. Jonson praises Penshurst for not having "polished pillars, or a roof of gold" (line 3); Pandaemonium features "Doric pillars overlaid / With golden architrave," "bossy sculptures," and a roof of "fretted gold" (*PL* 1.714–17). Nevertheless, Milton can also describe Pandaemonium admiringly. Its construction is likened to harmonious music, "with the sound / Of dulcet symphonies and voices sweet" (1.711–12). When the devils are finally assembled in their new headquarters, a famous simile transforms the "ample spaces" of Pandaemonium into a beehive (1.768–75). This simile unsettles the simple identification of Pandaemonium with the prodigy house; the devils suddenly occupy the "narrow room" of a natural physical space.

Even more troublingly, the devils' palace proves prodigious only to the extent that its opulence mirrors that of the heavenly court. Milton points out that Pandaemonium is designed by a prominent heavenly architect whose "hand was known / In heaven by many a towered structure high" (*PL* 1.732–33). Similarly, while the devils are censured for their ecologically destructive excavation of gold, Mammon is described as having acquired his love of the precious bane from "the riches of heaven's pavement, trodden gold" (1.682). In the country house genre, the rejection of the prodigy house negotiates currents in domestic politics; in an epic perspective, architectural prodigiousness also reflects global divisions. The devils' palace is repeatedly compared to the seats of Eastern despotism. Thus the opening lines of book 2 liken Satan's "throne of royal state" to "the wealth of Ormus and of Ind, / Or where the gorgeous East with richest hand / Showers on her kings barbaric pearl and gold" (2.1–4). Even the exoticized opulence of Pandaemonium has its counterpart in divine architecture. When Satan reaches the border between the chaotic and divine empires, he sees the lavish gate that God has erected, "with frontispiece of diamond and gold / Embellished." The decoration of this frontispiece is described in terms ("thick with sparkling orient gems") that recall the earlier descriptions of satanic and Eastern despotism (3.506–7).

Devilish parody proves especially acute in a cosmos governed by mimesis, where God's newest world is explicitly designed to resemble the imperial center. Milton's description of Pandaemonium suggests troubling connections between the satanic and divine kingdoms.[13] In a dismal outpost of divine creation, the devils occupy the "area between mimicry and mockery." Pandaemonium serves as a site of *"almost the same, but not quite"* that "problematizes the signs of racial and cultural priority"—and, in this case, the propriety of the divine kingdom in all of its splendor.[14] Satanic architecture also raises questions about Eden's perfection. If Pandaemonium mimics Heaven in a case of "court against the court," Eden's rural modesty should contrast with Heaven's opulent splendor. As a colony, however, Eden is explicitly designed to mirror the imperial center. As Christopher

Wortham observes, "Milton's divinely-built palace of nature has . . . its pillars of acanthus (later used in stylized form to decorate the capitals of Corinthian columns), its self-constructing artefacts of flowery mosaics, and its rich Tyrian carpetry. . . . [I]t all sounds very lavish and ornate, but who could accuse God of bad taste?"[15] But much more is at stake than the possibility of God's bad taste.

The connections between Heaven, Hell, and Eden prove less surprising, if not less fraught, in the context of Milton's monism, according to which "Heaven and Earth, like angels and men, are ontologically continuous."[16] Although Hell is a grosser branch of creation and its new residents have become debased, their continued existence in a monistic world confirms their ontological ties to the divine and human realms. Yet the monistic unity of Milton's cosmos coexists uneasily with the morally laden division between East and West, whereby the garish hellish realm proves at once foreign and uncannily similar to God's kingdom. At once a country house, Near Eastern garden, and colony designed to replicate the imperial center, Eden occupies an unstable middle ground in God's kingdom.

By locating supposedly exotic contagion throughout God's created order, *Paradise Lost* confutes the Jonsonian vision of harmonious insularity. The country house poem presents aristocratic landownership as natural in part by upholding a myth of self-sufficiency. Carew's "To My Friend G.N. from Wrest" describes the rural estate as an "Island Mansion" surrounded by a moat, a miniature image of England's supposed insularity (line 79). Robert Herrick praises "The Country Life" for rejecting both spices from the "Eastern Ind" and "the Ingot from the West."[17] The country house poem denies the cultural consequences of Eastern and Western expansionism. The happy rural seat of Eden, by contrast, uses the hospitality topos to display the goods of a global economy. When Eve gathers fruit to serve the angelic visitor, she picks

> from each tender stalk
> Whatever earth all-bearing mother yields
> In India east or west, or middle shore
> In Pontus or the Punic coast, or where
> Alcinous reigned.

> (*PL* 5.337–41)

As John Michael Archer notes, this "oddly global and domestic" moment registers "a primordial anticipation of world-economic exchange."[18]

The tension between the global and the rural has notable precedents. Accounts of blissful cultural insularity are presented as tenuous fictions even in Virgil's *Eclogues* and *Georgics*. In the Second Georgic, Virgil describes the farmers' happy unawareness of foreign luxuries; an expansive list of these foreign goods ironically underscores the disparity between the farmers' knowledge and the poet's.[19] Throughout the *Georgics*, Virgil's impassioned patriotism is defined within and against the knowledge of foreign nations, climates, and goods. Stella P. Revard reminds us that *Paradise Lost* borrows from the *Georgics* to describe both the idylls of rural life and the epic project. Part of "the epic potential of the *Georgics*" lies, I believe, in the interplay between the rural and the global.[20] Whereas the *Eclogues* explicitly resist the impulse to compose epic, passages such as the proem to the Third Georgic anticipate the imperial genre. Yet the Virgilian epic is centrally concerned with actions—seafaring, warfare, and conquest—that are inimical to the more insular worldview of the pastoral.

The known world had expanded tremendously between Virgil's time and Milton's; as we have seen, the latent pun in the word "Indies" enables Milton to transport the reader rapidly from East to West. Milton's New World imagery further debunks rural insularity by suggesting a complex pattern of similarity and difference between the center of God's kingdom and his latest colonial project. By the time Milton was composing much of *Paradise Lost*, Andrew Marvell had already associated with the Americas the cultural crises mediated by poems such as "To Penshurst." Writing during the Interregnum, Marvell tensely but wittily alludes to the revolutionary potential of agrarian class conflicts in his country house poem "Upon Appleton House."[21] In "Bermudas," Marvell puts the *locus amoenus* in motion, setting the poetry of paradisal gardens within the related contexts of sectarian conflict and New World colonialism. The poem takes as its occasion Puritans fleeing Laudian persecution and traveling west "in the expectation of some sort of practical Eden," as Rosalie L. Colie puts it.[22] Marvell's account of garden paradise, like Milton's, shuttles the reader between East and West: the pomegranates of the Bermudas are said to enclose "jewels more rich than *Ormus* shows's" (line 20). Annabel Patterson argues that "Bermudas" is a celebratory poem, and that Marvell's Protestant poetics achieves a "desirable poise" between acceptable devotion and excessive sensuality.[23] The poem, however, also invites ironic readings.[24] The "falling Oars" of the last line, for example, seem to carry an indistinct but ominous suggestion of a fallen paradise, much like the speaker's literal fall in the bountiful setting of "The Garden." In spite of the lucidity of "Bermudas," it is unclear whether the poem's tone celebrates a Puritan paradise or gently derides as misguided the quest for a colonial Eden.

In Milton's description of paradise, the interlace of Eastern, New World, and pastoral images advances a critique at once far more expansive and politically direct than Marvell's. Precisely at the same time that Milton describes Adam and Eve's bower as the seat of a rural estate, he also suggests that Eden is a colony: "it was a place / Chosen by the sovereign planter" (*PL* 4.690–91). Poets such as Milton and Marvell were certainly not alone in drawing imaginative connections between "plantations" at home and abroad. Radical dissenters compared domestic exploitation to imperial subjugation for polemical purposes. The Levellers Richard Overton and Charles Lilburne and the Digger Gerrard Winstanley traced unjust monarchies, private landownership, and the detested practice of enclosure to the Norman Yoke.[25] Yet there was a more literal link between the country house and the colony. J. Martin Evans describes the so-called purgative rationale, according to which the burdens of England's overpopulation could be relieved by shipping indigents, criminals, and other undesirables to the colonies. Richard Hakluyt the elder, for example, describes the necessity of "deliver[ing] our commonwealth from multitudes of loiterers and idle vagabonds . . . which, having no way to beset on work, be either mutinous and seek alteration in the state, or at least very burdensome to the commonwealth."[26] Hakluyt's proposal would fully take effect in the seventeenth century, when the clamor of the multitudes was turning revolutionary, especially in rural England.

The country house and the colony share strategies "to gain control of land and, subsequently, control over the dispossessed populations"; domestic and colonial plantations "begin to grapple in earnest with the project of enclosing and controlling space contested by 'outsiders,' usually those who used to inhabit and use it."[27] The country house poem was designed to quell the dissenting voices of the disenfranchised multitudes. It is now difficult to read "To Penshurst" without recalling Raymond Williams's imprecise but forceful argument that the poem conceals an exploitive economy "by a simple extraction of the existence of labourers."[28] Milton's Eden, by contrast, explicitly requires daily labor. *Paradise Lost* imagines a tenuous and ultimately unstable balance "between a *labor* of georgic and the *otium*, or leisure, of pastoral."[29] Edenic labor serves as a rejoinder to seventeenth-century country house poetry. Milton insists on the necessity of labor even in a perfect world, but the nonexploitive economy of Eden is genuinely "reared with no man's ruin, no man's groan" ("To Penshurst" line 46). In a case of unalienated labor, the lord and lady of the Edenic estate are also its only workers. Similarly, if Adam and Eve are described as colonists, the *terra nullius* argument fully applies, and their dominion does not dispossess.[30]

Yet Milton's critique runs deeper, for even this most perfect of rural estates requires forms of surveillance to maintain it. Even before Satan—and, through his eyes, the reader—arrives at Eden, *Paradise Lost* teaches a lesson about the political function of sight and its limitations. Milton's narrative suggests that domestic and colonial forms of subjugation rely on related forms of visual mastery; this shared mode of power is then deemed ineffective. The limits of vision become most acute at the end of book 3, when the angel Uriel, the overseer of God's latest creation, cannot see through Satan's disguise and instead helps direct the devil toward Eden. Satanic deception works because "neither man nor angel can discern / Hypocrisy, the only evil that walks / Invisible, except to God alone" (3.682–84). The qualification "except to God alone" may strike the reader as defensive. Only some thirty lines before, Milton has gone out of his way to remind us that Uriel (whose name means "light of God" in Hebrew) serves as God's active eyes (3.650). Earlier in book 3 God himself has taken pains to reconcile his omniscience and foreknowledge with the Fall that will occur. The Uriel episode raises a more specific version of such questions—namely, why God allows an innocent error to have such dire consequences. By bewailing the absence of a "warning voice," the opening lines of book 4 lead the reader to register the full emotional force of this question.[31] Divine omniscience remains unchallenged, yet it represents something to be explained rather than a source of comfort or aid. Milton's narrative challenges the reader to confront the painful question of why God's "permissive will" allows Uriel to fail at the most critical moment of his career as overseer (3.685).

Milton uses such theological questions to advance his political thought. The Uriel episode, despite its painful irony for the human reader, preserves Milton's theodicy by locating the fault within a fallible but innocent agent. At the same time, Milton displaces the temporal gap between divine foreknowledge and present action onto the spatial or geographical distance between the heavenly center and the peripheries of creation. God commissions Uriel as an administrator whose function is to "bear his swift errands over moist and dry / O'er sea and land" (*PL* 3.652–53). In the motif of Uriel's vision, theological issues converge with practical matters of management or administration. The sharp-eyed angel serves not only as an overseer of a distant outpost but also as a theorist of creation who describes border conflict as the first stage of genesis. Uriel relates to the disguised Satan what he empirically witnessed at the origins of the world:

> I saw when at his word the formless mass,
> This world's material mould, came to a heap:
> Confusion heard his voice, and wild uproar
> Stood ruled, stood vast infinitude confined;
> Till at his second bidding darkness fled,
> Light shone, and order from disorder sprung.

> (3.708–13)

Uriel emphasizes the defiant unruliness of matter and the necessity of God's forceful authority in the process of creation. Such an account tends to conflict with Raphael's cosmology. Raphael, as we have seen, does describe the purgation of chaotic dregs, but he underscores the harmonious and progressive movement of creation toward its divine source. "All things proceed, and up to him return," Raphael teaches. "If not depraved from good, created all / Such to perfection, one first matter all" (5.470–72). John Rogers shows that "chaology" provides Milton and his contemporaries a way to theorize the "metaphysical foundations of the state."[32] In Raphael's view of creation, Rogers finds the persistence of a liberal and egalitarian vitalism in *Paradise Lost*. Raphael goes on to depict the new world as an embryo and a womb that inseminates and gives birth to itself. Yet such a view of creation as natural, progressive labor partially independent of divine fiat coexists uneasily with Uriel's sense that God needs to subjugate matter and darkness. Whereas Raphael affirms a belief that the divine origin of the world predicts its future perfection, Uriel allows us to trace the instability of all homelands to the unruliness of primordial matter itself. Uriel's chaology is well suited to his occupation as vigilant overseer.

The Uriel episode begins to suggest the political significance of sight and visual epistemologies. By deceiving Uriel, Satan resumes his role as the primary eye through which Milton's reader sees creation, and the ensuing action clarifies Milton's critique of visual mastery—a critique that cuts against trends both at home and abroad. The politicization of sight as an instrument of surveillance is a common trait of travel narratives, descriptions of New World colonies, and seventeenth-century country house poetry. Marvell parodies this aspect of the country house genre when he describes the vertiginous loss of visual control over the potentially revolutionary workers at Appleton House. The poet initially views these workers from high above, "where Men like Grashoppers appear," but immediately his perspective plunges into the depths of "that unfathomable Grass" so that "Grashoppers are Gyants there: / They, in there squeking Laugh, contemn / Us as we walk more low then them" (stanza 47). Faced with such loss of control, the poet eventually flees the scene.

All country house poems offer a carefully guided tour through the perspective of the poet, which strives to be aligned with that of the estate's owner. The poet's eye oversees the laborers of the estate, squaring them into their prescribed roles and containing their unruly potential. "To Penshurst" inscribes hierarchical order onto the landscape: "The lower land, that to the river bends, / Thy sheep, thy bullocks, kine, and calves do feed: / The middle ground thy mares, and horses breed" (lines 22–24). James Turner observes that "the division of the grounds into 'lower land', 'middle grounds' and the haunts of gods corresponds precisely to the social divisions within the hall."[33] Jonson attempts to present Penshurst's economy as magically nonexploitive, but as Marvell's later country house poem suggests, the visual perspective of the genre is very much linked to the disciplinary control that maintains the rural economy.

Once we enter Milton's Eden, we learn that even this nonexploitive rural estate is designed for visual mastery. By providing access to Eden through Satan's eyes, *Paradise Lost* gestures toward distinctly postlapsarian concerns about estate management while suggesting that the impulse toward surveillance and visual mastery is a satanic habit. Satan surveys Eden's hierarchical landscape:

> A sylvan scene, and as the ranks ascend
> Shade above shade, a woody theatre

Of stateliest view. Yet higher than their tops
The verdurous wall of Paradise upsprung:
Which to our general sire gave prospect large
Into his nether empire neighbouring round.

(4.140–45)

The vegetarian Adam and Eve have no need of the animal husbandry that Jonson describes in Penshurst. Yet the forms of stratification present in Penshurst are also strikingly present in the soil and vegetation of Eden. These lines emphasize hierarchy both in their diction ("the ranks ascend / Shade above shade," "stateliest view") and in their movement toward ever higher ground. Milton signals the politicized nature of this sylvan scene by describing Eden as an "enclosure green," a phrase that would still have struck a chord of controversy in the 1660s and 1670s (4.133). The estate is indeed sealed off by a physical wall, and it is strategically elevated to give Adam a position of visual mastery despite the absence of unruly humans to monitor.

As these lines compel a visual ascent within the mind of the reader, they transform a sylvan scene into the seat of a "nether empire." This imperial language reminds us that rural poetry and colonialist discourses encode related forms of surveillance. The central role of visual perspective in early modern texts of discovery and conquest is a point that hardly needs to be belabored.[34] Ralph Hamor opens *A True Discourse of the Present Estate of Virginia* by explaining his God-given commission to write his account: "A taske I know by himselfe and others, meerely because I have bin *Oculatus testis*, thus imposed upon me."[35] As Hamor promises empirical knowledge and truthfulness, he expects the reader to accept Plautus's maxim "Pluris est oculatus testis unus, quam auriti decem. Qui audiunt, audita dicunt; qui vident, plane sciunt" (One eyewitness is greater than ten hearsayers. Those who hear, speak of what they have heard; those who see, know clearly). Milton's Satan agrees: disguised as a young cherub, he tells Uriel that he has chosen to visit the new world out of an "unspeakable desire to see, and know" (3.662).

In texts of travel and discovery, the eyewitness is often a scout or a spy, roles that Satan assumes when he enters Eden. In fact, Satan has a power that imperial explorers would have envied, as he can mimic (and even possess) the native's body to expedite his missions. Disguised as a cormorant, Satan chooses the Tree of Life, the "middle tree and highest," as his perch:

> yet not true life
> Thereby regained, but sat devising death
> To them who lived; nor on the virtue thought
> Of that life-giving plant, but only used
> For prospect, what well used had been the pledge
> Of immortality.

(*PL* 4.195–201)

Satan's actions suggest his role as a spy reconnoitering in a new world, but the setting reminds us that this particular new world shares traits with poetic terrain closer at home to Milton's audience. Shannon Miller has shown how Aemilia Lanyer's experiments with visual perspective in *Salve Deus Rex Judaeorum* should be read alongside Milton's poetry, ranging from his aborted poem *The Passion* to *Paradise Lost*. In "The Description of Cooke-ham," the country house poem that concludes *Salve Deus Rex Judaeorum*, "Lanyer highlights the political stakes of representing the garden."[36] The motif of visual mastery in "Cooke-ham" centers on a "comely Cedar straight and tall" whose towering height affords a strategic vantage point: "Where beeing seated, you might plainely see, / Hills, vales, and woods, as if on bended knee / They had appeard, your honour to salute, / Or to pre-ferre some strange unlook'd for sute."[37] Yet the poem then presents reli-gious meditation as the alternative and preferred mode of perspective that the tree offers: "What was there then but gave you all content, / While you the time in meditation spent, / Of their Creators powre, which there you saw" (lines 75–77). This is precisely the holy mode of "prospect" that Satan rejects in book 4, preferring instead the imperial mode of seeing. Milton divides the dual role of Lanyer's tree, for Adam, in the epic's final books, will ascend "a hill / Of Paradise the highest" in order to witness human history and, ultimately, the redemptive power of providence (11.377–78).

Attempts to align Milton with a pro-imperial position elide important differences between satanic and Adamic sight. Bruce McLeod thus talks about the poet's "satellite-like vision" but does not adequately account for his blindness. If Adam's mountaintop vision of human history supposedly constitutes "an imperial perspective," it is telling that Adam's sight falters.[38] Michael declares to him:

> but I perceive
> Thy mortal sight to fail; objects divine
> Must needs impair and weary human sense:
> Henceforth what is to come I will relate,
> Thou therefore give due audience, and attend.

(*PL* 12.8–12)

After laying down his supposedly imperial vision, Adam hears some of the most explicitly anti-imperialist lines in *Paradise Lost*. Michael proleptically censures Nimrod, who will "arrogate dominion undeserved / Over his brethren." (12.27–28). Sight is inculcated in dynamics of power and control, but *Paradise Lost* diffracts any stable relationship of viewing subject/viewed object. Regina Schwartz remarks that in the poem, "the temptation of voyeurism, the temptation to master, is never wholly achieved."[39] When even Uriel cannot successfully maintain visual mastery, it is unsurprising that book 12 underscores the limitations of human vision—a lesson that recurs in the work of a blind poet.[40]

Michael eventually gives Adam a clue about the significance of the failure of sight and the transition from seeing to hearing. He prophetically describes Abraham: "I see him, but thou canst not, with what faith / He leaves his gods, his friends, and native soil" (*PL* 12.128–29). This juxtaposition of sight, blindness (or aporia), and faith evokes a biblical definition: "Now faith is the substance of things hoped for, the evidence of things not seen" (Heb. 11:1). Milton, *pace* Plautus, asserts the supremacy of a certain kind of hearsay over being an eyewitness: only the former can be a basis of redemptive faith. This theological lesson in turn advances Milton's political commentary. J. Martin Evans argues that the modes of poetic inspiration in *Paradise Lost* correspond to two modes of colonial discourse, one aiming at empirical observation and the other (less common) mode based on secondhand information. He then claims that the epic presents a harmonious fusion of the two patterns. Yet the epic does not present "the two principal strategies of Renaissance colonial discourse" that Evans describes as equal alternatives, but suggests the necessity of one rather than the other.[41] Indeed, an excessive desire to see is a satanic temptation: "your eyes that seem so clear, / Yet are but dim, shall perfectly be then / Opened and cleared, and ye shall be as gods" (9.706–8). The triumph of mediated faith over eyewitness knowledge helps to undermine the perspective of power assumed both by rural poetry and by texts of discovery and conquest.

The political ramifications of sight and knowledge allow us to read anew the differences between Uriel's and Raphael's cosmologies. *Paradise Lost* does not deem either angel wrong in any simple fashion. Rather, the poem challenges the reader to weigh the weaknesses and strengths of each perspective. Uriel's inability to detect satanic hypocrisy highlights how his God-given visual function ironically aligns him with a satanic desire to see and know. Raphael, by contrast, eventually admits to Adam that he was away during the last day of creation. Although this admission does not necessarily call into question Raphael's narrative of the first days of Genesis, his lesson that we should "know to know no more" (4.775) suggests a tendency to accept received wisdom rather than to insist on firsthand knowledge. Uriel and Raphael thus offer both sobering and hopeful reflections on the contradictions at the heart of Milton's universe. Uriel locates in the origins of creation a wild uproar of chaotic forces; such a view, however accurate, leads to a mode of supervision that can never be vigilant enough. Raphael's account of an ever-improving universe may strike fallen readers at naïve, yet it serves as a powerful corrective lesson about faith in things unseen. Disquieting knowledge of unruly origins must coexist with hopeful anticipation of a better end. In Milton's divided world, however, these views cannot be synthesized into the outlook of a single angel.

Yet Unspoiled Guiana

Uriel's narrative of creation as confrontation does not explicitly register the gendered nature of the Miltonic cosmos. We have seen that Raphael, by contrast, provides a vivid account of the abject dregs of chaos. When Raphael subsequently describes the earth as a womb and a great mother, however, the account of creation as natural birth shepherds the reader away from the conflict between God and chaos. In Raphael's optimistic cosmology, a felicitous process of birth can take place in a world purged of abject traces. Adam, meanwhile, experiences intimately the persistent tension between gendered agon and conjugal love. In Eve, Adam finds a female counterpart who should be the mother of all mankind, but who also proves recalcitrant and potentially excessive in her fertility. As John Rumrich has shown, Eve is aligned with chaos in being "constitutionally unpredictable and resistant to easy explanation."[42] To reproduce, Adam must at once tame the excesses of a chaotic female body and maintain a loving, natural union with her. The tendency toward both abundance and wild excess associates Eve with the Edenic landscape, which must be tamed and pruned daily. Satan's initial impressions of Eve capture the organic bond— at once precious and threatening—to the landscape around her. Eve's disheveled hair "in wanton ringlets waved / As the vine curls her tendrils, which implied / Subjection, but required with gentle sway" (*PL* 4.306–8). Adam's roles as husband and as lord of Eden are thus intertwined, and his failure to maintain control over his wife leads to the loss of paradise.

Milton's encomium to Edenic marriage suggests its uniquely important role in property relations: "Hail wedded love, mysterious law, true source / Of human offspring, sole propriety, / In Paradise of all things common else" (*PL* 4.750–52). Grammatically, "sole propriety" may refer to "offspring," whereas the sense may indicate "wedded love" as the referent. The relatively imperceptible effect of this slippage suggests the strong link between marriage and reproductive politics. Even in paradise, conjugal love must be proprietary for the sake of familial property. As the original command to be fruitful and multiply suggests, reproduction exists to spread dominion over all the earth. This is a distinctly patriarchal economy: as Adam learns after the Fall, Eden would have been his capital seat, to which his offspring would have returned "to celebrate / And reverence . . . their great progenitor" (11.345–46). The father alone, as sole progenitor, would have received such homage. Milton's encomium to marriage, however, underscores the tension between patriarchal marriage and Edenic communalism—a tension that persists to disquiet the poem's concluding vision of Adam and Eve's redemptive marriage.[43]

I turn now to the question of how *Paradise Lost* comments critically on the reproductive politics of the country house genre and of colonialist discourse. Whereas the Jonsonian country house poem affirms the harmony between birthright and ownership, Milton's narrative of the Fall leads us

to question primogeniture and dynastic succession. The epic perspective of
Paradise Lost in turn allows the poem to show that the cultural logic of expansionism shares with country house poetry a troubled politics of sexual
reproduction, both literal and metaphorical.

In the Second Epode, Horace sets a precedent for describing the virtuous family as central to the virtuous rural life. According to Jonson's translation, titled "The Praises of a Country Life," the happy Horatian farmer
has "a chaste wife meet / For household aid, and children sweet" (lines
39–40). "To Penshurst" preserves this motif, but the concern shifts to the
lady's role in the succession of estate property: "These, Penshurst, are thy
praise, and yet not all. / Thy Lady's noble, fruitful, chaste withal. / His
children thy great Lord may call his own: / A fortune, in this age, but
rarely known" (lines 89–92). These lines invoke Barbara Gamage not as
the wife of Robert Sidney but as the lady of Penshurst; her primary duty
is not "household aid" but the perpetuation of the family's landownership.
Jonson wryly remarks, however, that wifely chastity is "rarely known." He
acknowledges the pervasive anxiety that arises from a patriarchal system of
succession, turning the lady's sexual virtue into the focus of uneasy scrutiny.

Before Jonson composed "To Penshurst," Lanyer's "Cooke-ham" had
already revealed the precarious position that ladies of country estates occupied. Lanyer opens with a farewell to the estate that she praises. What
makes Cookham untenable, and what makes its loss particularly poignant,
is its fleeting status as female domain, populated by "that Grace," Margaret
Clifford, Countess of Cumberland, her daughter Anne, and Lanyer herself.[44] Lanyer anticipates the Jonsonian country house poem when she
describes the countess's organic connection to and power over the estate.
Unlike Lady Sidney, however, the countess cannot maintain the bond of
ownership through the work of childbearing. Lanyer describes the countess as a guest at an estate that does not belong to her. Her relationship to the
landscape turns agonistic as she is depicted as a Diana-like huntress: "The
little creatures in the Burrough by / Would come abroad to sport them in
your eye; / Yet fearefull of the Bowe in your fair Hand, / Would runne away
when you did make a stand" ("Cooke-ham" lines 49–52). Lanyer suggests
that the countess's procreative powers had gone for naught. Because her
only surviving offspring was a daughter, the countess could not perpetuate
her family's connection to the landscape. The opening lines of *Salve Deus
Rex Judaeorum* anticipate the indirect allusion to Diana by invoking the

late Elizabeth I as Cynthia. Lanyer goes on to endorse virtuous celibacy as a way to transcend exploitive gender relations. In "Cooke-ham," Anne Clifford's marriage to "noble Dorset" is at best a bittersweet event, one that the poet must celebrate even though it marks the end of her blissful stay at Cookham. Writing several decades later, Marvell also elevates chastity to express ambivalence about the structures of succession.[45] "Upon Apple-ton House" attempts to achieve poetic closure by celebrating the virginal youth of Thomas Fairfax's aptly named daughter Mary. Nevertheless, the poem acknowledges that Mary's marriage will result in her loss of sexual innocence and in her removal from the family line. As a result, the happy bond between Mary and the landscape proves transitory: "Mean time ye Fields, Springs, Bushes, Flow'rs / . . . Employ the means you have by Her" (stanza 94).

The narrative of the Fall in *Paradise Lost* seems to revolve around a similarly vexed drama of reproduction and landownership. Milton fol-lows biblical and Horatian precedent when he describes Eve as Adam's "fit help" in the tasks that even paradise requires (8.450). As in the country house genre, however, the importance of the wife's role in reproduction as-sumes prominence. Milton echoes the biblical commission to "be fruitful, multiply, and fill the earth, / Subdue it, and throughout dominion hold" (7.531–32). Only by being fruitful will mankind populate the new creation, thus fulfilling God's imperial design to repair his kingdom and ultimately to unite Heaven and earth. Eve, who is created "female for race," is instru-mental to this plan (7.530). In the separation scene of book 9, the events immediately leading to the Fall revolve around questions of reproduction. Eve first proposes a separation from Adam by describing their childless-ness: "but till more hands / Aid us, the work under our labour grows / Luxurious by restraint" (9.207–9). When Adam eventually concedes, the departing Eve is compared to a nymph of Diana's (or "Delia's") train, and then to Diana herself (9.386–89). Milton goes on to compare Eve to Po-mona fleeing from Vertumnus, "or to Ceres in her prime / Yet virgin of Proserpina from Jove" (9.395–96). Like Lanyer's countess, Eve is described as a paradoxical married virgin whose ability to propagate familial domin-ion is suspended. When Eve departs, she rejects the patriarchal economy of marriage and eventually turns to the Tree of Knowledge. In book 5, an earlier allusion to the Ovidian Pomona-Vertumnus episode describes trees as metaphorical husbands: the masculine elm is barren but provides support for the fertile vine (5.215–19). In Lanyer's "Cooke-ham," the "comely Cedar" acts as a kind of surrogate husband, offering the countess a joyous embrace. The Tree of Knowledge, by contrast, appeals to Eve as a maternal body that needs no husbandly support. Satan tempts Eve both by addressing her as a sovereign "Queen of this universe" (9.684) and by hailing the tree as the "Mother of science" (9.680).

Whereas Jonson inscribes aristocratic continuity onto the landscape he celebrates, Lanyer, Marvell, and Milton deal with rupture and instability. Milton attempts to subvert aristocratic designs even more strenuously than other writers working through the country house genre. Milton's Eve shares with country house ladies her vital link to the landscape. Because Milton writes of Eden, though, he invites the reader to believe that he accurately depicts what the country house poet can only suggest hyperbolically. Eve's unity with Eden is not a flattering conceit but an aspect of unfallen monism. As Stephen Fallon puts it, Milton's vitalist animism "turns the pathetic fallacy on its head—it is no longer an illusion to speak of nature sharing thoughts and emotions."[46] Sin, however, results in the related curses of death and dualistic modes of thought and action.[47] Adam articulates his nascent dualism in a speech about the fears that plague the otherwise comforting prospect of death. Adam reasons that his spirit will die because it is guilty of sin, and that his body will die because it never "properly" had life (*PL* 10.791). Fallon points out that mortalism is the "inevitable concomitant" of Milton's monism and animist materialism.[48] In *De Doctrina Christiana*, Milton bases his heretical mortalism upon the dictum that man "is not double or separable" (*CPW* 6:318). Adam's speech, by contrast, reaches a mortalist conclusion ("All of me shall die") through a sharp division between spirit and flesh.

The full context of Adam's speech reveals a specifically gendered and reproductive logic of dualism: "How gladly would I meet / Mortality my sentence . . . / how glad would lay me down / As in my mother's lap!" (*PL* 10.775–78). At once Hamletesque and reminiscent of Job's lament— "Why died I not from the womb? why did I not give up the ghost when I came out of the belly?" (Job 3:11)—Adam's soliloquy registers a sense of the maternal body as both comforting and lethal. The man born from clay imagines the earth as his womb and rightful tomb.[49] Adam prefaces his dualist and mortalist remarks with anguished thoughts about reproduction: "Oh voice once heard / Delightfully, *Increase and multiply*, / Now death to hear! For what can I increase / Or multiply, but curses on my head?" (10.729–32). After the Fall, the commission to propagate life and dominion carries the ironic possibility that Adam and Eve may be able to reproduce only moribund life and corrupted power. Adam's gendered dualism leads to misogyny and the fantasy of a wholly male world. His concern is for the "patrimony" that he will leave exclusively to his sons (10.818–19). When Adam laments, "Ah, why should all mankind / For one man's fault thus guiltless be condemned," he describes his guilt as an internalized feminized deficiency and, at the same time, longs to deny Eve's role in sinful procreation (10.822–23). Out of his sole fault Adam bequeaths to his sons the patrimony of death. The heavy burden of sin might be "divided / With that bad woman," but Adam also wishes to divide himself from the partner he once claimed as his own flesh, heart, and soul (10.836–37). Adam openly expresses his revulsion toward Eve and the concomitant desire to arrogate to himself all reproductive powers. When Eve approaches penitently, he furiously rejects her and wishes that God had provided a way to populate the world without females.

Even in its blustery confusion, Adam's thinking about postlapsarian reproduction points to important principles in Milton's critique of patriarchal succession. Adam's soliloquy, according to Rachel J. Trubowitz, reveals how "after the Fall, birthright and bloodline no longer guarantee the dynastic nation's corporate perpetuity, as royalist rhetoric of the king's two bodies proclaimed they did."[50] Trubowitz demonstrates how Milton shifts between monistic and dualistic rhetoric to support his antimonarchical position. Birth-based forms of succession and primogeniture rely on the mere fact of reproduction. In a potentially dualist world, biological ties do not ensure the continuity of spiritual worth.[51] Challenges to birthright arise even before the Fall; Eden is, in fact, a product of the very first such challenge. The war in Heaven begins when Lucifer challenges God's elevation of his Son as heir and vice-regent. Even before Raphael's narration of the war in Heaven, the reader is assured that the Son is elevated "by merit more than birthright" (*PL* 3.309). There should never have been any cleavage between birthright and worth in this unique case of dynastic reproduction, in which the Son perfectly reflects his Father without the mediation of any baser matter. Nevertheless, the poet's postlapsarian perspective still leads him to make the contrast, and his republican principles lead him to privilege merit. By volunteering to redeem mankind, the Son decisively confirms that Satan was wrong ever to have doubted his merit as heir. Yet the proof manifests itself retroactively, as a response to the damaging results of the original war of succession.

In God's new world, the problems besetting reproduction become more conspicuously gendered. Adam, in his postlapsarian misogyny, simultaneously blames Eve for these problems and denies her role as mother, even if this means arrogating all fault to himself. Lanyer, in a dedicatory poem to Anne Sackville (née Clifford), registers the unstable position of women in a patriarchal economy. As a poet seeking patronage, Lanyer must praise but also anxiously enjoin the noble union of biological and spiritual succession: "You are the Heire apparent of this Crowne / Of goodnesse, bountie, grace, love pietie, / By birth its yours, then keepe it as your owne" ("To the Ladie *Anne*" lines 65–67). Yet Anne Clifford must assume her role not just as the deserving daughter of a noblewoman but as a wife. Lanyer's country house poem reveals the instability and unfairness of patriarchal economies, yet the poet cannot prevent marriage from dissolving her cherished female community. Milton, as a fervently anti-aristocratic poet, can afford to be more openly critical of dynastic structures. As an ardent defender of conjugal love, however, he also seeks to redeem marriage and childbearing. Eve's proposal of celibacy must first be overcome as a false solution to the problems of postlapsarian reproduction (*PL* 10.979–991). (Eve herself suggests that willfully refusing sex will lead to suicidal despair.) When the Son arrives in Eden, he announces the redemption not only of mankind but also of reproduction and, more specifically, of motherhood. The incarnation of "Jesus son of Mary second Eve" will restore the spiritual integrity of biological reproduction after the Fall; his conception will grant the "second Eve" access to God without male mediation (10.183).

Milton emphasizes, however, that this familiar solution does not undo the systematically inequitable practice of marriage. The Son's promise to Eve is accompanied by the twin curses of pain in childbirth and increased subjection to her husband. The newly chastened Eve accepts her condition. Even before the Son arrives in Eden, Milton adds to the Genesis account Eve's speeches offering to accept more than her share of blame; her humility, too, must be corrected by Adam before it becomes effective. Although Milton mounts a theological and poetic critique of dynastic succession, patriarchal patterns of thought persist in a state of tension with egalitarian politics.[52] On the one hand, the gendered politics of marriage seem to limit

Milton's theories of both pre- and postlapsarian equality; on the other, his views seem far afield of such committed apologists of patriarchy as his opponent Robert Filmer.[53] Eve's final speech in the poem reveals the compromise that Milton attempts to stabilize. She declares satisfaction in her role as dependent wife but adds that she finds "further consolation" in the Marian prophecy of an independent motherhood: "*By me* the promised seed shall all restore" (*PL* 12.620–23, emphasis added).

The ending of *Paradise Lost* attempts to surmount any lingering tensions with its appeal to both inward and conjugal forms of happiness. Yet these lines are beautiful partly because they share with "Cooke-ham" an elegiac sense of the loss of the "happy rural seat." Indeed, the *felix culpa* appeal to a happier paradise within underscores the loss of a monistic paradise where spiritual and physical bliss are integrated. John Rogers has described the "monistic description of the expulsion," whereby the garden itself responds "to the Fall by ejecting the tainted human body from the garden's harmonious air."[54] Even before the expulsion, the Fall and its consummation result in bodily shame: Adam and Eve use leaves as "broad as Amazonian targe" to "gird their waist, vain covering if to hide / Their guilt and dreaded shame" (*PL* 9.1111–14). The singular form of "waist" emphasizes the couple's sinful unison, and it also heightens the pun on "waste," which suggests the corruption of the reproductive organs of God's latest creation. This shield is "vain" because outer coverings cannot conceal the couple's spiritual guilt. Both "dreaded shame" and an inadequately physical reaction to it signal Adam and Eve's broken link to the monistic purity of Eden.

Milton makes explicit the connection between sexual shame and colonial politics. Before the reference to the Amazons, the leaves that Adam and Eve don are compared to the leaves of the Indian banyan tree; the couple are then compared to the natives of the Indies in the Western Hemisphere. This compact sequence rapidly expands a domestic, conjugal narrative into a global one. Originally commissioned to spread dominion throughout the earth, Adam and Eve now find themselves likened to the dispossessed—the "wild" natives discovered by Columbus. Paul Stevens describes the rhetoric of holiness that structures colonialist discourses: according to what he terms "Leviticus thinking," the "*quid pro quo . . .* becomes land for sexual purity."[55] English apologists for expansionism appeal to a sense of national holiness to defend the subjugation of supposedly impure peoples.[56] In the great English epic, however, the narrative of loss reflects a conviction that sinful debasement heavily qualifies the commission to possess and to expand. Milton relies on Leviticus thinking but suggests that the link between sexual purity and ownership—central to a monistic landscape—can neither ensure nor fully justify dominion in a fallen world.

The lost vital connection between untainted body and Edenic landscape allows us to trace how Milton broadens his critique of the aristocratic strains of rural verse into a commentary on the logic of expansionism. Paradise is lost because of a struggle over the body of Eve, who is organically linked to the land, and over the territory of Eden, which is often evoked in bodily terms. When Satan first approaches Eden, its "enclosure green" is described as a "rural mound" with "hairy sides." (*PL* 4.133–35). (These lines led C. S. Lewis to remark, "The Freudian idea that the happy garden is an image of the human body would not have frightened Milton in the least.")[57] Satan's ability literally to penetrate this garden/body through the rivers that fertilize it prefigures his ability "to reach / The organs of [Eve's] fancy" (4.801–2) and, later, to enter "into the heart of Eve" with his words (9.550).

The simultaneous contestation over land-as-woman and woman-as-land reminds us that the discourses of nascent empire link territorial rights to reproductive sexuality. Such writings imagine lands as maternal bodies. Columbus, in the account of his third voyage, describes the world as pear-shaped, featuring "something like a woman's nipple."[58] This nipple marks the location of paradise, and the potential for reclaiming it leads Columbus to imagine the lands he has reached as the focus of sexual and infantile longing. As Anne McClintock has remarked, Africa and the Americas became "a porno-tropics for the European imagination—a fantastic magic lantern of the mind onto which Europe projected its forbidden sexual desires and fears." Fears as well as desires, because "if, at first glance, the feminizing of the land appears to be no more than a familiar symptom of male megalomania, it also betrays acute paranoia and a profound, if not pathological sense of male anxiety and boundary loss."[59] Few English writers express the sexual energy of conquest with the disturbing concision of Walter Raleigh, who declares that "Guiana is a countrey that hath yet her maydenhead" (*PN* 10:428). Milton admired Raleigh's writings and, in 1658, published a collection of aphorisms titled *The Cabinet-Council* under the mistaken belief that Raleigh was its author.[60] Milton also includes a quotation from Raleigh's *History of the World* in his commonplace book (under, appropriately enough, the heading "Of Marriage").[61] In *Paradise Lost*, when Adam sees a vision of "yet unspoiled / Guiana," the geographical reference almost certainly contains a recognition of Raleigh's exploits (11.409–10).

The image of the Amazonian targe in book 9 bridges the reproductive concerns of rural verse and of colonialist writings. In the *Discovery of Guiana*, the link between conquest and reproduction is highlighted by Raleigh's curiosity about the Amazons, which leads him to venture into an uncharacteristic digression. At the heart of his description is an account of the Amazons' highly ceremonial mode of procreating, which allows them "to increase their owne sex and kind" (*PN* 10:367). As Louis Montrose remarks, "the conceptual shift from *the land as woman* to *a land of women*" implies "the possibility of representing women as collective social agents."[62] The Amazons represent similar concerns in country house poetry. Marvell relates the history of Appleton House as a convent where "*Suttle Nunns*" tempt Isabella Thwaites to remain a virgin and to reject her betrothal to William Fairfax (stanza 12). One of these nuns invokes the Amazons to describe the joys of a militant virginity: "'Here we, in shining Armour white, / Like *Virgin Amazons* do fight'" (stanza 14). Unlike Raleigh's Amazons, these Catholic Amazons do not reproduce. Like Adam and Eve's "Amazonian targe," this "shining Armour" is designed to deflect the reproductive demands of patriarchal succession. Before Marvell praises the temporary chastity of young Mary Fairfax, he describes the Catholic threat of permanent virginity. Appleton House had originally been a convent, and only William Fairfax's triumph over the nuns allows him to join the Fairfax and Thwaites bloodlines and to establish Appleton as a familial estate.

In Raleigh's *Discovery*, the Amazons successfully maintain an exclusively female domain. They reemerge at the text's conclusion, which makes explicit the ideological link between dynastic succession and expansion abroad. Raleigh again asks Queen Elizabeth to be commissioned with an excursion into Guiana: the Amazons "shall hereby heare the name of a virgin, which is not onely able to defend her owne territories and her neighbours, but also to invade and conquer so great Empires and so farre removed" (*PN* 10:431). Whereas the Amazons maintain possession through ritualized reproduction, Elizabeth's status as the Virgin Queen raises pervasive concerns about succession. Yet Raleigh uses this concern as a final spur to expansion as an alternate form of childbearing. The Virgin Queen will be able "not onely . . . to defend" but also to expand her territories. Despite her ostensible virginity, Elizabeth can trump the Amazons. Raleigh hopes to be the virile agent of such expansion, but events would soon prove him politically impotent. As much as any explorer, Raleigh had cause for male anxiety and a sense of boundary loss while mediating between the Virgin Queen and maiden territory.

In book 8 of *Paradise Lost*, Adam relates to Raphael his struggle to maintain authority over Eve. Although Adam insists that sex is not the primary source of Eve's charm, the description in book 9 of Eve's "virgin majesty" eroticizes her disarmingly regal presence (9.270). Albert Labriola argues provocatively that Milton's (and, quite often, Satan's) descriptions of Eve evoke the imagery of the Elizabethan cult.[63] Eve, like the Virgin Queen, attempts to preserve her sense of sovereignty by resisting the demands of marriage and dynastic reproduction. Even without this specific connection, Satan's fawning address to Eve as "Queen of this universe" contains a kernel of truth about Eve's challenge to and Adam's insecurities within a patriarchal system. Faced with Adam's dilemma, Raphael cannot maintain the egalitarian vitalism expressed in his cosmology. On the contrary, Raphael teaches that Eve is fulfilling her natural role, and that Adam should strive to maintain his sanctioned position of superiority. Adam's struggle with his unruly female counterpart may ultimately confirm that he was created in God's image. This mimetic dilemma can only be half acknowledged: fallen Adam upholds both Milton's theodicy and his own place as the head of mankind by declaring that his wife's fault derives not from God or from nature but from himself. This painful admission may shield Adam from the even more dangerous possibility that his contested status as lordly husband merely reflects that of an entire cosmos in which God labors to become all in all. Any new world arising out of such a universe can never be a stable home, but must remain a domestic space that bears signs of geographical and gendered divisions.

Allusions to both country house poetry and colonialist writings reveal the historical and literary links between Adam's failure to control his other, female self and the loss of Eden. The conjugal narrative of *Paradise Lost* mirrors the suspicious fascination with the female body in such seemingly disparate texts as "To Penshurst" and *The Discovery of Guiana*. Whereas writers like Jonson and Raleigh appeal to the link between reproduction and dominion, Milton associates dynastic structures with the loss of Eden. Through descriptions of Eden as country estate, Near and Far Eastern destination, and New World colony, Milton's narrative works to unsettle both insular myths and expansionist ambitions. *Paradise Lost* integrates political thought within an expansive artistic and theological framework, articulating its cultural commentary poetically, through the interplay between pastoral and epic modes, and prophetically, within a biblical narrative that claims access to the very origins of the world.

3

PARADISE LOST AND THE QUESTION OF IRELAND

> But if it was incumbent on England to force upon Ireland the maintenance
> of the Union for her own sake, and for England's sake . . . it was at any rate
> necessary to England's character that the bride thus bound in a compulsory
> wedlock should be endowed with all the best privileges that a wife can enjoy.
> Let her at least not be a kept mistress. Let it be bone of my bone and flesh of
> my flesh, if we are to live together in the married state.
>
> —Anthony Trollope, *Phineas Finn*

In *Paradise Lost*, questions about the loss of humanity's first homeland converge upon questions about Adam and Eve's unstable union. The
answers offered by the poem must be explored in greater detail, not only
because their psychological density marks the poem as a key moment in
early modernity, but also, as I aim to show in this chapter, because they
open onto a profound political meditation. Adam and Eve fall at different
times and for different reasons. Any question about Eve's motives will invariably lead to what William Kerrigan and Gordon Braden cite as perhaps "the most reflective, even philosophical account of courtship in all of
Renaissance literature,"[1] the account of her first waking experience:

> As I bent down to look, just opposite,
> A shape within the watery gleam appeared

Bending to look on me, I started back,
It started back, but pleased I soon returned,
Pleased it returned as soon with answering looks
Of sympathy and love; there I had fixed
Mine eyes till now, and pined with vain desire,
Had not a voice thus warned me, What thou seest,
What there thou seest fair creature is thyself,
With thee it came and goes: but follow me,
And I will bring thee where no shadow stays
Thy coming.

(4.460–71)

In the *Metamorphoses*, the Ovidian speaker interrupts the story of Narcissus to warn the protagonist. The poet declares the reflection a mere shadow (*umbra*) in which nothing of Narcissus genuinely inheres ("nil habet ista sui").[2] In Milton's adaptation, by contrast, the disembodied voice reinforces Eve's imaginary identification, affirming that what she sees *is* her very self. Eve's self is thus divided and doubled: "With thee it came and goes." The incongruity between the past-tense "came" and the present-tense "goes" suggests that the spatial division between Eve and her reflected self becomes a temporal one. Line breaks stress the split between action and reaction: "I started back, / It started back"; "I soon returned, / Pleased it returned as soon." Eve's adverbial phrase "as soon" attempts to describe simultaneity, but her narration undermines itself. It is impossible to capture simultaneity in language, and the image that *is* Eve's self is doomed to be belated, its action deferred.

The possibility of visual signification tantalizes the human reader, who will learn from the angel Raphael the incompatibility between the immediate acts of God, "more swift / Than time or motion," and the "process of speech" required for human comprehension (*PL* 7.177–78). But whether or not Eve's actual experience with her own image was marked by a temporal lag is impossible to ascertain fully, for the lesson of the disembodied voice is also Eve's entrance into language. Eve must thus assume what psychoanalytic thought describes as the split between the subject of enunciation and the subject of the statement.[3] Yet as I argued in the previous chapter, the breakdown of vision and the necessity of mediated knowledge become for Milton the possibility of faith in things unseen. By rewriting the Narcissus episode, Milton takes up Ovid's assertions of the superiority of verbal over visual or plastic arts.[4] Narcissus's fatally flawed vision serves as the first confirmation of the powers of Tiresias, who has received in recompense for his blindness the truth of prophecy.

Milton, a self-styled Christian Tiresias, redeems language from the temptations of sight. The goal of mediated knowledge turns out to be love. The warning voice teaches Eve to turn away from herself and to avoid temporal splitting by uniting with Adam in a union "where no shadow stays / Thy coming." (The relevance of the temporal sense of "stays" as "delays" is highlighted by yet another meaningful line break.) Only then can she become "our general mother." Though initially unwilling, Eve internalizes this lesson, condemning her previous actions as a display of "vain desire." Yet marriage is a dubious solution to the split between a present-tense self and a deferred self. Seamless union with Adam relegates Eve to the condition of permanent belatedness. "But I suffer not a woman to teach, nor to usurp authority over the man, but to be in silence," the first epistle to Timothy teaches, "For Adam was first formed, then Eve" (1 Tim. 2:12–13). Marriage confirms that Eve is in fact "after made / Occasionally" for Adam's satisfaction (*PL* 8.555–56).

Adam's marriage manifests the contradictions of the Miltonic cosmos at a personal level. Eve has a different experience of love as a dilemma, one that arises not from an unruly partner but from an innate desire to identify herself. She is initially taught to identify with her own image, but only so that she can assume her proper role as the image of another. This story enacts a patriarchal fantasy of the woman as a blank slate receiving language and self-knowledge—her name and her maternal destiny—by uniting with her husband. Yet fantasies reveal the anxieties that produce them, and Eve's narrative bears witness to a conviction that she is "in herself complete," potentially happier without either marriage or language (*PL* 8.548). The separation scene in book 9 represents Eve's attempt to escape from the belatedness she suffers in marriage. Adam's response to Eve's request for separation is revealing: "O woman, best are all things as the will / Of God ordained them, his creating hand / Nothing imperfect or deficient left / Of all that he created, much less man" (9.343–46). Adam conveniently omits his own profound sense of deficiency, but his early experiences help to explain his fear that Eve is growing weary of his company: "Go; for thy stay, not free, absents thee more" (9.372).What matters more than the propriety or impropriety of Adam's capitulation is the re-emergence of the word "stay," the word that plays an important part in Eve's scene at the pool. When fallen Eve decides to return to her husband, her first words are "Hast thou not wondered, Adam, at my stay?" (9.856). By falling, Eve activates within marriage the "stay"—absence and temporal splitting—that was within her from the beginning, and the shadow of mortality falls upon her.

The irony of the Fall lies in the fact that Eve performs her belatedness precisely by attempting to supersede it. The biblical account suggests the epistemological temptation as a visual one: "For God doth know that in the day ye eat thereof, then your eyes shall be opened, and ye shall be as gods, knowing good and evil" (Gen. 3:5). One of Milton's major additions to the Genesis account is connecting this epistemological/visual motif with Eve's account of her primary narcissism. When the poet tells us "Fixed on the fruit she gazed" (*PL* 9.735), he echoes Eve's narration of the reflecting pool: "there I had fixed / Mine eyes till now." The fruit appeals to Eve as an alternate reflection, a way of bypassing temporally split language with recourse to immediate knowledge ("then your eyes shall be opened, and ye shall be as gods") and a way of overcoming her own status as a secondary addition. The unspeakable desire to see and know proves to be a fully satanic temptation. After eating the fruit, Eve suffers a different sort of temporal dilemma. By offering obeisance and "low reverence" to a tree, she regresses into what Protestant iconoclasm would deem primitive idolatry (9.835).[5]

In this chapter I read Eve's belatedness and the story of her uneasy union with Adam as condensing complex thinking about the contradictions of colonialist power, which proves at once ineffective, undeserved, and yet sanctioned by God. Theorists of nation and empire have alerted us to the political significance of temporality within language.[6] In *Paradise Lost*, the temporal disjunction at the heart of Adam and Eve's marriage cannot be suppressed, and ultimately reveals forms of barbarism as being not only foreign intrusions but also native possibilities in Eden. Through the motif of belatedness both prompting and fracturing unity, Milton's conjugal narrative speaks to his conflicted thought about Anglo-Irish relations, and about what this history reveals about the English as much as about the unruly Irish. Raphael teaches Adam to maintain his superiority out of the belief that Narcissus-like Eve will eventually yield her shows to manly

realities. The advice, then, is to foster a sense of divinely sanctioned superiority by insisting on it precisely when it feels most undeserved. Adam's
embattled masculinity is of a piece with Milton's political thinking, which,
in the words of Linda Gregerson, locates "the modern nation as a back-
formation, part of the retroactive logic of empire."[7] A sense of national
ascendancy both acknowledges and suppresses the fact that it is defined at
the embattled borders.[8] The story of Adam and Eve's union crystallizes in
a personal register the experience of an intimately familiar menace, of suppressed internal potential that arrives as a second self.

Reading *Paradise Lost* in the light of Anglo-Irish politics will be at times
a willful practice, inquiring into ideas and implications that Milton may
prefer to conceal. I excavate a political allegory that exists only as a latent,
fragmentary possibility within the epic poem. Milton's late writings es-
chew the troubling questions about nationhood, sovereignty, and cultural
ascendancy that the Irish context continues to raise after the Restoration.
On the one hand, his inability to reconcile his critique of unjust force with
his ingrained suspicion of the Irish and of Catholicism creates a notewor-
thy silence. On the other hand, *Paradise Lost* does offer the reader genuine
clues about an altered understanding of the relationship between England
and Ireland. The most explicit hint lies in the Nimrod episode of book 12,
which describes one consequence of Nimrod's "dominion undeserved" as
"the hubbub strange" (12.60); the word "hubbub" carries a profound implication that England's role in Ireland has taken part in the paradoxically
tyrannical but necessary mode of postlapsarian dominion.

After first tracing the implications of the Irish hubbub, I return to the
central human narrative of *Paradise Lost*. Matters raised by Anglo-Irish relations serve to answer questions about the instability of Eden. Of particular importance is the way *Paradise Lost* relates to a body of writings about
Ireland that deploys two related tropes: Ireland as a potential paradise that
has been spoiled, and Ireland as a woman, either treacherously seductive
or humbled and fertile. By situating *Paradise Lost* within a long history of
representing Anglo-Irish affairs—spanning from the medieval period to
the very end of the seventeenth century—I show how the epic takes part
in a fraught conversation that would continue to evolve after its composition. Milton's conjugal narrative describes how reconciliation can occur
after betrayal and moral failure. The end of *Paradise Lost* presents Eve as
an erstwhile rebel who renounces her former deeds. She directs Adam out

of despair and toward divine favor by prostrating herself humbly. Only by volunteering to take more than her share of blame does Eve guide her husband out of his suicidal despair. Indulging in a fantasy that is at once masculinist and political, Milton depicts a penitent temptress who is willing to debase herself and to seek mercy. Such a trajectory offers little practical insight about the contestations in and about post-Restoration Ireland. Yet even as a fantasy, the narrative of Adam and Eve's union, Fall, and reconciliation registers an urgent need for a politics of grace that would replace lapsed dominion with mutual cooperation.

The Hubbub Strange

Milton's anti-Irish sentiments had deep roots in his religious, political, and literary thinking. In his commonplace book, Milton records his knowledge of Edmund Spenser's *View of the State of Ireland*: "The wicked policies of divers deputies & governours in Ireland see Spenser dialogue of Ireland" (*CPW* 1:465).[9] Like Spenser, Milton had insisted on England's God-given right and duty to impose civility upon the Irish. It is unsurprising that Milton's second *Defense* (1651) praises Cromwell for breaking "the power of Hibernia" when "all Ireland was lost" (*CPW* 4:670). After the Restoration, however, Milton would have a profoundly different sense of England's cultural mandate. The English had, in Milton's eyes, proved themselves unfit for spiritual and political reform.[10] It would seem that such momentous developments would have altered Milton's thoughts about Ireland. Yet his later work says very little about the topic, and Milton certainly never seems to abandon his suspicions of Irish backwardness. *The Ready and Easy Way*, published on the brink of the Restoration, mentions the "*Irish* massacre" to repeat the old argument that Charles I had fomented rebellion (*CPW* 7:410).[11] This utterance serves less to suggest fresh thinking than to reiterate allegiances.

By the 1660s, there were reasons for Milton to seem less concerned about the Irish. Ireland was more firmly in subjection to England than before. Cromwell's settler-soldiers had largely supplanted the Old English, many of whom remained disenfranchised after the 1662 Act of Settlement and the 1665 Act of Explanation. Yet in part owing to this very fact, the political climate in Ireland was far from settled. Grievances over landownership, bitter accusations in print, and sectarian rifts continued to proliferate. In a pamphlet battle with the Franciscan Peter Walsh, Roger Boyle, Earl of Orrery, denounces Old English Catholics and declares the need to "rub up" the memories of the 1641 uprising against English Protestants.[12] He goes on to enumerate old grievances against Irish Catholics but strains against a fact that his opponent emphasizes: Irish Catholics had loyally fought against the regicides. Orrery's rhetoric is in part a defensive reaction to his own assailable actions. Orrery had appealed to Parliament for assistance during the Civil War and had fought on Cromwell's side in Ireland.[13]

The year 1641 remained a cynosure of Protestant identity in Ireland well into the 1670s and 1680s. Especially telling is the publication history of Sir John Temple's 1646 treatise *The Irish Rebellion,* which advances the popular interpretation of the Confederate Wars as the result of an insidious Catholic conspiracy. After the Restoration, the Duke of Ormond had blocked its republication. In London, however, *The Irish Rebellion* was reprinted on multiple occasions in the 1670s. Charles II, whose Irish agenda was at least officially one of reconciliation, lamented that Temple's work "already has done much harm by increasing the present animosity betwixt the English and the Irish with old ones. Sure there needeth not much pains to make men remember that which all the addresses of the government hath not as yet been able to make men forget."[14] In a climate of "present animosity," silence is not always a sign of forgetfulness. In 1677 Orrery addressed *A Treatise on the Art of War* to Charles II, encouraging the king to pursue continental war. Despite Orrery's military experience, *A Treatise* excises any mention of Ireland and the author's previous service to Cromwell. Although, as Deana Rankin puts it, "Ireland remains only a shadowy presence" in the *Treatise,* Orrery "remained haunted by the ghosts—and the lessons—of his own semi-legitimate Irish experience."[15]

Milton had not been actively involved in Irish affairs, nor were his personal fortunes at stake in the struggle over property in Ireland.[16] Yet given the strident attitudes toward Ireland expressed in Milton's earlier work, the relative lack of reference to the Irish in his post-Restoration writings might represent a meaningful silence, one that points to the painful lessons that he could not fully articulate. Milton briefly but powerfully gestures toward such lessons in book 12 of *Paradise Lost.* For early modern English writers, seemingly arcane speculations about Nimrod's identity staged pressing debates about the nature and origins of sovereignty. In Milton's account, the story of Nimrod underscores the dilemma of political authority: in a fallen world, sovereignty must begin with wrongful conquest and its dire consequences. Upon seeing the proud attempt of Nimrod and his minions to reach Heaven, God "in derision sets / Upon their tongues a various spirit to raze / Quite out their native language, and instead / To sow a jangling noise of words unknown" (12.52–55). The result, which prompts "great laughter" in heaven, is "the hubbub strange." "Hubbub" is a rare word in the Miltonic lexicon, occurring nowhere in his prose and only twice in his poetry. The word certainly alludes to Ireland, especially in the context of a story about linguistic confusion. Spenser describes the hubbub in his *View* as "a terrible yell as if heaven and earth would have gone together."[17] This savage custom links the Irish to the Scythians in their challenge to civility.[18] Barnabe Rich devotes an entire tract to the hubbub. According to Rich, the hubbub had originally been used as an alarm, "that when any Rebels or Theeues came to doe any robbery in the Countrey, they should then raise the Crie (which they call the *Hubbub*) therby to giue notice to the Inhabitants." The hubbub, however, has come to be used "upon other sleight occasions. If a couple of drunkards doe chance to fall together by the eares. If a man being drunk . . . doth fortune to strike his wife."[19] The hubbub has thus become almost meaningless, not unlike Milton's "jangling noise of words unknown."

Spenser's writings make conspicuous the impossibility of maintaining cultural boundaries in the name of English ascendancy. As David J. Baker argues, the *View* both conceals and reveals the inefficacy of English law in Ireland, but failure only serves to call for an ever more forceful English intervention.[20] Rich's treatise bears further witness to the failures of linguistic nationalism, the project to impose English culture and language upon Ireland.[21] Writing in Dublin in 1618, Rich is keenly aware of the English colonists' inability to suppress cultural crossbreeding. The title of his tract reveals that the Irish custom is a variant of a familiar English practice: *The Irish Hubbub, or, The English Hue and Crie*. Rich performs the condition of cultural contamination when he declares in his dedication that he has "borrowed an Irish mantle" (the piece of native clothing that Spenser denounces as dangerous and savage).[22] Rich explains that he will not only describe but also deploy the Irish hubbub: "The *Irish* have wit and discretion, both to weep when they list, and to laugh at their pleasure. And I am glad

of it: for I will make a little bold to borrow some of their agilitie." Laugh-
ing ironically and "giving the hubbub" become appropriate responses to a
world in which corruption, vice, and popery go unchecked. The hubbub
is a travesty, but it is thus perfectly suited to the deplorable conditions of
Anglo-Irish culture. Rich raises the hubbub at English vices as much as at
those of the Irish. Late in the treatise he declares that the Irish are predis-
posed to sin but also learn from the "ill example of the *English*."[23] Rich's
chief response is not didactic but almost gleefully derisive. He repeatedly
invokes a dark laughter that functions like God's laughter in Milton's account of Babel: the scornful response distances the viewing subject from a
world gone awry.

In *Paradise Lost*, Nimrod's ambition threatens to introduce forms of
debasement reminiscent of chaos into a world temporarily cleansed by the
Flood. Nimrod starts his project to reach heaven in "the plain, wherein
a black bituminous gurge / Boils out from underground, the mouth of
hell; / Of brick, and of that stuff they cast to build / A city and tower"
(12.41–44). By tracing this gurge that erupts from the earth to hellish origins, the angel Michael invites a comparison between earthly and hellish construction projects. Whereas the devils find ribs of gold under the
surface of Hell and erect Pandaemonium, Nimrod makes use of stickier,
filthier stuff.[24] Bitumen may not be identical with the tartareous dregs of
chaos, yet its effects are described as specifically chaotic. Michael calls the
unfinished Tower of Babel a work of "Confusion," recalling God's primordial confrontation with chaos both in *Paradise Lost* ("Confusion heard
his voice" [3.710]) and in *De Doctrina* ("a confused and disordered state"
[*CPW* 6:308]). Adam, having witnessed Eden groan and tremble after his
and Eve's act of sinful eating, intuits the gustatory logic of the abject matter that undermines creation. After declaring Nimrod an "execrable son,"
Adam asks,

> What food
> Will he convey up thither to sustain
> Himself and his rash army, where thin air
> Above the clouds will pine his entrails gross,
> And famish him of breath, if not of bread?

(12.64, 74–78)

Michael politely ignores this peculiar question. Yet Adam is perceptive in imagining Nimrod's body as the site of abjection. Respiration (and, by implication, spirit) and digestion blur into each other as lack of breath and bread corrupts the body at the moment of its transgression.

Adam imagines the confusion that Michael describes as bodily corruption, but the chaos ensuing from Babel attaches not to the entrails but to language and meaning. Milton's description of the "jangling noise" emanating from Babel anticipates his condemnation of rhyme as a "jingling sound." Nimrod introduces into the world wretched matter that results in debased speech. For early modern English writers, the association of Babel, Nimrod, and Ireland serves to explain the murky origins of the island's turmoil. Edmund Campion argues in his *History of Ireland* that one of the languages arising from the fall of Babel must have been imported into Ireland because the island "was inhabited within one yeare after the devision of the tongues."[25] Later, Campion describes Bastolenus, one of Japheth's progeny, traveling westward after being inspired by Nimrod's success at expansion. A more concrete connection between Nimrod and Ireland obtains: "Together with *Bastolenus*, arrived in Ireland certain godlesse people of the stocke of *Nemrod*."[26] These descendants of Nimrod "began to kicke at their Governours, and taking head, set up a King of their owne faction. . . & every day bred a new skirmish" until "the lawfull Kings prevayled, the miscreants done to death."[27] Meredith Hanmer's *Chronicle of Ireland* describes the island as populated first by the descendents of Japheth, with the "cursed seed of *Cham*" arriving later. Following "the example of *Cham* or *Zoroastres* the Magician, and *Nimrod* grandfather to *Ninus*," the children of Cham resist "lawfull rule and dominion" and start a pattern of strife.[28]

In *Foras Feasa ar Éirinn* (*The History of Ireland*), Seathrún Céitinn (Geoffrey Keating) presents a more tenuous but felicitous connection between Ireland, Nimrod, and the Tower of Babel. He relates how the legendary Scythian king Feinius Farsaidh (Fenius Farsa) tries to recover the *lingua humana* that had existed until "Nimrod and his kinsfolk were building the tower" and "the confusion of tongues set in."[29] Fenius Farsa travels to Shinar, commissions linguistic scholars, and eventually appoints Gaedheal, son of Eathor, to regulate the Gaelic language and divide it into five dialects. The Gaelic tongue, according to Keating, takes its name from Gaedheal, whose own name may mean "all noble," "great," or "lover of wisdom." For Campion and Hanmer, contemporary Irish affairs testify to Nimrod-like rebellion that must continue to be suppressed. For Keating, the Gaelic language is established in an effort to mend the cultural divisions produced in the wake of Nimrod's prideful actions; Keating's choice to compose Ireland's history in Gaelic thus takes on an even greater resonance.

For Milton and his contemporaries, Nimrod's story reveals how the origins of multiple tongues in the world are linked to the birth of sovereignty. The Irish shadow that falls upon Milton's description of Babel leads us to reexamine the political message of the entire Nimrod episode. The angel Michael proleptically describes Nimrod as one

> Of proud ambitious heart, who not content
> With fair equality, fraternal state,
> Will arrogate dominion undeserved
> Over his brethren, and quite dispossess
> Concord and law of nature from the earth.

> (*PL* 12.25–29)

Milton relies on a long exegetical tradition that had described Nimrod as the world's first king and tyrant.[30] In the *Antiquities*, Josephus declares that Nimrod had become a tyrant in contempt of divine authority; indeed, in arrogating divine authority to himself, Nimrod had also become an idolater. Following suit, Augustine interprets the description of Nimrod in Genesis as a "mighty hunter before the Lord" to mean a mighty hunter of men against (*contra*) the Lord. On this point, *Paradise Lost* equivocates: "A mighty hunter thence he shall be styled / *Before* the Lord, as in despite of Heaven, / Or from heaven claiming second sovereignty" (12.33–35, emphasis added). About Nimrod's unjust ambition and his "empire tyrannous," however, Milton is unambiguous. Even without being specifically against the Lord, Nimrod proves an execrable tyrant who tries to usurp divine forms of authority.

Elizabeth Sauer has examined the ways in which Milton's description of Nimrod registers a complaint with the restored monarchy and also with the failures of the Commonwealth.[31] Milton perceives in post-Restoration England both political and linguistic dissonance. The implications of

Nimrod's eventual punishment—the "hubbub strange"—sharpen Milton's commentary about intertwined developments in domestic and colonial affairs. Michael's description of Nimrod advances not only an antimonarchical but also an anti-imperial position. Nimrod tyrannizes after he conquers peoples. The description of Nimrod in Genesis makes such a claim plausible: "And the beginning of his kingdom was Babel, and Erech, and Accad, and Calneh, in the land of Shinar" (Gen. 10:10). In book 4 of *The Faerie Queene*, "the name of *Nimrod* strong" is memorialized next to that of "*Alexander*, and his Princes fiue" on the walls of Ate's infernal home (*FQ* 4.1.22). Like Spenser, Milton describes Nimrod as an emperor whose ambition spreads discord. Confusion and hubbub serve as fitting punishments for Nimrod's pride. Given the origins of the word "hubbub," this is provocative. Milton's earlier prose had rehearsed the familiar claim that the debasement of the Irish called for their subjugation. In *Paradise Lost*, however, "the hubbub strange" is the appropriate result of (not the justification for) conquest: before Nimrod, piety, peace, and linguistic unity characterized the postdiluvian world.

The double bind of necessary but undeserved subjugation applies not only to individuals but also to entire nations that

> will decline so low
> From virtue, which is reason, that no wrong,
> But justice, and some fatal curse annexed
> Deprives them of their outward liberty,
> Their inward lost.

(*PL* 12.97–101)

This resembles the logic that Milton and other English writers had used to inveigh against the backward Irish. Here, however, Michael's pronouncement falls squarely upon the English, who have proved themselves unfit for liberty. When writers such as Campion contrast the rule of Japheth's progeny to the seditiousness of the sons of Cham, they suggest that from the very start, the distinction between rightful authority and rebellion had been ordained by God. Michael's lesson, by contrast, shows that rulers are as culpable in God's eyes as the conquered. The angel cites the "fatal curse" of Cham and "the shame / Done to his father" (12.102–3) as an example of a people who deserve tyrannical oppression. Milton seems to reiterate the long-standing view of Ham's African descendants as cursed. Yet Michael has just finished describing Cham's grandson Nimrod as the original tyrant. Michael teaches that the curse of political oppression falls upon the oppressor and his seed.

Earlier writings about Nimrod had revealed the difficulties involved in thinking about his identity as a fable of sovereignty. In *Polimanteia* (1595), William Covell, *pace* Augustine, describes Nimrod as a strong hunter *of* the Lord. Even as Covell denies that Nimrod is a tyrant, however, he refers to Nimrod's actions as tyrannical. Covell surmises "that Common wealths had their beginnings by violent Tyrannies, & that *Nimrod* by force & violence obtained the soveraigntie. Notwithsta[n]ding we find in scripture, that he was a most heroicall King and no Tyrant: (howsoever some do intend otherwise) because that by his means was established the forme of a Common wealth."[32] "Notwithstanding" registers the paradox of the heroic and divinely sanctioned establishment of commonwealths deriving from tyrannical force. Covell continues with an uneasy, partial defense of tyranny, which serves a role in the providential plan to establish laws and sovereignty.

Walter Raleigh writes of Nimrod with less ambivalence in *The Historie of the World*. Raleigh does not describe Nimrod's acts as even potentially tyrannical. On the contrary, his Nimrod establishes political sovereignty through the just acts of exploring and settling postdiluvian *terra nullius:* "This charge was rather given him, than by him usurped."[33] Raleigh suggests how expansion and sovereignty—the two senses of "empire"—are inextricably linked. He makes an especially telling statement in the course of arguing that Ninus, Belus, and Nimrod were three distinct persons. This argument encounters a problem: Augustine declares that Belus first governed in Nineveh for sixty-five years. Genesis, according to Raleigh's explication, designates Nimrod as "the establisher of that Empire."[34] Are we then to conclude that Augustine identifies Belus as Nimrod? Raleigh thinks not, and he makes a distinction between Nimrod's establishment of the Babylonian empire and Belus's first rule over it. He clarifies his point by drawing an analogy: "For although *Iulius Caesar* overthrew the liberty of the *Romane* Commonwealth, making himselfe perpetuall *Dictator*, yet *Augustus* was the first established Emperor." Nimrod "first brake the rule of Eldership and Paternitie, laying the foundation of sovereign Rule, as

Caesar did; and yet *Belus* was the first, who peaceably, and with a generall allowance exercised such a power."[35] From a republican standpoint, this is a troubling story about the origins of sovereignty, which is established and then practiced on the ruins of the republic.

In the 1640s and 1650s Milton had maintained an optimistic account of the origins of sovereignty. The *First Defense* describes how "even at the very beginning of nations the paternal and hereditary power had given place to strength of character, and soon afterwards to the rights of the people. This is the source, justification, and true natural cause of royal power." Contrary to Raleigh and Covell, Milton does not locate Nimrod's tyranny at the transition from paternal to political rule. Rather, the origins of monarchy are described as being compatible with republican meritocracy. Milton accuses Salmasius of confusing legitimate kingly power with Nimrod's brand of tyranny: "Perhaps you are thinking of Nimrod, who is said to have been the first tyrant" (*CPW* 4.1:472–73). *Paradise Lost*, however, articulates a darker view not only of monarchy but also of sovereignty in general. Michael agrees with Adam that Nimrod assumes over his brethren "authority usurped, from God not given" (12.66), but he also explains that in a fallen world, "tyranny must be / Though to the tyrant thereby no excuse" (12.95–96). This is the most succinct formulation of the crisis of power in Milton's later writings. As Annabel Patterson observes, "Milton invests his clearest statement of political theory in precisely those figures, differently deployed, on whom the apologists for monarchy relied." Patterson argues that the Nimrod episode in *Paradise Lost* functions more coherently as a theory of conquest than strictly as one of tyranny.[36] In Milton's account, in fact, the differences between republican and monarchist depictions of Nimrod tend to contract in surprising ways. Michael, like Covell and Raleigh (or even like the Salmasius whom Milton impugns), describes sovereignty as necessarily originating in Nimrod's violation of republican ideals and the law of nature.[37]

Milton's description of Nimrod functions as a complaint against Caroline monarchy, as a warning against the consequences of conquest, and as a lesson about the inevitability of tyranny. These registers seem complementary. After the Restoration, Royalists invoked the name of Nimrod to deride Cromwell as a usurper and tyrant. Thomas Shipman, in "The Restauration and Welcome. 1660" (published in *Carolina, or, Loyal Poems*), calls Cromwell "that *bloody Rebell*" and refers to the remnants of the Cause as "those *Blood-hounds* which the *Nimrod-Cromwel* bred."[38] Milton's description of Nimrod turns the tables on this kind of Royalist rhetoric: the tyrant derives his own name from rebellion, "though of rebellion others he accuse" (*PL* 12.37). Thomas Newton's gloss on this line seems sensible enough: "This was added by our author probably not without a view to his own time, when himself, and those of his party were stigmatiz'd as the worst of rebels."[39] The Irish undertones of the Nimrod episode tend to confirm its antimonarchical complaint by alluding to Milton's claim in *Eikonoklastes* that Charles I had covertly encouraged the Irish rebels. As *The Ready and Easy Way* reminds us, Milton had already declared that the king himself had been the true rebel.

For reasons of censorship, the name of Charles cannot be uttered. Michael, however, also painstakingly avoids the names of Babel and of Nimrod. Instead of the tyrant's name, the angel gives an etymological clue; exegetes had incorrectly speculated that Nimrod's name derived from *mârad*, "to rebel." Michael's speech actively emphasizes an indeterminacy regarding the identity of this rebel against God and nature: the reader must fill in the blanks. If we were to insist on identifying Nimrod with a contemporary figure, Cromwell serves as suitably as Charles. Milton anticipates a Nimrod-Cromwell comparison when, in *The Ready and Easy Way*, he frets about how Royalists will mock the unfinished "tower of a Commonwealth" (*CPW* 7:423). The image seems to be borrowed from the parable of the unwise builder, but Milton's imagined antagonist then compares the Commonwealth to the Tower of Babel. Yet Royalists were joined by radical republicans in opposing Cromwell and calling him a Nimrod. As David Loewenstein reminds us, John Lilburne had done so as early as 1649, after Cromwell's suppression of the Levellers at Burford.[40] We are well aware of the fears of tyranny harbored by republicans after Cromwell became Lord Protector. As Cromwell's seventeenth-century biographer (who is far less radical than Lilburne and makes clear his allegiance to the Cause) asks, "Nothing could satisfie *Caesars* Ambition, but a perpetual Dictatorship; nor *Alexander's*, but to have more worlds to conquer; and why then should our *Cromwel*, having the same aspiration . . . be satisfied with less then a perpetual Protectorship?"[41] In book 12 of *Paradise Lost*, Cromwell's betrayal of republican values may roughly correspond to Nimrod's despoliation of "fair equality, fraternal state."

Identifying literary characters with contemporary personages—what early moderns called "application"—is surely a crude interpretive device. Yet deploying this mode heuristically highlights how the rhetorical force of the lines "And from rebellion shall derive his name, / Though of rebellion others he accuse" exceeds the occasion of straightforward antimonarchical complaint. These lines acknowledge that those who accuse others of rebellion might be lying or deluded in God's eyes. Such an admission does not merely turn the tables on Royalists but may also cut close to Milton's allegiances.

The latent relevance of Anglo-Irish politics underscores the problems of legitimacy. Cromwell and his supporters had certainly relied heavily on accusing others of rebellion. The Commonwealth had consolidated its political strength in part through Cromwell's incursions in Ireland and by justifying this action as a divinely sanctioned punishment of Irish rebels. After the Restoration, the renewed debate about Ireland revealed that the question of who the actual rebels were had not lost its currency. Cromwell had done little to establish lasting concord, despite his claim—after the siege of Drogheda—that his actions would prevent the effusion of blood for the future. Back at home, the eventual failures of the Commonwealth would produce political faction and confusion. As Sauer shows, Milton's representations of multiple voices and linguistic disunity correspond to the political tumult that marked the end of the Commonwealth and the Restoration period. England, too, would prove full of the hubbub strange.

All of this remains half-spoken. The Nimrod episode does not provide conclusive evidence for Milton's later views about Cromwell. The opening vignette of book 12 keeps open as interpretive possibilities antimonarchical complaint and critique of the Cromwellian agenda. Milton could not openly publish his antimonarchical opinions, nor would he ever offer an explicit and unequivocal recantation of Cromwell. Yet this very open-endedness conveys a powerful lesson. Milton's description of Nimrod and its tacit allusion to the Irish situation locate the basis of all sovereignty in unjust conquest, which must be in a fallen world. Left to its own devices, human action can only produce what *Paradise Lost* describes as a hellish phenomenon: "a universal hubbub wild / Of stunning sounds and voices confused" (2.951–52). When strife becomes all-encompassing, language turns into a hideous gabble that imperils the most basic distinctions—between Cromwell and Charles, between lord and rebel.

Natives, and Not Forreigners

Before we return to Milton's Eden, it will be useful to establish some relevant questions by examining a moment in Milton's last prose work, *Of True Religion* (1673). This treatise responds to the debates surrounding Charles II's 1672 Declaration of Indulgence, which had repealed penalties against Nonconformists, thus acknowledging the inefficacy of imposing religious uniformity. *Of True Religion* extols toleration among Protestants, echoing the convictions voiced in *Areopagitica* that a plurality of voices facilitates the search for truth. Yet Milton excoriates the stipulation of Charles's declaration that had also been offensive to the Cavalier Parliament: the toleration of private Roman Catholic worship. Milton argues that Catholicism is dangerous to the state; even though *Of True Religion* repeatedly appeals to the individual conscience as the best defense against "popery," it calls for state intervention in the case of Catholicism.

In the course of making this argument, however, Milton makes a potentially revealing qualification: "Having shown thus, that Popery, as being Idolatrous, is not to be tolerated either in Public or in Private; it must be now thought how to remove it and hinder the growth thereof, *I mean in our Natives, and not Forreigners*, Privileg'd by the Law of Nations" (*CPW* 8:431, emphasis added). Elizabeth Sauer argues that this concession to international law is a minor one as she emphasizes how anti-Catholicism shapes the Protestant toleration that Milton characterizes as definitively English.[42] The actual number of non-Protestant foreigners in England protected by the law of nations (merchants or ambassadors, for instance) may have been relatively insignificant, but the distinction between natives and foreigners signals key questions. The parliamentary debates about the Declaration of Indulgence had touched upon such weighty issues as the limits of monarchical sovereignty, but they had opened with the contention that "the end of this declaration was to invite people into the nation . . . [W]e want people, and this will bring them in."[43] Sir John Vaughan had objected to the declaration on the grounds of the "dispensation with Merchant-strangers . . . by law of nations," fearing that "all sorts and manners of people are dispensed with by this Declaration, Turks, Jews, &c."[44] In Vaughan's slippery-slope argument, the status of Turks and Jews lies halfway between that of actual foreigners and well-worn tropes for cultural backsliding. Milton's earlier writings had repeatedly warned that cultural and political debasement would cause the English to be no better than Turks and Jews. In *Of True Religion*, however, Milton is willing to concede that foreigners protected under international law should be able to practice Roman Catholicism in England with impunity. Milton's call for inner regeneration in his last prose work does not appeal to the xenophobia that characterizes his earlier arguments.

Milton's brief concession to international law in *Of True Religion* gestures obliquely toward larger questions that the text does not address: Who counts as a native? Who counts as a foreigner? For generations, the conditions in Ireland had been the staging ground for such questions. A decade before Charles II invited "strangers in this conjuncture to come live under us" in the Declaration of Indulgence, the Irish Parliament had passed an Act for Encouraging Protestant-Strangers and Others, to Inhabit and Plant in the Kingdom of Ireland. Responding to economic and political necessity, the act (introduced by Ormond) decrees that foreigners who take Oaths of Allegiance and Supremacy will become "to all Intents, Constructions, and Purposes, Your Majesties natural and liege subjects of this Kingdom."[45] Although the act aims to attract such Protestant groups as the Huguenots, its full title accommodates concerns that even non-Protestant "Others" might covertly settle in Ireland.[46]

Ireland tests the conceptual limits between kingdom and colony. In *Of Reformation*, Milton describes England and Scotland as "dearest Brothers both in *Nature*, and in CHRIST," but calls Ireland "our free Denizon upon the back of us both" (*CPW* 1:596). As a nation of Catholics, Ireland cannot attain the status of Christian brother, but only of denizen, "a foreigner admitted to residence and certain rights in a country."[47] Historians continue to debate the accuracy of descriptions of Ireland as "kingdom," "colony," or "marcher region."[48] Such debates would not strike early modern writers as unfamiliar. Blood ties had become tenuous as the Anglo-Norman Old English lapsed into Irish customs. Many readers have noted that Elizabethan English writers such as Spenser denounce the Old English as being more dangerous and barbarous than the Gaelic Irish. The web of local and national political allegiances, sectarian rifts, and differences of custom and language complicate any simple dichotomy of Irish and English. The aftermath of Cromwell's Irish campaigns and the attempts to restore equilibrium after the Restoration would only intensify questions of cultural and national origins. As we have seen, debates about how to redistribute expropriated lands stirred up vitriolic memories of past bloodshed.

The topic of Ireland seems far removed from Milton's brief concession to the law of nations. Yet the distinction between natives and foreigners points to broader questions about the rights and status of the populations in Ireland, which fit neatly under neither category. Such questions, in turn, generate vexing problems for models of national sovereignty and autonomy. Spenser's *View of the State of Ireland* registers the problems of international law raised by the Irish context. Eudoxus recalls that Lord Grey de Wilton had been accused of excessive cruelty against both the Irish and the Spanish. Irenius defends Grey's actions, denying the applicability of "either custome of Warre, or law of nations" in this case. The Spanish, Irenius argues, were mercenaries without commission from the pope or a king, and "the Irish themselves . . . were no lawfull Enemies; but rebels and traytours, and therefore they that came to succour them, no better then rogues and runnagates."[49] The use of categories like "rebels" and "traitors" allows Irenius to deny Ireland any measure of autonomy and legal protection.[50]

At the end of the seventeenth century, William Molyneux would appeal to the law of nations to argue for a degree of Irish autonomy from acts of English Parliament. He argues that one nation cannot justly levy force against another for economic advantage. Molyneux anticipates the objections that Ireland is not a foreign nation but a colony. He responds not only by contrasting England's treatment of Scotland with that of Ireland, but also by declaring that Ireland is "a *Compleat Kingdom* within it self," as evinced by its constitution.[51] After a rhetorically heightened passage appealing to natural law and the equality of mankind, Molyneux returns to the law of nations as a support for his case, citing the writings of Hugo Grotius, Samuel von Puffendorf, and John Locke. Arguments like Molyneux's reveal how the topic of international law leads to long-standing questions about the relative status and freedoms of the Irish peoples. These questions in turn reveal how, for centuries, interactions between the English and Irish laid bare the instability of cultural, sectarian, and national identities.

In *Of True Religion*, Milton must avoid such problems to advance his political cause. Only by pushing Ireland and the concomitant questions about native origins and citizenship to the margins can he create the space to articulate his position about English religious freedom. Milton does not impugn any specific Catholic nations, and despite his claim that faction can reveal truth agonistically, he remains hors de combat: "I will not now enter into the Labyrinth of Councels and Fathers, an intangl'd wood which the Papist loves to fight in" (*CPW* 8:418). To pursue the logic of natives and foreigners in Milton's later writings, we must return once more to the "intangl'd wood" of his poetry.

And from Thy State Mine Never Shall Be Parted

Questions about the native and the foreign encompass political and military rule, concerns about linguistic coherence, and intimate matters of personal identity. Such problems become particularly acute in the context of Anglo-Irish relations. Explicit attention to Ireland may overwhelm Milton's attempts to shore up England's religious and political integrity. By alluding to the hubbub, however, the Nimrod episode of *Paradise Lost* comes far closer than *Of True Religion* to signaling a meaningful political meditation about Ireland. In isolation, however, this episode cannot explore the full implications of conquest that is deemed unjust, ineffective, and yet sanctioned by God. Adam's question about the fate of his "execrable son" seems jarring in part because Nimrod is almost wholly without meaningful personhood, and Milton has no interest in turning this mythic figure from Genesis into a full-fledged character. By contrast, in Adam's own narrative Milton can embed a sophisticated commentary—at a microcosmic, intimate level—about the politics of the native and the foreign and about the ensuing challenges to language and personhood.

By the time Adam hears Michael's lesson about human history, his marriage has already suggested the workings of undeserved dominion. Unfallen Adam knows that his divinely sanctioned role as lordly husband is peculiarly out of sync with his experience. Eve seems complete within herself; Adam has felt his single imperfection. Adam's innate defectiveness proves consistent with Milton's earlier writings about marriage, but it also signals a change in his conception of the political body. In *Of Reformation*

(1641), Milton had relied on the familiar trope of the nation as a single person to argue the need for guarding England's integrity: "for looke what the grounds, and causes are of single happines to one man, the same yee shall find them to a whole state" (*CPW* 1:572).[52] In *Eikonoklastes*, Milton had turned the rhetoric of the king's two bodies to his advantage in order to argue that Charles I had been far too lenient toward (and in fact had been secretly allied with) the Irish "rebels": "for he lookt upon the blood spilt, whether of Subjects or of Rebels with an indifferent eye, *as exhausted out of his own veines*; without distinguishing as he ought, which was good blood and which corrupt; the not letting out whereof endangers the whole body" (*CPW* 3:485). Milton's metaphorical prescription for more selective blood-letting appeals to the need to protect the integrity of the political body. In *Paradise Lost*, by contrast, there can be no "single happines to one man." Even the impeccable man's self originates not with a wholeness to be defended but with a need to be fulfilled by another.

This need gives rise to conjugal love, which Milton consistently upholds as beneficial both for the individual and for the nation. In *The Doctrine and Discipline of Divorce*, Milton advises Parliament to see that "as a whole people is in proportion to an ill Government, so is one man to an ill marriage" (*CPW* 2:229). Happy marriage, by contrast, lays the foundations of a healthy commonwealth. In reading *Paradise Lost*, Christopher Hill insists that "we must recall what no one in the seventeenth century would ever forget, the analogy between marriage and the state."[53] This analogy allows Hill to identify Adam's husbandly authority over Eve with Parliamentarian leadership over majority opinion in the 1650s. Adam's inability to divorce himself from fallen Eve should thus be read in light of the shortcomings of the leaders of the republican cause.

Recent emphasis on the need to understand the English Civil War within the context of the War of the Three Kingdoms reveals how mid-seventeenth-century strife concerns both domestic sovereignty and colonialist power. Interpreting *Paradise Lost* with the relevance of Anglo-Irish relations in mind complicates any straightforward analogy between conjugal and political relations. At the same time, this revised reading suggests new reasons for Adam's inability to exercise proper authority over Eve and over his Edenic home. The contest over such categories as native versus foreign and authority versus rebellion emerges within Adam and Eve's marriage. Their union is precarious from the outset because of a logic of power that calls Adam to be a civilizing vanguard and relegates Eve to the status of a belated addition. The ensuing narrative of separation, hostility, and reconciliation imparts a lesson about the need to replace a colonial mindset with a politics of grace. Yet this lesson can operate only at the level of poetic myth, where gracious cooperation coexists with a divinely sanctioned imbalance of power. Milton's critique of colonialist power can be expressed even as its full implications remain out of view, as revised forms of undeserved dominion remain accepted at the level of conjugal politics.

A younger Milton had already practiced the fusion of political and erotically charged familial dramas. *A Masque Presented at Ludlow Castle* ambivalently commemorates Lord Egerton's promotion to the presidency of the Council of Wales. Egerton is described as a "noble peer of mickle trust, and power" who has been called upon "to guide / An old, and haughty nation proud in arms" (lines 31–33). Young Alice Egerton, temporarily separated from her parents and then from her brothers, endures Comus's sexual temptation, as Richard Halpern puts it, in "the spiritual as well as the physical darkness of the Welsh landscape," which "provides a barbarian setting . . . where 'savage' marital practices release the dangers of feminine sexuality."[54] Even as the masque enacts fears about Welsh-English relations, it does so in part by referring to Irish forms of barbarism. Philip Schwyzer observes that Comus's background (that is, his having roved "the Celtic, and Iberian fields" before arriving at "this ominous wood") "closely resembles Spenser's genealogy of the Irish race."[55] Schwyzer notes that Comus's mother, Circe, often symbolized the beastly, degenerate forces of Irish culture.

In book 2 of *The Faerie Queene*, such forces are figured in Spenser's Circean witch Acrasia, who offers a sensuous but dangerously convincing simulacrum of paradise. Spenser describes the Bower of Bliss as

> A place pickt out by choyce of best alyue,
> That natures worke by art can imitate:
> In which what euer in this worldly state
> Is sweete, and pleasing vnto liuing sense,
> Or that may dayntest fantasie aggrate,
> Was poured forth with plentifull dispence,
> And made there to abound with lauish affluence.

(2.12.42)

When Milton describes Adam and Eve's "blissful bower" as "a place / Chosen by the sovereign planter, when he framed / All things to man's delightful use" (*PL* 4.690–92), he responds directly to Spenser's comparison of the Bower of Bliss to "*Eden* selfe, if ought with *Eden* mote compayre" (*FQ* 2.12.52). *The Faerie Queene* contains numerous *loci amoeni*. Redcrosse restores Eden to Una in the first book, but the poem's pattern of reduplication ensures that the story cannot end there. It falls upon the Garden of Adonis in book 3 to overcome the dichotomy between the true and the false, the Christian and the pagan versions of Eden. Spenser stretches his Edenic thought across the horizontal axis of his allegorical narrative; Milton's account of the one true Eden relies on the vertical stratification of a literary landscape that compresses numerous layers of allusion.

The relationship between the terrain of Spenser's Faeryland and the "salvage soyl" of Ireland that the poet inhabits has become a topic of critical scrutiny. Readers have noted Spenser's fear of and fascination with the wooded Irish landscape and its menacing Gaelic and Old English inhabitants. Such attitudes help to account for the vital importance of the settings in which Spenser's heroes undergo moral temptation. The Bower of Bliss is designed to achieve an ominous combination of offense and defense; it is "enclosed rownd about, / Aswell their entred guestes to keep within, / As those vnruly beasts to hold without" (*FQ* 2.12.43). Milton's bower has no need to fence its inhabitants in, but it is still designed for exclusion: "other creature here / Beast, bird, insect, or worm durst enter none" (*PL* 4.703–4). When Satan first intrudes into Eden, he encounters a landscape "whose hairy sides / With thicket overgrown, grotesque and wild, / Access denied" (*PL* 4.135–37). Later, however, the ease of Satan's trespass—"At one slight bound high overleaped all bound / Of hill or highest wall" (*PL* 4.181–82)—turns into a joke the previous lines about the fortress-like quality of Eden. Spenser explains that physical defenses are never reliable: "Yet was the fence thereof but weake and thin; / Nought feard theyr force, that fortilage to win, / But wisedomes powre, and temperaunces might" (*FQ* 2.12.43). For Spenser's Guyon as for Milton's Adam and Eve, true defense lies in the vigilant maintenance of virtue.

Guyon's destruction of the bower manifests Spenser's politics of conquest. Yet the arrestingly spectacular nature of this episode derives its energy from the intemperance of Temperance personified. Stephen Greenblatt has described Guyon's act as one of cultural overcompensation that reflects in part the ambivalent mixture of attraction and loathing that iconoclastic Protestant colonists felt in the face of Irish, Catholic practices.[56] Book 2 of *The Faerie Queene* thus conjoins an Edenic theme of erotic temptation with pressing concerns about Irish affairs. Other texts apply such dynamics more explicitly to this cultural context. A long history of writings describes Ireland as paradise and frames political debates through questions about its fall and possible reclamation. These tropes are worth surveying at some length because they provide the historical matrix in which *Paradise Lost* can be called upon to speak about the Irish question.

   In the opening chapter of *The Ecclesiastical History* (AD 731), Bede describes Ireland as an island abounding in milk and honey ("diues lactis ac mellis"), suggesting not only that it is more fertile and pleasing than Britain but also that it recalls the biblical promised land.[57] Bede helps to promulgate the importance of the absence of snakes in Ireland; he declares that were snakes to exist there, the island would naturally render their poison ineffective. Giraldus Cambrensis (Gerald of Wales), in the *Topography of Ireland* (1186–87), describes Ireland as a separate world not only because of its geographical isolation but also because of its many wonders. Gerald agrees with Bede that Irish soil neutralizes poison and drives venomous creatures away. Gerald deems as fanciful conjecture the story of Saint Patrick driving the snakes from Ireland; he considers the island's natural attributes a far likelier explanation for the absence of snakes.[58] Yet the Irish prodigies that Gerald describes range from natural blessings (the most temperate climate of all nations) to fantastic myths (a sacred island where animals and women cannot set foot) and unnatural debasement (a goat that copulates with a woman). The overall impression conveys Ireland's potential to be a place of marvels or of nightmares. Once Gerald turns to Irish history and culture, he strongly suggests that the latter possibility has prevailed because the Irish have proved unfit stewards of the island. In *The Conquest of Ireland* (1189), Gerald continues to detail how and why the Norman monarch Henry II should subjugate Ireland fully and reclaim this potential paradise from savagery. The late sixteenth century would give rise to a return to Gerald's writings, which were translated and reprinted in major texts such as the 1587 edition of Holinshed's *Chronicles* and William Camden's *Britannia*.[59] Gerald's presentation of Ireland as a place of wonderful bounty and monstrous prodigies set the terms for the New English settlers' colonialist imagination.

Paradisal logic could be conscripted for very different political aims. In 1625 the Irish Franciscan Robert Rochford compiled and translated biographies of Ireland's three patron saints from medieval sources. In the dedicatory epistle Rochford repeats his wish that the work might kindle patriotic and sectarian fervor. The primary hero of the volume is Saint Patrick, who planted "a Paradise of pleasures, whether Elias would not disdaine to be transported in his fiery Coach . . . as it were a third heaven, whether S. Paul would willingly be rauished to contemplate her delightfull maruayles." Unlike the histories of Bede and Gerald, the biography of Patrick, originally compiled by the hagiographer Jocelyn of Furness, affirms the familiar lore of the patron saint driving "serpents, scorpions & other venemous animals" from the island. For the Catholic apologist, the intrusion of Protestantism spoils this mystical paradise. Hagiography turns polemical, as Patrick is cast as a Catholic hero who will stand up to "the proudest of Achilles of the Protestant side."[60] (The irony of Achilles belonging to the winning side is matched by the fact that Saint Patrick was, according to his own *Confessio*, born on the British mainland and arrived in Ireland only after being kidnapped and sold into slavery there.)

English Protestants, of course, blamed Old English and Gaelic Catholics for spoiling paradise. In *A Briefe Declaration of the Barbarous and inhumane dealings of the Northern Irish Rebels* (1641), the author, "G.S. Minister of Gods word in Ireland," draws a direct connection between the original Fall and the 1641 uprising: "There was a blessed Union betwixt God and man, till mans sin broke the Peace. . . . And this generall Rebellion of ours against our gracious God, hath much occasioned this particular Rebellion of the envious Papists in *Ireland* against us."[61] Defeating the Confederates, shoring up English rule, and settling Ireland with an influx of Protestants are described as ways to fulfill Ireland's potential. So too are projects of husbandry designed to harness Ireland's impressive natural resources. Samuel Hartlib prefaces Gerard Boate's *Irelands Naturall History* (1657) by emphasizing the spiritual rewards of agricultural and commercial projects. Hartlib anticipates not merely the resettlement of Ireland by English and continental Protestants but "*the Restauration of all things*," which will undo "the works of the Devill, whereby he hath brought us, & the whole Creation, under the bondage of Corruption."[62] Local developments in Ireland assume an eschatological significance, turning the island into a focal point of a drama stretching from Genesis to Revelation.

Writings about Anglo-Irish relations frequently turn territorial and cultural contestation into stories of erotic contact and marriage. Although intermarriage between the English and the Irish had been officially illegal since the 1366 Statutes of Kilkenny, writers such as Spenser and Barnabe Rich would continue to decry the phenomenon as a source of debasement. In Spenser's *View*, the oft-cited passage about the dangers of Irish wet nurses declares that "these evill customes of fostering and marrying with the Irish" are "most carefully to be restrayned."[63] In *A New Description of Ireland* (1610), Rich relates the story of a young wife who consents to an affair with her friend as long as he refrains from kissing her or touching her lips. Preferring letter to spirit, she reasons that she will thereby be able to claim to have kept "what my mouth hath Religiously vowed." Rich immediately turns the story into an allegory of the general untrustworthiness of Catholics: "I think of my conscience, this Woman was as firme in the promise she made to her husband, as a number of Papists in their Oaths they do make to the king."[64]

Intermarriage, however, could also be a vehicle of redemption. In 1655 an anonymous anti-Catholic pamphlet about the persecution of Protestants narrates the story of Owen Mac-Connel, an Irish servant in Dublin with a Protestant English wife. During the 1641 uprising Mac-Connel foils a local plot against Protestants. When Mac-Connel asks his master "what should become of his wife and poor Children, he replyed in these words, *Hang her English Kite, we will get thee a better Wife.*"[65] Fortunately for the English Protestants, Mac-Connel spoils the plot, betraying master, country, and religion out of loyalty to his wife. In post-Restoration Ireland, where reconciliation and resettlement were official desiderata, marriage between the Irish and English could become, at least in theory, a more programmatic project. William Petty, in *The Political Anatomy of Ireland* (1672), estimates that there are 600,000 poor Irish and "not above 20 M. of unmarried marriageable Women." He proposes that if these women were transported to England "and as many *English* brought back and married to the *Irish* . . . the whole Work of natural Transmutation and Union would in 4 or 5 years be accomplished."[66] Petty's almost comically implausible assertion ascribes to marriage a tremendous power to expedite cultural and political union.

The history of representing Ireland through the tropes of Edenic imagery and of familial or erotic relationships—a history that spans from medieval texts to writings after *Paradise Lost*—provides a robust context to the literary exchange between Spenser's description of the Bower of Bliss and Milton's account of the Edenic bower. Concerns about sexual boundaries, territory, and religious belief converge in these epic Edens. Spenser's Guyon witnesses sexual temptation in a false paradise created by the witch Acrasia; readers continue to debate the propriety of his single-minded response within the framework of the poem and its Christian ideals.[67] In Milton's account, the bower is the site of what Adam memorably calls "transported touch," which leaves him "weak / Against the charm of beauty's powerful glance" (*PL* 8.530–33). What is required of Adam becomes less and less clear. As Adam struggles to explain to Raphael, Eve's challenge to husbandly dominion is not simply sexual but based on her numerous "decencies." Even in fallen Eve, Adam encounters not a wicked enchantress—or at least not *merely* a wicked enchantress—but flesh of his flesh and bone of his bone.

In the opening moments of this chapter I offered some reasons behind Eve's choice to fall. Adam's decision to join his wife in sin advances Milton's simultaneously political and psychological investigation. When fallen Eve first approaches, what Adam feels is not the threat of a foreign temptation but the fear of the uncanny. Adam

> Astonied stood and blank, while horror chill
> Ran through his veins, and all his joints relaxed;
> From his slack hand the garland wreathed for Eve
> Down dropped, and all the faded roses shed:
> Speechless he stood and pale.

> (*PL* 9.890–94)

Freud's notion of the *unheimlich* has everything to do with doubling and the repetition of "the primary narcissism which dominates the mind of the child and of primitive man. But when this stage has been surmounted, the 'double' reverses its aspect. From having been an assurance of immortality, it becomes the uncanny harbinger of death."[68] Replacing "it" with "Eve" in this last sentence provides a rough summary of the conjugal narrative of *Paradise Lost*. Through Eve, Adam is to produce "like of his like, his image multiplied"; this redoubling is meant to relieve Adam's sense of solitary deficiency (8.424). Eve herself is, in fact, Adam's double but with the difference of gender, "manlike, but different sex" (8.471). Attached to Adam, Eve is called the mother of mankind; when she has fallen, however, she fully realizes her threat as a female who denies Adam his sense of primacy. Adam indeed "must feel that [her] intentions to harm us are going to be carried out with the help of special powers."[69] Adam's horror is the immediate reaction to the newly malign intentions of his female double.

For the current discussion, the most salient feature of the uncanny is its relation to a sense of what is "home" and what is "native." Homi Bhabha has described the work that Freud's concept can do to evoke "something of the estranging sense of the relocation of the home and the world," or "unhomeliness."[70] Unhomeliness reveals the systems of suppression and disavowal that underwrite political units like the imperial nation. The unhomely reveals that a "coherent national culture" is fractured by "double-time" and thus needs to be "redeemed and iterated" continuously.[71] Eve's uncanniness speaks to the fissures within Milton's Eden, and these fissures bring us back to one of the primary definitions of *heimlich*: "native." Eve becomes a chilling spectacle because her act reveals the intrinsic belatedness and potential for degeneration that Adam has been called upon to suppress. Adam's inability to do so leads him to confront, in the figure of Eve, his estrangement both from his Edenic home and from his other self. Coherence and language itself fail before this particular kind of threat. Like so many Spenserian heroes and heroines, Adam finds himself astonied into silence.

In the preceding chapter I discussed how Milton uses New World imagery to describe the dislocation of Eden. Adam and Eve in their naked shame are compared to Americans discovered by Columbus, "so girt / With feathered cincture, naked else and wild" (*PL* 9.1116–17). Paul Stevens argues that "Adam and Eve become Americans only at their most intense moment of shame," and goes on to describe the political function of shame in "defining the nation as a godly community" by "inhibiting any kind of radical engagement with cultural alterity."[72] As the example of John Rolfe and Pocahontas shows, shame can fail, but prohibitions and customs should normally maintain boundaries between the proper and improper. At the decisive moment of choosing to sin, however, this particular kind of shame has little bearing on Adam, for Eve is dangerous by virtue of her intimate familiarity. Only after consummating sin sexually (and after the intoxication of lust wears off) will Adam be compelled by shame to attempt belatedly and ineffectively to separate himself from his fallen wife.

Both the connections and the differences between Ireland and America in the English imagination help to account for the cultural logic of Adam's fall. The Irish had often been compared to Americans since the sixteenth century; both peoples could represent a form of cultural atavism.[73] Pernicious comparisons in turn facilitated a more concrete connection. As Elizabeth Sauer reminds us, "during the 1650s, Irish priests, Tories, and 'vagrants' were exiled to the colonies, including Jamaica and Barbados," where they were sold to planters for less than the price of black slaves.[74] In *The Irish Colours Folded, or the Irish Roman-Catholick's Reply* (1662), the Old English Peter Walsh alludes fearfully to this phenomenon. Responding to the Earl of Orrery's charge that the hubbub continues to bear witness to Irish degeneracy, Walsh implores the Duke of Ormond, "I hope your Grace, without sending the Natives to the *Barbadoes* . . . will not only suppress the *Ditty*, if any such be used, but ever abrogate the *Tune*."[75] The Cromwellian practice of sending recalcitrant Irish to the Americas continues to be a source of fear and resentment after the Restoration.

Yet the differences between Native Americans and the Irish were as obvious as they were significant. If the Irish were frequently accused of being savage, they were also near and familiar enough that the prospect of union could be endorsed rather than simply interdicted. Even more dangerously, the Irish could challenge England's sense of cultural primacy even at home within the British Isles; a very long tradition of writing could claim that that the Irish had helped to bring civilization and Christianity to the English.[76] Rochford, the translator of Jocelyn's biography of Saint Patrick, cites Bernard of Clairvaux, according to whom "*swarmes of Saints did breake out*" from Ireland and proselytized not only on the Isles but also on the European continent.[77] Early modern English writers had long been acutely aware of the challenge to primacy that Ireland posed. Richard McCabe points out, for example, how Spenser's *View* anxiously registers the "fragility of England's civility" which "is exacerbated by its relative novelty."[78] Such fears are distinct from the challenge to English explorers and colonists in the New World. At the simplest level, the complexity of the Irish situation was compounded then as it would be for centuries afterwards "by the absence of the visual marker of skin colour difference which was used to legitimate domination in other colonized societies."[79] Irish culture threatens the colonialist imagination as an image of debasement.

Despite being a menace, however, the familiarity between Irish and English peoples accommodates hope for reconciliation and union even after bloody feuds. The final books of *Paradise Lost* dramatize (in miniature and yet at the grandest level) the process of reconciliation after rebellion. When the Son arrives in Eden in book 10, he comes not only to forgive and to prophesy future grace, but also to mete out appropriate punishments for man, woman, and the serpent. In this last we find a meaningful point of contact between Milton's theological narrative and political thinking about Anglo-Irish affairs after the Restoration. The humble serpent plays an indispensable role in the cultural myths both of Eden and of Ireland. In the works of writers ranging from Bede and Gerald of Wales to Robert Rochford, we have seen that snakes help to define Ireland by their very absence. Yet the question of whether snakes were indigenous to the island is a long-standing one that accrues political and sectarian implications. *Paradise Lost* makes deft use of the interpretive problems posed by the serpent in Genesis to investigate questions about identity, place, and the contested logic of native origins.

The biblical serpent raises troubling questions: What does it mean that it is called more subtle than any other beast in Eden, where all creatures should have been completely innocent before the Fall? If the serpent was indeed innocent and thus merely a vehicle for satanic temptation, why does it receive harsh punishment from God? John Calvin's commentary stages a series of arguments in order to render the third chapter of Genesis reasonable and inoffensive. Calvin argues against any definition of subtlety as a negative trait by declaring that the Hebrew word *aroom* means something like "prudent."[80] He goes on to explain that the snake's prudence or intelligence made it a convenient vessel for Satan, whom Moses never explicitly mentions because his original audience was unprepared for such truth. Calvin must then proceed to argue how the serpent, even as a victim of satanic agency, merited a divine curse by becoming noxious rather than beneficial to mankind.[81]

Paradise Lost amplifies questions about the fairness of the serpent's punishment, applying topical cultural logic to this theological problem. Once in Eden, Satan finds a fit vessel for cunning and deception,

> for in the wily snake,
> Whatever sleights none would suspicious mark,
> As from his wit and native subtlety
> Proceeding, which in other beasts observed
> Doubt might beget of diabolic power.

> (9.91–95)

The phrase "native subtlety" adds a charged tag to the questions surrounding the subtlety of the snake. Joan S. Bennett was one of the first readers to suggest the relevance of the Irish rebellion for the plot of *Paradise Lost*. According to her reading, Satan plays a role analogous to the one that Milton previously attributed to Charles I by becoming the "Author of that rebellion" in Eden.[82] In *Eikonoklastes*, Milton describes the Irish rebels as being led not only by the "many suttle and *Italian* heads of the Romish party" but also by the closet Catholic Charles I (*CPW* 3:470). Ingrained fears of Catholic rebellion in Ireland, kept alive in collective memory after the Restoration, invests the narrative of *Paradise Lost* with political energies. Having led an unsuccessful rebellion in Heaven, Satan usurps the body of the native serpent to stir up new enmity against God in Eden.

Far more than the Catholics in Ireland who were stirred to rise up against English Protestants, the serpent in the Edenic narrative seems to represent an innocent pawn caught in a larger clash. At the moment when Satan possesses the serpent, the poet describes the animal as "not yet in horrid shade and dismal den, / Nor nocent yet" (*PL* 9.185–86). The phrase "nor nocent yet" seems to echo Calvin's argument that the serpent merited punishment after being manipulated by Satan; its innate innocence would be short-lived.[83] In book 10, however, God draws a sharp distinction between Satan's and the serpent's guilt. Whereas the former is "rebel to all law / Conviction to the serpent none belongs" (10.83–84). In the very same book, the Son decrees against the snake the familiar curse from Genesis: "thou art accursed / Above all cattle, each beast of the field; / Upon thy belly grovelling thou shalt go" (10.175–77). The poet acknowledges the

discrepancy with a bristly declaration that the serpent was "justly then accursed / As vitiated in nature: more to know / Concerned not man (since
he no further knew)" (10.168–70).

On the matter of the guilt or innocence of the native snake, the Son
comes dangerously close to disagreeing with God. The difficulty of distinguishing between guilt and mere association with rebellion in Restoration
Ireland suggests one reason why Milton underscores the questions raised
by the serpent's punishment in Genesis. "Nocent" is, like "hubbub," a rare
word in Milton's writings which signals a potential topical reference to
Irish affairs. After 1641, the "nocent Catholic" was targeted as the agent
culpable for unjust violence. The 1642 political pamphlet *An Alarum to
Warre* declares in its full title the need *To Subjugate Savage cruelties, and
inhumane Massacres Acted by the Nocent Papists*.[84] In the post-Restoration
effort of reconciliation, distinguishing between innocence and nocence
proves an urgent but difficult task. According to the 1662 Act of Settlement, the distinction became the basis, at least in theory, of restoring
property to Catholics. "And least any Ambiguity or controversy might
arise," the act declares that "first all innocent Protestants, and those persons termed innocent Papists . . . be first restored."[85] Ambiguity and controversy were inevitable, given the twists of recent history whereby some
who had participated in the 1641 uprising went on to fight for the Royalist
cause. Although the 1662 act opens by proclaiming that the crown abhors
the "unnatural insurrection" begun in 1641, it later goes out of its way to
acknowledge Irish subjects who had been loyal to Charles I.[86]

The matter would remain contested long after the Explanation Act of
1665 set more stringent criteria for Catholic innocence. In 1672 William
Petty declares coolly but tendentiously, "Of those adjudged Innocents, not
1/20 were really so."[87] Yet this troubling indeterminacy would afford later
writers the space to maneuver rhetorically. In 1680 James Tuchet, the third
Earl of Castlehaven, published a memoir defending his actions in the wars
in Ireland. During this tense time in the aftermath of the Popish Plot,
Castlehaven's writings again turn memories of Ireland in the 1640s and
1650s into a flashpoint. In 1682 Edmund Borlase published a rebuttal of
Castlehaven's memoirs, addressing his work to Charles II. To Castlehaven's claim that he had joined the so-called Irish rebels in the 1640s
partly because English forces were killing indiscriminately, Borlase responds that in Ireland at the time, "the Infection seemed to have polluted

the whole Kingdom, so as an enraged Army, justly incensed by many (who at first had suffered by the Rebels) could hardly distinguish betwixt the Nocent and Innocent."[88] In the years immediately after the Restoration, the perplexing work of establishing innocence had been meant to create a basis for restoration. Borlase, however, reads this ambiguity back into the earlier conflict and uses it to justify bloodshed.

The lasting fallout from the Confederate Wars in Ireland points to one way in which contemporary political affairs bear upon the theodicial questions of Milton's epic. The latter books of *Paradise Lost* turn the question of the nocent serpent into a dominant leitmotif. Colubrine destiny becomes linked to the fate of the human species and to the unfolding of redemptive history. Adam, Eve, and Satan repeatedly ponder the meaning of the protoevangelion that the Son has delivered: "Between thee [the snake] and the woman I will put / Enmity, and between thine and her seed; / Her seed shall bruise thy head, thou bruise his heel" (10.179–81). Between the snake and the woman the Son will put enmity. This will be a necessary correction, for in the most misogynistic tirade of the poem, Adam declares Eve a serpent: "that name best / Befits thee with him leagued, thyself as false / And hateful" (10.867–69). Though full of bluster, this accusation is of a piece with the way the entire poem applies its cultural logic to the other theological question about the Edenic snake: Why was it subtle even before the Fall?

When book 9 initially describes the "native subtlety" of the serpent, it traces a potentially ominous trait to Eden itself. Adam's accusation that Eve is leagued with the serpent and is a serpent herself shows how questions about the snake lead to questions about Eve's origins. Earlier in book 9 Adam appeals to a different sense of "native." When he finally assents to a temporary separation, he admonishes Eve, "Go in thy native innocence, rely / On what thou hast of virtue, summon all" (9.373–74). When Adam refers to Eve's "native innocence," he most likely has in mind her birth from his body; he has already reminded her that she is "daughter of God and man" to persuade her to stay by his side. Yet Eve has a different genealogy as well. In describing Milton's God as a colonial planter, J. Martin Evans states that God "'plants' (1.652) the human pair in the terrestrial paradise," but this is not completely accurate.[89] Adam, in both Genesis and *Paradise Lost*, is indeed created outside of Eden and later planted there. Milton, however, follows the Yahwist account of creation in the second chapter of Genesis when he describes Eve as having been created in Eden. Adam alone is planted in Eden; Eve is born there. Surprisingly, the tension of *Paradise Lost*'s conjugal narrative derives in part from the fact that Adam and Eve are paradoxically flesh of each other's flesh while at a same time a couple of mixed origins. As a native of Eden, Eve shares a special bond to the landscape that represents the potential both for fertility and for dangerous excess. In the final books of the epic, exile from Eden allows Adam to return to his native origin, the dust from which he was created. Eve, however, bewails the loss of her birthplace and must be taught to consider her husband as her native home.

Adam and Eve's separation in book 9 presents in highly condensed form the perturbing questions about cultural kinship raised by the messy and bloody drama of recent Irish history. When Eve strikes off on her own, she confronts a dilemma with cultural and political resonances: caught between competing origins, she must choose between allegiance to her "planted" husband ("native innocence") or the unruly potential that she inherits as a daughter of Eden (sharing, perhaps, the "native subtlety" of the snake). According to Adam's bitter accusation after the fact, Eve reveals her snakelike identity by eating the forbidden fruit and then tempting him to do the same. Despite having received instruction from Raphael, Adam (not unlike the original audience of Genesis in Calvin's estimation) cannot fully comprehend that the serpent is merely a vehicle for the true, satanic source of sin. Yet the point is rendered partially moot in book 10, when Satan literally finds himself transformed into a serpent. Part of this work has already been accomplished much earlier, when the opening lines of book 1 brand Satan a serpent. By the time the narrative turns to the literal serpent, two possibilities emerge. Perhaps the reader cannot help but impose a fallen perspective on Eden by associating an innocent creature with Satan. Yet a more troubling possibility persists: perhaps the serpent has always been suspect, and its troubling characteristics are native to Eden itself. The former possibility is more logical because it preserves Milton's theodicy, but the narrative gains vitality from the interplay between the two.

Rebel and author of rebellion thus come to assume (or, in retrospect, seem always to have assumed) the same shape. This suggests a political meaning to Adam's accusation that Eve has been "leagued" with the serpent. Eve has ostensibly forsaken her true origins by allying herself with the flora and fauna of the landscape of her birth. Adam's tirade against Eve continues by imagining the kind of external transformation that Satan undergoes: "nothing wants, but that thy shape, / Like his, and colour serpentine may show / Thy inward fraud, to warn all creatures from thee" (*PL* 10.869–71). In the end, only the Son of God can clear Eve's name by placing enmity between the serpent and the woman, thus denying her a share in the snake's native subtlety and reclaiming her innocence.

Eve must undergo her share of punishment as well. Not only will she feel pain in childbirth, but also her willful independence must be subjected more securely to husbandly dominion: "and to thy husband's will / Thine shall submit, he over thee shall rule" (*PL* 10.195–96). It would seem that the Son's punishment forces Eve to become a humble and penitent supplicant. What qualifies such a reading, however, is one of Milton's telling acts of omission. In Genesis, God tells Eve, "Thy desire shall be to thy husband, and he shall rule over thee" (3:16); there is no corresponding clause in *Paradise Lost*. Milton's Arminianism, not to mention his own experiences of marriage, lead him to believe, contra Genesis, that Eve's desire cannot be dictated even when she is placed into a position of subservience. As a result, Eve's gracious actions in the final books of the poem testify not to her subjugation to God and to Adam, but to her free response to divine grace after her rebellion.

The narrative of Adam and Eve's reconciliation with each other and with God works to elevate Eve's worth at Adam's expense. When Adam lapses into suicidal despair, only Eve's response can snap him out of it. After volunteering to ask for the brunt of sin to fall upon her shoulders, Eve pleads, "Let us no more contend, nor blame / Each other . . . but strive / In offices of love" (*PL* 10.958–60). Such gestures prompt Adam to resume his place in the relationship by taking over and correcting Eve's suggestions. By the end of the epic, full reconciliation becomes possible once Eve communes directly with God in a mysterious dream. After Adam receives his long history lesson from the angel Michael, he returns to Eve only to learn that she has had access to a higher, less mediated form of divine knowledge. "Whence thou returnst," Eve declares to Adam, "and whither wentst, I know; / For God is also in sleep, and dreams advise, / Which he hath sent propitious" (12.610–12). Anticipating the role of Mary, who is repeatedly invoked as the second Eve, the first Eve utters a *magnificat* as her final words of the poem: "Such favor I unworthy am vouchsafed /

By me the promised seed shall all restore" (12.622–23, emphasis added). What will ultimately redeem mankind is not husbandly dominion—which even unfallen Adam had found questionable—but Eve's acceptance of her maternal role after direct and mysterious contact with God. As a restored wife, Eve can finally satisfy her original desire for unmediated knowledge; rather than looking down into a pool to commune with herself, however, she now has ineffable contact with God.

In Me Is No Delay

Eve, whose erotic charms and quotidian decency generate intense affection, proves to be both the dangerous temptation that leads to Adam's loss of paradise as well as the vehicle of reconciliation after the Fall. The trajectory of writings about Irish affairs before and after the Restoration bears upon the narrative of Eve's transformation from recalcitrant partner turned rebel into the maternal agent of divine grace. Post-Restoration Irish writers personify Ireland as a humbled but dignified partner, marshaling both epic and biblical models for their rhetorical aims. In a 1661 *Panegyrick* to the Earl of Ormond, Francis Synge makes complex use of the Aeneas and Dido story. The full title of the *Panegyrick* calls Ormond "the faithful Achates of our royal Charles" and thus depicts the king as Aeneas. After decrying the regicide and the ensuing travesties, however, Synge suddenly blurs any simple identification. Synge compares his own situation as a writer of past woes to Aeneas's when asked by Dido to narrate the events that have brought him to Carthage: "*Infandum, Regina, jubes* [renovare dolorem]" (You command me, Queen, [to revive grief]).[90] By this point it is completely unclear whom Aeneas and Dido are called upon to represent. Synge goes on to refer to Ormond's shipwreck, turning him into the Aeneas figure. The Irish speaker then seems to resume the role of Aeneas as narrator, but he also plays the part of Dido by loving Ormond for his sufferings. Palpably relevant is the fact that the Aeneas and Dido story is centrally one of deep betrayal, but all of these rapid oscillations work to render unclear who has been (or will be) to blame. More optimistically, the passage works to split the experience of love between speaker and reader, between Irish subject and English governor, between Aeneas and Dido. Synge implores Ormond—initially invoked as Achates but deputized as

Aeneas himself—to rewrite this political narrative as a case of lasting love rather than one of abandonment.[91]

Whereas Synge echoes Virgil, Ruaidhrí Ó Flaithbheartaigh (Roderic O'Flaherty) turns to scriptures in *Ogygia* (1685), a history of Ireland. O'Flaherty writes as the last leader of a clan that had lost its property to Cromwell's confiscations in the 1650s. In a conciliatory gesture, O'Flaherty dedicates *Ogygia* to the future James II. The dedication personifies Ireland as a woman who "prostrates her venerable person at your highness's feet." Ireland, "with dishevelled hair and tears trickling down her cheeks, presents a book, in which are written, lamentations and mourning and woe, *Ezekiel* 2.10."[92] O'Flaherty initially seems to represent Ireland as a penitent harlot, evoking the image of the woman (often taken to be Mary Magdalene) who wipes Jesus's feet with her tears and hair. Yet this feminized Ireland suddenly becomes a powerful divine agent. The second chapter of Ezekiel does indeed tell the story of "a rebellious nation that hath rebelled" (Ezek. 2:3), but in the verse that O'Flaherty cites, it is God himself who presents a book to the prophet. The citation implies a parallel between Ireland presenting her book of lamentation to James II and God spreading a book before Ezekiel. *Ogygia*'s dedication goes on to ascribe to feminized Ireland a maternal role. O'Flaherty frames his project of tracing Irish history from ancient biblical origins to his present day as the history of the Stuart monarchy, one that affirms James's claim to the throne. Ireland has suffered much, but "her only remaining solace at present is, that one family, your paternal stock . . . wields the scepter of the British dominions."[93] Despite its humbled status, Ireland should thus command respect as a "proto-parent" of English monarchs.

Through epic and biblical modes, writers such as Synge and O'Flaherty turn the treacherous figure of feminized Ireland into a powerful agent. No straightforward allegory obtains in *Paradise Lost*, yet I have attempted to show how Eve's roles—recalcitrant partner, rebel, penitent, and conciliatory agent—imagine a politics of grace as an alternative to conquest and subjugation. Even at its most appealing, however, the political dimensions of this fantasy cannot break free from the contradiction whereby undeserved and ineffective power is still authorized. Eve's original impulse for independent wholeness will be fulfilled through the Virgin Mary. This second Eve will successfully escape the economy of "he for God only, she for God in him" by playing a central role in redemptive history largely independent of her husband. The Virgin mother, however, remains for Eve a singular anomaly to arrive in a distant future. In the meantime, the first Eve can only anticipate the full redemption of motherhood by assuming more voluntarily than she ever had before her role as subservient wife: "but now lead on; / In me is no delay; with thee to go, / Is to stay here; without thee here to stay, / Is to go hence unwilling" (*PL* 12.614–17). Both the temporal and spatial logic of Eve's last declaration bear upon the poem's cultural thinking. Eve finally accepts marital union with Adam as a means to overcome her belatedness. The rhyme between "delay" and "stay" not only returns us to the original scene of temporal splitting at the reflecting pool but also points to the very last lines of the epic, in which, indeed, "no shadow" comes between the couple: "They hand in hand with wandering steps and slow, / Through Eden took their solitary way" (12.648–49). Yet Eve can only assert her newfound optimism about marriage by denying her connection to her native Eden. Her identity must now be based on Adam's presence, which will serve as a surrogate homeland.

At the same time, Eve's declaration of willingness to follow her husband echoes Anchises' speech to his son Aeneas in book 2 of the *Aeneid*: "Now, now there is no delay; I follow, and where you lead, there am I."[94] The allusion seems to offer Eve a way to accept exile not only as a trailing wife but also as the parent of a greater empire to come. Yet Eve's alignment with Anchises remains subordinated to the more explicit confession of humble wifely obeisance. The conclusion of book 2 of the *Aeneid* sunders patriarchal commitments and conjugal love: when Aeneas takes Anchises on his shoulder and his son by his hand so that they can travel with no delay, he unwittingly turns his wife, Creusa, who trails behind the men, into a victim of war. Whereas writers like Francis Synge work to blur the distinction between Aeneas and Dido to plead his case for political union and cooperation, Milton's allusions to the *Aeneid* reveal the limits to his egalitarianism and thus the limits of his critique of national and sectarian ascendancy.

To the crisis of undeserved but necessary dominion, *Paradise Lost* posits a Protestant and largely defanged Mariology carefully confined within marriage. The maternal figure of Mary, the second Eve, poses an internal challenge to the male-centered economies of Christian belief and of reproduction.[95] Yet Milton works to exorcise Mariolatry from his Mariology: the desire for female abundance without male mediation has already been relegated to the status of idolatrous tree worship. Milton's poetic solution reveals the sharp limits of any politics of grace that seeks to overcome the politics of dominion. The recognition that Adam's husbandly lordship is undeserved leads, paradoxically, to the fantasy that contact with God will cause Eve to submit graciously even as she recognizes her original desire to be her own image. The political resonances of this narrative show the precise intersection of gender and national or colonial politics. Milton's inability to articulate a sustained or practical line of thought about Irish affairs can best be understood as the result of a clash between his unremitting anti-Catholicism and his hard-fought political insights. The crisis of dominion undeserved generates Milton's intellectually probing and morally urgent art precisely to the extent that it poses an impasse with no clear resolution. The history of the so-called British mainland would replicate this deadlock on a larger scale, for centuries to come.

4

GEMELLE LIBER: MILTON'S 1671 ARCHIVE

The latter end of his commonwealth forgets the beginning.

—William Shakespeare, *The Tempest*

For a reader who knows the entire corpus of Milton's writings, *Paradise Lost*'s concluding vision of conjugal love is compromised. In book 9 Adam and Eve consummate the Fall, and the poet likens the couple to the figure of Samson: "So rose the Danite strong / Herculean Samson from the harlot-lap / Of Philistean Dalilah, and waked / Shorn of his strength" (9.1059–62). If Adam and Eve maintain their bond as one flesh after the Fall, that flesh is now likened to that of Samson, whose sexual transgression undoes his heroic valor. By invoking the biblical Delilah, the image of unity in sexual congress reverts to division across gender.[1] In *Samson Agonistes*, Milton transforms the Philistine harlot Dalila into Samson's estranged wife, and the couple's explosive confrontation stages a breakdown of marital and political reconciliation. Samson's exchange with Dalila forms the middle of a dramatic poem about the confrontation between God's elect nation and its idolatrous oppressors.[2] Samson's own arguments generate an interpretive challenge for modern readers. Affirming Israel's ascendancy over the Philistines requires agreement that wives should be subject absolutely to their husbands.[3] The discord of *Samson Agonistes* lays bare the ideologies of gender that the conclusion of *Paradise Lost* renders lovely through Eve's gracious speech.

For Milton, the division of gender harkens back to the challenge that feminized chaos, the womb and tomb of creation, poses for God's primacy. Such problems cannot be resolved decisively by Samson's heroism or by Adam and Eve's union. Only the body of Christ can serve as the unifying and all-encompassing agent. As the apostle Paul writes to a church divided by the question of Jewish versus Gentile worship, "There is neither Jew nor Greek, there is neither bond nor free, there is neither male nor female: for ye are all one in Christ Jesus" (Gal. 3:28). This passage may strike us as genuinely revolutionary, describing the messiah as obliterating cultural identities previously adjudicated by Hebraic law, social classifications according to Roman law, and even the fact of gender difference. The consequences are at once political and cosmological, advancing the world toward its final destiny of being all in all. Yet such a conviction jars with other moments in which Paul strictly upholds gender norms. "But I suffer not a woman to teach, nor to usurp authority over the man," Paul writes to Timothy, "for Adam was first formed, then Eve" (1 Tim. 2:12–13).

Milton desires a radical universality, but he never lets his readers forget about the persistence of regulated differences. This ineluctable tension prevents Milton's Jesus from fully overcoming the politics of undeserved dominion despite proving his merit time and again. In *Paradise Regained*, Jesus repeatedly rejects all available forms of power. He rejects the satanic temptation of liberating God's nation politically, choosing instead to offer spiritual liberation to Israel and to all the nations. In chapter 1 I argued that, according to *Paradise Regained*, war imperils rather than edifies a people by producing forms of cultural chaos associated with the Tartars. Jesus considers "it more humane, more heavenly first / By winning words to conquer willing hearts, / And make persuasion do the work of fear" (1.221–23). Yet even as he anticipates a politics of grace, Jesus both adopts the language of conquest and reserves the ultimate right to subdue those who stubbornly resist a new messianic regime (1.224–26). At stake is the continued existence of national and cultural boundaries:

> Know therefore when my season comes to sit
> On David's throne, it shall be like a tree
> Spreading and overshadowing all the earth,

Or as a stone that shall to pieces dash
All monarchies besides throughout the world,
And of my kingdom there shall be no end.

(4.146–51)

Jesus initially describes his reign as a season, an organic turn to plenitude. The image of the tree, however, gives way to that of the stone. In a
world beset by a central dilemma, the decisive shift toward universalism
and peace requires both the humane art of persuasion and earth-shatter-
ing force.

In *Paradise Regained*, such matters of global significance converge upon
the story of one man in the wilderness. Because Milton was famously unable to narrate the crucifixion, the poem's central question is not how Jesus
dies but rather how he comports himself in life. For Milton's Jesus, the first
step in building an endless kingdom lies in clarifying his personal identity;
within the integrity of his being, the divine and the human can converge.
At this personal level, Milton's brief epic relates the tension between the
nation versus universality (there is neither Jew nor Greek) to Jesus's attempt to define the contours of his gendered self (there is neither male nor
female). At neither the cultural nor personal level does a clear path to the
all in all present itself. The category of abjection serves to link the mythic
division between divine and chaotic realms, the cultural mandate to separate from impurity, and the intimate challenges to individual integrity.
According to Kristeva, Christ effects a shift from abjection to incorporation. Whereas Israel's holiness is predicated on separation, the Christian
seeks redemption by acknowledging the internal presence of abjection—
now termed sin. The function of the mouth changes from refusing the
unclean to speaking a language that gains beauty even as it gives voice
to unclean impulses. Christian speech expresses the possibility of grace.
In Milton's cosmology, replacing abjection with incorporation marks an
advance toward a world of complete plenitude. Yet the transition from
the living Jesus to a new Christian subject remains incomplete in *Paradise
Regained*. Milton assiduously avoids calling his hero Christ, choosing instead to tell the life of Jesus as a young Jewish man who seeks above all to
obey. Jesus must fulfill Hebraic law and resist all impurity, even though his
ultimate mission is to admit unclean Gentile members into his holy body.

This paradox will eventually be resolved in death and resurrection, but as a living man, Milton's Jesus can find no solution.

The conclusion of *Paradise Regained* underscores how abjection tests not only a nation's limits but also the primacy and wholeness of an individual subject who traces his origins to a maternal body. Insofar as Milton's second epic has a plot, it is largely the story of a hungry young man who finally finds a suitable meal before returning to his mother's home.[4] In the final moments of the final book, Jesus takes part in a heavenly feast, at which angels hail him as the Son of God and man. Yet Milton's narrative cannot describe how this incorporation of the divine and the human becomes fully effective for salvation. *Paradise Regained* famously ends in suspension, with Jesus returning obscurely and privately to his mother's house. Even in triumph, Milton's Jesus does not find a way to leave his mother's side to assume full control of his Father's house, the Temple, which he seeks to open as a place of redemption for all the nations.

In this chapter I aim not only to describe the contradictory demands of Jesus's dilemma—Hebraic purity versus universal incorporation, identification with the heavenly Father and human mother—but also to show how this impasse occasions new poetic and religious communication. The difficulty of Jesus's position becomes amplified by the initial 1671 publication of Milton's gospel narrative. The original title page calls the publication *Paradise Regain'd. A Poem. In IV Books. To which is added Samson Agonistes*. The incomplete narrative of Jesus's messianic mission is followed by a tragedy in which self-annihilating heroism upholds the chosen nation against its enemy. In recent decades, the basic meaning of *Samson Agonistes*—whether it upholds Samson as a heroic type of Christ or reproves his actions as those of a dark, shadowy type—has been hotly contested.[5] Tracing the dilemma of Miltonic creation allows for a reading that negotiates the differences between the orthodox and revisionist positions. As I have argued, Milton reveals that conquest proves ineffective or even unjust without surrendering his conviction that force against chaotic unruliness is sanctioned by God. These chaotic forces are distant forms of contagion that nonetheless strike surprisingly close to home. In *Samson Agonistes*, the Philistine Dalila registers such a threat. Milton displays the problems besetting Samson's militant and masculine form of heroism, knowing that Israel is not effectively liberated at the end of the book of Judges. At the same time, however, Milton's dramatic study does not in any simple or straightforward way deny that Samson's heroism derives from God. Samson calls Jesus's mission to account precisely because the marked failures of his heroism have already been deemed acceptable as part of Jesus's own history, as the eleventh chapter of the epistle to the Hebrews teaches. Milton's divided thinking about force and conquest continues to produce conflicted understandings of *Samson Agonistes* and its hero.

It has not gone unnoticed that the initials of the printer of Milton's 1671 poems are the same as those of the author, but the printer J.M. was most likely John Macocke, and the exact conditions that led to these two works being bound together remain uncertain.[6] Tobias Gregory has argued against reading *Paradise Regained* and *Samson Agonistes* as linked. "The idea to print the two poems together," Gregory points out, "could have just as well come from the stationer John Starkey as from the blind poet, the better to make up a saleable volume."[7] Yet numerous critics have described the need to examine these poems together, as they were initially published, in order to understand Milton's formal, theological, and political engagements.[8] Doing so complicates the typological relationship whereby Jesus and Samson respectively stand for "perfection and fallibility" or "clarity of the completed understanding and the darkness through which the design is seen in fragments."[9] The experiences of Milton's last poetic protagonists undermine the typological settlement of past, present, and future. *Samson Agonistes* adds to *Paradise Regained* the troubling knowledge that the internal contradictions of creative power lie at the heart of Jesus's cultural legacy—a legacy that he struggles to overcome as a living human being.

This culminating chapter shares the central concerns of the entire book: abjection as the manifestation of undeserved dominion at the levels of the divine kingdom, the nation, and the self. Nevertheless, it cannot (because Milton's writings cannot) offer any prescriptive solutions. Rather, such concerns are reoriented to ask how Milton's intractable problem becomes the basis of a Christian poetry that mediates between past experience and present-day knowledge. *Paradise Regained* meditates upon how its poetic narrative transmits Jesus's lived experience across time through the printed word. My analysis of Milton's 1671 poems relies not only on the category of abjection but also on Jacques Derrida's late work *Archive Fever* (*Mal d'archive*). This theory of the archive provides a robust account of how the body governs the transmission of cultural knowledge. Through an engagement with the Freudian archive, Derrida comments on a Hebraic sense of the future and the past. The archive troubles the distinctions between a discrete mind and the cultural tradition that lays claims upon it; the latter must always be in excess of the former without being necessarily external to it. Rites such as circumcision turn the body into one of many media for preserving the archive. In *Paradise Regained*, Jesus seeks to possess the Hebraic archive and turn it into a universal seat of redemption. He finds, however, that this archive lays a claim upon him, body and mind.

I read Milton's 1671 poems as an archive in miniature, as two linked works that enact sustained thought about the Hebraic, Christian, and Miltonic archives. The archive, as Derrida reminds us, is always directed to the future. Milton knows that his archive arises out of the imperfections of the past. *Paradise Regained* declares that it seeks to "tell of deeds / Above heroic, though in secret done, / And unrecorded left through many an age" (1.14–16). This audacious claim receives sanction from the gospel of John, which ends by surrendering to the overwhelming narrative demands of its protagonist: "And there are also many other things which Jesus did, the which, if they should be written every one, I suppose that even the world itself could not contain the books that should be written." (John 21:25). Milton seizes on this opportunity to make his mark on the open-ended project of knowledge. As much as it is entangled in multiple histories— early modern, New Testament, Hebraic, and mythic—Milton's archive presents itself as a resource for the future reader who continues to seek, against all prior evidence, a world free of dominion. In the meantime of history, however, the intractable political and theological crises of undeserved dominion serve as the grounds of communication between Milton and his future readers.

Of Whom They Spake I Am

Reading Milton's 1671 poems together does not necessarily assume that Milton actively bound these works together. On the contrary, the contingencies of the printing house and of the marketplace demarcate the limits of the poet's agency and control over his archive. Stephen B. Dobranski's scholarship on the book trade emphasizes how even an individualist like Milton could publish his works only as "a social writer who depended on others—especially printers and booksellers—to construct the perception of his autonomy."[10] In a 1646 Latin poem, Milton (then a published poet with unfulfilled epic ambitions) voices concerns about the author's loss of control in the transition from verse to printed book, from private work to public archive. Milton composed "Ad Joannem Rousium, Oxoniensis Academiae Bibliothecarium" (To John Rouse, Librarian of Oxford University) after a copy of his 1645 poems was lost en route to the Bodleian.[11] Rouse had asked Milton for a copy of his poems, providing an occasion for the poet to be enrolled in a distinguished space. Deploying a common metaphor, Milton refers to his missing book as his wayward child. The two halves of Milton's English and Latin poems constitute his twin book, a *gemelle liber*, but this twin also has many brethren in the book's multiple copies.

In the coda to chapter 1 I argued that the shared logic of wretched matter links Milton's attempt to banish rhyme with God's purgation of chaotic dregs from creation. "Ad Joannem Rousium" describes literal filth invading Milton's poetry, but the ode also uses images of physical defilement to suggest broader concerns about cultural abjection in England. The poet imagines that his lost book will be perused by a low-born bookseller with calloused hands (lines 41–42). But because this bookseller can, despite his low status, actually read Milton's verse, the poet can instruct his book to have hope of transcending its materiality. The ideational content of the book, the author hopes, will fly from Lethe to Jove. Later in the poem, Milton conflates the lost book with the new one he sends to Rouse. He describes the new book's destination, Oxford's library, as a home safe from vulgar tongues, "Quo neque lingua procax vulgi penetrabit" (line 79). The poem's full title calls the Bodleian a "biblioteca publica," but this relatively exclusive archive proves a safer shelter than the imagined bookshop.

Milton's writings are threatened not only by mere mishap but also by pervasive cultural upheaval in a time of civil war. The turbulent present makes the future reception of Milton's writings all the more uncertain. The second strophe of "Ad Joannem Rousium" expresses a wish that the current situation might be rectified by a god or an "editus deo," one begotten by a god. These lines invite a Christian interpretation of these Latin words in their Greek ode form, whereby God through his Son and Word would rescue England from strife. The strophe describes how the divine power may use the arrows of Apollo, god of poetry, to drive away the impure birds ("immundas volucres") that harass Phineus. Milton refers to the second book of the *Argonautica*, in which Zeus punishes the prideful prophet Phineus by sending harpies that take food out of his hands and mouth and pour over him a foul stench. Milton thus likens the Civil War to defilement, and he hopes that God or the Son of God will use the arrows of poetry to undo cultural abjection. Yet such a desire cannot be fulfilled within the poem, and "Ad Joannem Rousium" leaves undecided the fates of Milton's country and of his legacy in publication.

Milton would return to "Ad Joannem Rousium" decades after its composition by publishing it in the 1673 edition of his *Poems*. As the last poem in the volume (followed only by the treatise *Of Education*, also "written above twenty years since"), "Ad Joannem Rousium" occupies a privileged place in a volume that encapsulates Milton's poetic career and anticipates his future reputation. The ode concludes with the hope that Milton's book will find not a vulgar throng but what *Paradise Lost* calls fit audience though few. Although Rouse has already recognized Milton's talent, the poet's public legacy remains uncertain. Milton hopes that "the children of the future, in some distant and wiser age" will evaluate his poetry (lines 81–84). The poem ends conditionally, with both the soundness of future judgment and the poet's own merits remaining indeterminate: "Si quid meremur sana posteritas sciet" (line 86). Contingency crystallizes in the poem's final line, an ablative absolute ("Rousio favente") that ascribes to Rouse the agency to fulfill Milton's desire for recognition.

"Ad Joannem Rousium" both foreshadows (in 1646) and recalls (in 1673) some of the central concerns of Milton's 1671 poems: knowledge and the body, purity versus defilement, and the past's claim on the future. Whereas Milton's early ode describes the problem of transmitting artistic truth in an impure world, his later poetry ascribes this dilemma to Jesus. *Paradise Regained* tells the story of the true *editus Deo*, the word of God turned flesh. Yet Jesus does not simply announce himself as a new truth, but rather claims an existing Hebraic archive as always having been his own. The opening chapter of *De Doctrina Christiana* declares that all scriptures properly belong to Christian doctrine. Milton directs the reader to understand "the name Christ as meaning also Moses, and the prophets who foretold his coming, and the apostles whom he sent" (*CPW* 6:126). The original Latin is even more emphatic, teaching that the writings of all the prophets before Christ and of the apostles after him are subsumed by his name ("sub nomine Christi"). "Christian" thus designates an archive, one that unifies and reorganizes a body of old materials and designates space for ones to come under the authority of Christ.

Jesus, in Milton's view, fully deserves to claim Hebrew scriptures for his own. Yet Jesus finds that he must labor to fulfill this calling. Annabel Patterson reads *Paradise Regained* as "an essay on the importance of reading the Scriptures," in which the hero is "an ardent scriptural exegete."[12] Milton's hero cannot act in the manner of Boiardo's Orlando, who forgets he has a book of all answers and farcically overthrows the Sphinx with sheer strength, thus ignoring the Sphinx's oedipal riddle rather than solving it. Seeking to "publish his godlike office," Jesus prepares himself by reading and rereading assiduously. "I again revolved / The Law and prophets," Jesus recalls, "searching what was writ / Concerning the Messiah" (*PR* 1.259–61). This is how he realizes that the archive has been his all along: "of whom they spake / I am" (1.262–63). This good news must be disseminated to be made effective; Jesus seeks ways to "publish his godlike office now mature" (1.188). Yet the Word of God leaves behind no writings of his own, leaving the work of transmitting his story and teachings to his followers. As Patterson points out, however, *De Doctrina Christiana* admits that the New Testament is less reliable than Hebrew scriptures "because it has been committed to the care of various untrustworthy authorities."[13] The Bible itself is a bifurcated collection of ancient writings, and the textual history of the Christian half may call into question its claim upon Hebrew scriptures.

Collecting, preserving, and disseminating textual knowledge is the work of an authority and an exercise of power. The archive, as Derrida points out, originates as the privileged place from which archons legislate. The power of the archon is one of consignation, which "aims to coordinate a single corpus, in a system or a synchrony in which all the elements articulate the unity of an ideal configuration."[14] More specifically, the archive is originally a house, a dwelling that eventually becomes a public resource.[15] The archive marks a transition from private and familial to public knowledge. *Paradise Regained* narrates a decisive moment in textual history through a biography of the Word of God. The site of the archive is the Temple, the Father's house, where, even at the age of twelve, Jesus had demonstrated his proficiency at reading the Law. Yet the means of taking control of his Father's house and then opening its doors to all the nations prove difficult. By the end of the epic, Jesus stands triumphantly atop the Temple, but he does so only momentarily before returning to his mother's private house.

Jesus's vocation begins at his baptism, a public affirmation that he is indeed the proper heir to the Father's house. In an extended internal monologue, Jesus recalls this same event as a scene of recognition that enacts a momentary confusion of identity: "but he [John the Baptist] / Straight knew me, and with loudest voice proclaimed / Me him (for it was shown him so from heaven) / Me him whose harbinger he was" (*PR* 1.274–77). The repeated phrase "me him" could potentially suggest that John the Baptist identifies Jesus as himself. (The New Testament alludes repeatedly to the troubling confusion between Jesus's and John's identities, which persists even after the death of both men. In the gospels, Jesus speaks somewhat passive-aggressively about his forerunner.)[16] After the parenthetical delay, however, Jesus clears up this potential ambiguity decisively with the phrase "whose harbinger he was." If John the Baptist's status as harbinger suggests his temporal primacy, the genitive "whose" declares Jesus's mastery. The past tense "was" accords with Jesus's narration of a prior event, but it also emphasizes the obsolescence of John the Baptist after the messiah's arrival.

As a watery scene of potential doubling and recognition, Jesus's baptism at the Jordan effectively replaces Eve's narcissistic mirroring at the Edenic reflecting pool. As I argued in the preceding chapter, Eve's narcissistic impulses condense into psychological form the structural instabilities that trouble Eden. Jesus must excise unhomeliness from creation, and baptism begins this work by clarifying the singular identity of the Son of God at the threshold of the promised land. It is John the Baptist who arrives first at the Jordan and could potentially treat Jesus as his reflection. If, according to Jesus, John "proclaimed / Me him," John would devolve into a version of Ovid's Narcissus, whose declaration of self-realization identifies his ego with a third-person pronoun ("iste ego sum"). This possibility is foreclosed almost as soon as it appears. John the Baptist humbly and willingly accepts his position as Jesus's inferior. Yet like Eve's lesson at the reflecting pool, Jesus's lesson at the Jordan reveals him to be a reflection—not of John the Baptist but of God the Father. John humbles himself but performs a baptism that allows divine narcissism to express itself fully: "And last the sum of all, my Father's voice, / Audibly heard from heaven, pronounced me his, /

Me his beloved Son" (*PR* 1.283–85).[17] "Me his" replaces "me him." Public recognition of Jesus as the one greater man turns into divine recognition of Jesus as "the express image" of God (Heb. 1:3).

Yet this demonstration of Jesus's relationship to his Father leaves central questions unresolved. As the conclusion of *Paradise Regained* underscores, Jesus's identity may remain bound up with his mother's, and a return to the mother's house amounts to a deferral of Jesus's full publication. In book 1 Jesus recalls his early experiences and describes how Mary intuits and responds to her young son's plans for future heroism by informing him of his unique birth and infancy. This story culminates in Simeon and Anna's confirmation of his birth as the King of Israel. Jesus then continues:

> This having heard, straight I again revolved
> The Law and prophets, searching what was writ
> Concerning the Messiah, to our scribes
> Known partly, and soon found of whom they spake
> I am.

> (1.259–63)

It is Jesus who returns to the Law and prophets after hearing his mother's story, but the reader does not gain absolute certainty that the "I" in line 259 refers to Jesus and not to Mary until the momentous "I am" of line 263. (This line hints at a equation of Jesus and Yahweh, but the lack of contradiction in verb tense makes it far less emphatic than passages from the gospels such as John 8:58. Milton's "I am" formula accommodates Trinitarian readings even while leaving room for anti-Trinitarian views.) In book 2 Mary narrates her and her son's lives in an internal monologue; she concludes that her "heart hath been a storehouse long of things / And sayings laid up" (2.103–4). Mary, most likely illiterate, does not point to her brain or mind, but her heart also archives knowledge of the messiah in the medium of affective intensity.

Bibles allow individual families to enroll their names within the covers of a sacred book. Yet a patriarchal archive can neither deny nor fully acknowledge the female hands that reproduce knowledge and the female bodies that give birth to future recipients.[18] Milton's familial archive suggests as much. John Milton Sr. bequeathed to his son a King James Bible that marked the father's break with Catholicism. Milton would continue to list the names of family members in this Bible, but as William Kerrigan notes, Milton's inscriptions "suggest a bias. . . . His daughters are born, but his wives merely die . . . [and] his sister joins the family record only through her male children. This is the bookkeeping of a patriarch."[19] The daughters whose births are recorded in this Bible would go on to serve as Milton's amanuenses, but they were expected only to record their father's words passively, not to speak either in their own name or in his.

Paradise Regained seems to stage the relationship between the maternal and the patriarchal archive ideationally, through Jesus's and Mary's intertwined thoughts. Yet the reference to Simeon and Anna suggests the importance of Jesus's and Mary's bodies. Only the gospel of Luke records Simeon and Anna's recognition of Jesus at the Temple. This scene occurs as Mary enacts postpartum rites: "And when eight days were accomplished for the circumcising of the child, his name was called JESUS, which was so named of the angel before he was conceived in the womb. And when the days of her purification according to the law of Moses were accomplished, they brought him to Jerusalem, to present him to the Lord; (as it is written in the law of the LORD, Every male that openeth the womb shall be called holy to the Lord;) and to offer a sacrifice according to that which is said in the law of the Lord, a pair of turtledoves, or two young pigeons" (Luke 2:21–24). Luke makes a revealing conflation. Initially, what seems to be described is the *pidyon ha'ben*, the redemption of the firstborn son. Yet this ritual requires a monetary offering (Numbers 3:47 calls for five shekels per firstborn), whereas turtledoves and pigeons are sacrifices for the purification of the mother. According to Leviticus 12:8, a mother who cannot offer a lamb must offer "two turtles, or two young pigeons; the one for the burnt offering, and the other for a sin offering." Whether accidentally or deliberately, Luke's conflation of maternal purification with the redemption of the firstborn makes apparent multiple ironies. The Son of God, sent to redeem the world, must himself be ritually redeemed; Mary brings to the Temple the very Lamb of God, but she must offer a substitute sacrifice to purify her body after giving birth to him.[20]

As Luke 2 points out, Jesus is known and named by God before being conceived in the body of his Jewish mother.[21] Yet in the eight days between birth and circumcision, Jesus remains nameless, without any legible identity. Only circumcision reveals his name and renders it effective for salvation. The brief episode in Luke raises compelling questions about the Jewish messiah—about the need for his circumcision and ritual redemption and for his mother's purification. Such questions would vex the earliest Christians, as debates about circumcision would create tensions and divisions alluded to in the other canonical work attributed to Luke, the Acts of the Apostles. A familiar recourse in Christian thought is to dismiss Jewish rites as mere formality, in contrast to the deeper truth that Christ initiates. The Geneva Bible notes in response to Luke 2:22, "*This is meant, for the fulfilling of the law: for otherwise the virgin was not defiled, nor uncleane, by the birth of this childe.*"[22]

For early modern thinkers, concerns about the purity of Jesus's Hebraic body and about his relationship to his mother bear on political thought about nationhood and universality. This is apparent in the work of the Dutch humanist Hugo Grotius. In *On the Truth of the Christian Religion* (originally published in Dutch in 1622 and in Latin in 1627), Grotius differentiates the nation-specific covenant with the Israelites from "a new one, and this common to all Nations."[23] Grotius notes that Jesus was circumcised and "used Jewish meats," but he emphasizes that "that part of the Law, which was dissolved by Christ, contained nothing good in its own nature, but consisted of things themselves indifferent."[24] Only an ecumenical covenant can bring the spiritual meaning of the circumcision to the physical action. These commonplaces about Christianity and Judaism help form Grotius's influential thought about universal and international law. In *On the Laws of Warre and Peace* (1625), Grotius attempts to establish natural law—founded on universal human values—as the basis of international law, the law of nations. The possible cleavage between divine will and natural law is problematic. Grotius cautiously comments that "many things in [the 'Old Law'] proceed from the free will and pleasure of God, which yet is never contrary to the true Law of Nature."[25] Grotius maintains this uneasy space between natural law and God's covenant with a single nation as he seeks a basis for international agreement. He expresses his admiration for Christian Roman rulers who had attempted to formulate an international law, but he faults them for having mistaken Roman for genuinely universal principles. Grotius attempts to go further.

Most relevant to the current discussion is how Grotius's theological and legal positions had been expressed earlier in his 1608 tragedy *Christus*

Patiens, translated into English by George Sandys. The climactic fourth
act, which narrates the crucifixion, ends with a seventy-line speech by a
chorus of Roman soldiers. The speech begins with an apostrophe to the sun
and goes on to describe in pagan, mythological terms the recent calamities
("What new Phaeton / With feeble hands to guide thy Charriot strives, /
And farre from the deserted Zodiack drives!").[26] Yet these soldiers draw
closer to Christian truths that surpass their pagan beliefs. They come to
pray not to the sun but to the "Great Father of us all," and they conclude
that salvation cannot be achieved by "the Religion of the Samian, / Nor
Thracian Harpe . . . / Nor that Prophetick Boy" (4.411, 419–21). Sandys's
gloss identifies the Samian as Pythagoras, and the prophetic boy as Tages.[27]
Through seemingly unaided reason, the Roman soldiers come to an understanding that both Greek and Latin religions have been rendered obso-
lete by a greater truth.

The final act begins by dramatizing the meeting of Nicodemus and
Joseph of Arimathea, who conclude that both Romans and Jews are guilty
of Christ's death—but especially the Jews. The last words in the tragedy
belong to Mary, who laments her son's death by remembering the intimate bond between mother and child ("Thy milk from these two foun-
tains sprung: / These armes about my neck have hung" [5.211–12]). Mary
concurs with a view of Israel's special guilt: "Aegypt, so just to thy exile, /
Hath now redeem'd her former Curse; / Our Jews then those of Memphis
worse" (5.214–16). In her final speech, Mary turns from despair and bit-
terness to joy and hope, in part because she recognizes her son's mission
as universal and not bound to a single nation that has proved itself unfit.
"A holy people shall obey thy Throne," she declares, and goes on to explain
the capacious nature of this people: "A thousand Languages shall thee
adore: / Thy Empire know no bounds" (5.287, 295–96).By surrendering
her intimate maternal claim on Jesus, Mary speaks for the entire tragedy
and expresses this shift between Jewish, Roman, and then truly universal
paradigms.

Milton engages with commonplace typological modes of interpretation,
but in a way that tends to devote more attention to the historical reality of
the Old Testament.[28] In *De Doctrina Christiana* he asserts, "Each passage of
scripture has only a single sense, though in the Old Testament this sense is
often a combination of the historical and the typological" (*CPW* 6:581). Initially, Milton's insistence on a single sense seems to preclude the possibility

of both "historical and typological" interpretations, until the caveat insists that the two can join into one. Yet this union is not easy to maintain. Jeffrey Shoulson has described how, for Milton, "the Jew's body represents that element of the text, that element of lived experience, which is necessarily unassimilable."[29] Because of Milton's intense desires to unite body and spirit and to assign a real historical value to "lived experience," Judaism cannot be relegated to the status of mere types and forms.[30]

At the end of *Paradise Lost*, Michael provides a pithy account of typology as he evokes the fallen world to come. He describes to Adam the transition "from shadowy types to truth, from flesh to spirit" by contrasting Moses "though of God / Highly belov'd, being but the minister / Of law" to "Joshua whom the gentiles Jesus call" (12.303, 307–10). Milton expresses a Christian view of typology that Deuteronomy partly resists: "And Joshua the son of Nun was full of the spirit of wisdom; for Moses laid his hands upon him.... And there arose not a prophet since in Israel like unto Moses" (Deut. 34:9–10). The first Joshua is explicitly inferior to Moses, yet the second must prove superior. Milton's brief account further suggests how, in the double helix of typology, the Jewish and Christian strands are kept in place by pagan bonds. It is the Gentile's naming that transforms Joshua the second-order lawgiver into Jesus the universal messiah. Only with his Gentile name can this second Joshua bring what Milton calls "large grace" to the nations. In the gospels, Jesus makes the transition from Jewish to pagan to Christian possible at his death, whereupon the Temple's veil is torn asunder. Yet Milton's narrative emphasizes how in life, Jesus must remain Jewish and avoid contact with pagan defilement.

Milton's views about Jewishness are far more vexed than those of a thinker like Grotius. For Milton, the uneasy kinship between Judaism and Christianity stages a foundational test case for the relationship between national exceptionalism and international agreement. Milton's 1671 poems focus such problems on the bodies of their heroes, and this pattern of thinking reveals specific difficulties in preserving lived experience within typological forms. "Upon the Circumcision" describes the infant Jesus's circumcision as a foreshadowing of the crucifixion, an act that will fully satisfy "that great covenant which we still transgress" (line 21). In Milton's sonnet on his "late espoused saint," Jesus is invoked implicitly as the one who will fulfill both the pagan and Hebraic forms of redemption imagined in the poem.[31] Milton's late wife returns to him in a dream, as Alcestis rescued by Hercules and as one "washed from spot of childbed taint" by "purifica-tion in the old Law" (lines 5–6). Atop the Temple in *Paradise Regained*, Jesus will fulfill his Herculean role (already attributed to Jesus by Milton's early Nativity Ode) by defeating Satan, "As when Earth's son Antaeus (to compare / Small things with greatest) in Irassa strove / With Jove's Alcides" (4.563–65). Thus begin the two sole epic similes in *Paradise Regained* that compare Jesus to classical figures. These similes have been described as impressive examples of a Christian perspective fulfilling and reorient-ing pagan myths.[32] Yet Milton leads his readers to question this fulfill-ment even while celebrating it. To prove himself the one greater Hercules, Jesus must fully conjoin the divine nature of his Father and the human nature of his mother. According to Ovid, Hercules does not suffer from the fires of the underworld upon his death, "save in the part his mother gave him"; only the part he inherits from Jove remains invulnerable.[33] In *De Doctrina*, Milton complicates or even contradicts his anti-Trinitarian logic (based on the conviction that a single God could not be plural in per-son) by describing "the union of two natures in Christ (*CPW* 6:423).[34] Like Hercules, Jesus is the son of God and man, but unlike the pagan hero, Jesus should not be divisible into discrete parts.

In Milton's Jesus the question of how to preserve the lived experience of Jewish bodies within a typological view of history coincides with the equally difficult question of how to conceptualize the union of human and divine natures. In what sense Jesus is both fully divine and human serves as the most basic question of *Paradise Regained* for Satan, Jesus, and the reader alike, forming what Barbara Lewalski has called the brief epic's identity motif.[35] My argument primarily concerns the relationship between Jesus and his human mother. The climactic Temple scene of *Paradise Re-gained* reminds us again of the maternal imprint on both mind and body. Antaeus draws strength from "his mother Earth" and needs to be sepa-rated from earth before he can be defeated. Jesus's Herculean feat lies in his ability to separate fully grown child and mother. Milton's sonnet on his deceased wife suggests that, both as the greater Hercules and as the one who fulfills the Hebraic Law, Jesus will restore the purity of the maternal body. The second epic simile recasts Jesus's Herculean victory by likening him to Oedipus. Jesus defeats Satan by solving the Sphinx's riddle anew, and his redefinition of man must clarify his relationship with his mother.

If attachment to the mother is an Antaean and satanic trait, Jesus, as a latter-day Oedipus, must learn to overcome it.

This is a lesson that Milton does not—perhaps cannot—narrate to completion, and the poem concludes with Jesus's return to his mother's house. This is in distinct contrast to the conclusion of Grotius's *Christus Patiens*, in which Mary learns to leave behind the memories of the infant attached to her body and to celebrate his role as the initiator of God's universal kingdom. Grotius's Mary recalls nursing as an intimate bond with her son. In Milton's imagination, eating and drinking assume far more prominence as acts of psychosexual and theological significance. Christian exegetes such as Calvin had argued that the temptation to turn stones into bread was a temptation not of hunger but of lack of trust in God. Milton's narrative adds a wholly new dietary temptation in the banquet scene of book 2, and the question of whether Jesus feels real hunger becomes a source of debate between Satan and Jesus and of some confusion for the reader.[36]

The category of abjection helps us connect dietary, sexual, and theological concerns in Milton's depiction of Jesus. As a subject living under the Law, Jesus seeks to fulfill not just heterogeneity but, ultimately, a radical monistic unity of body and flesh, of Jew and Gentile, perhaps even of male and female. In his focus on the living, Jewish Jesus rather than the resurrected and corporate body of Christ, Milton complicates any straightforward reading of Judaism—including Kristeva's—as a foil to the capacious standards of Christianity. Faced with the temptation of a satanic banquet, Milton's Jesus does not declare that nothing entering into him can defile him. Barbara Lewalski has described the dilemma that Satan generates— a dilemma that compels the reader to consider "the double perspective of the past and the future."[37] Jesus himself must look forward to fulfilling and abrogating aspects of the Law such as dietary restrictions. As an obedient Jewish subject, however, he cannot act in the name of Christian liberty. Jesus resists Satan's Comus-like temptation by echoing the response of the young Lady.[38] In *Paradise Regained,* as in both *A Masque* and *Paradise Lost,* the temptation of eating is also one of erotic knowledge: Satan presents Jesus with an elaborate banquet of "far-fet spoil" attended by youths fairer than Ganymede or Hylas as well as nymphs and naiads. Rejecting the twinned threat of food and erotic temptation, Jesus insists on his purity by keeping any potential contaminants at bay.

The dream that precedes this temptation illustrates how bodily purity impinges on the transmission of knowledge and, specifically, on the relationship between Christian and Hebraic archives. After admitting real hunger, Jesus dreams and sees "the ravens with their horny beaks / Food to Elijah bringing even and morn, / Though ravenous, taught to abstain from what they brought" (*PR* 2.267–69).[39] Elijah partakes twice of this food, which sustains him for his forty-day fast. Elijah clearly serves as a type of Christ, especially in his prophetic role; both old and new prophets will receive enough sustenance from God to endure their trials. Yet Jesus's dream reveals the multiplicity of roles that he must assume. Jesus, unlike Elijah, nears the end of his fast and feels hunger. In his abstinence from food, Jesus is identified in part with the ravens, who suppress their "ravenous" nature to bear divine sustenance without consuming it themselves. Jesus is also to fulfill the role of the food itself, as he will become the food that sustains his followers. The biblical source for this vision may support a typological reading whereby Elijah's food foreshadows the bread of communion: the first book of Kings records that the ravens brought to Elijah "bread and flesh" (1 Kings 17:6). Jesus's tripartite identification is complicated by the fact that ravens are deemed abominable (Lev. 11:15). A younger Milton had longed for an *editus deo* who could fend off the *immundas volucres* of cultural abjection. In the work of the mature Milton, Jesus maintains his own purity but also dreams of being conveyed by and even identifying with unclean birds. Jesus thus faces the more difficult task of incorporating within himself the divisions besetting creation while maintaining his Hebraic holiness.

At the end of *Paradise Regained,* Jesus finds "celestial food, divine" and "ambrosial drink" that he can properly accept (4.588–90). Milton specifies that while Jesus partakes of this food, the angels sing, and they begin by declaring him "true image of the Father," the Son of God, and the second Adam who founds a "fairer Paradise . . . / For Adam and his chosen sons" (4.596, 613–14). By resisting forbidden food, Jesus has both rejected the narcissistic mode of eating that led to Eve's loss of paradise and successfully weaned himself from the body of the second Eve. Jesus has prepared himself for nourishment from his Father, a meal that decisively confirms his place in divine and human patriarchal lineages as the Son of God and the second Adam. It is telling that the angels reach their climactic but obvious conclusion about Jesus's identity ("Hail Son of the Most High, heir of both worlds" [4.633]) only after foreseeing his conquest over physical uncleanness and spiritual confusion: the angels sing of how Jesus will command the demons into the herd of Gadarene swine. In the gospels, these demons represent a teeming confusion of identity as they collectively name themselves Legion. Once Jesus casts Legion into nearby swine, the unclean beasts immediately plunge to their death in the sea.

Despite the angels' triumphant song, the elevation of Jesus as the Son of God and man who remains heterogeneous but pure cannot be made fully public within the time frame of the poetic narrative. Jesus arrives at the scene of the heavenly banquet not on the wings of ravens but on the "plumy vans" of the angels. Yet this downward journey enacts the poem's greatest abomination, as a grammatical confusion conflates Jesus and Satan: "So Satan fell and straight a fiery globe / Of angels on full sail of wing flew nigh, / Who on their plumy vans received him soft" (*PR* 4.581–83). The reader can only deduce gradually that "him" in line 583 refers to Jesus, not to Satan.[40] From the reader's perspective, the setting of the divine banquet coincides precisely with the emergence of Jesus's identity from the murky "him."

In the acts of communion that will follow Jesus's death and resurrection, however, sinful and unclean Gentiles will partake of the heavenly banquet. In book 3 of *Paradise Lost*, the Son volunteers to die for mankind and foresees his resurrection: "Thou wilt not leave me in the loathsome grave / His prey, nor suffer my unspotted soul / For ever with corruption there to dwell" (3.247–49). Before his incarnation, the Son may not yet realize that even if God preserves his "unspotted soul" in death, the cleanliness of his body presents a problem. The biblical source of these lines suggests as much. Paul, trying to convince a Jewish audience that Jesus was indeed the messiah, appropriates the words of the psalmist to describe Jesus's purity even after death: "Thou shalt not suffer thine Holy One to see corruption" (Acts 13:35; cf. Ps. 16:10). Unconvinced, the Jews leave the synagogue, but "the Gentiles besought that these words might be preached to them the next sabbath" (Acts 13:42). Even after trial and triumph, Milton's Jesus faces the dilemma of having proven himself the Son of God and man by maintaining his purity, only to anticipate a future in which unclean peoples enter into and partake of his communal body. This dilemma proves intractable, and rather than publish his office, Jesus retires as an obscure figure to his mother's house at the end of the poem. There he will remain for the time being, a Jewish man by his mother's side.

My Riddling Days Are Past

The addition of *Samson Agonistes* to *Paradise Regained* amplifies the question of how Jesus, as a Jewish subject, can fulfill history and begin annulling the divisions that hinder the unity of God's kingdom. In a compelling reading of *Paradise Regained*, James Nohrnberg describes Milton's Jesus as being "tried by the future" and "summoned by the future," his ego "formulated and reformulated as if it were the recipient of a series of callings."[41] Yet the pairing of Jesus and Samson suggests that Jesus is called not only by the future—a future that will culminate in the divine all in all—but also by the past, the cultural legacy inscribed upon his body on the same day he received his divinely ordained name (Joshua, whom the Gentiles Jesus call). Milton's Samson, by contrast, is summoned by a Christian future that will both affirm his life and overshadow it. If this is a future Milton believes in, it is one that Samson resists. The addition of *Samson Agonistes* to *Paradise Regained* presents a series of unresolvable challenges. On the one hand, the unified Hebraic archive may exist not only to guard against but also to appropriate neighboring cultures. On the other hand, the past also deems Jesus's attempt to arrogate the Hebraic archive for an ecumenical future an unjust act of usurpation.

The pairing and ordering of the 1671 poems thus reopen the question that Milton attempts to settle in *De Doctrina*: how Hebraic writings can be reinterpreted as looking ahead to the Christian archive that will assimilate them. For Derrida, the archive looks to the future even as it houses the past. Derrida reveals the cultural politics of the archive by following Yosef Yerushalmi's attempts to claim Freudian writings for Judaism. Although Yerushalmi wants to insist upon the Jewish heritage that Freud only partly assumed, the project remains contingent on the future paths of Judaism and of science. Yerushalmi claims openness to the future as not just the essential but the unique feature of Jewishness. Elsewhere, however, Yerushalmi argues, "Only in Israel and nowhere else is the injunction to remember felt as a religious imperative to an entire people."[42] For Derrida, such contradictory claims about openness to the future and memory reveal the paradoxical place of the archive. More troubling is the claim that such traits are exclusively Jewish. This claim reveals the violence involved in "the archontic injunction to guard and to gather." Archontic violence is not simple exclusion. Rather, the archive guards against the other while also keeping some of the other, and "in the movement of this jealous violence, it comprises in itself, thus guarding it, the self-otherness or self-difference." The command both to remember and to be open to the future "orders to promise, but it orders repetition" and thus reveals the operation of the death drive, "the violence of forgetting."[43] The archive defines integrity for an individual, a culture, or a religion by excluding and usurping, storing and suppressing.

Samson Agonistes enacts, on multiple levels, archontic violence and the ambivalent status of the archive. Its characters initially espouse an elegantly simple conception of the archive, of past and future, of Jewish and non-Jewish. Early in the poem Samson describes himself as having been "like whom the Gentiles feign to bear up heaven."[44] If "like whom" threatens to set the typological wheel spinning, the word "feign" fixes it and declares the primacy of Hebraic truth. The mythological Atlas can only dimly resemble the true historical personage of Samson. Yet the impulses of the Christian author and his Hebraic characters may be at odds with each other. In shaping a biblical narrative into tragic form, Milton conjoins the godly and the pagan, the Hebraic and the Hellenic.[45] As William Riley Parker has noted, the ode form of "Ad Joannem Rousium" recurs only once more in Milton's writings, in *Samson Agonistes*, and the note on verse at the end of "Ad Joannem Rousium" deploys terms very similar to those of *Samson*'s prefatory note.[46] In both works, the union of truth and pagan form can be achieved through a Christian perspective: the preface to *Samson* cites as justification for its artistic project Paul, who is recorded quoting Euripides in the Acts of the Apostles. Milton also cites as a precedent *Christos Paschon*, the original *Christus Patiens* tragedy, which he attributes to the church father Gregory Nazianzen (rather than Apollinarius of Laodicea, who was commonly thought to be the author). This attribution, Joseph Wittreich argues, aligns Milton with Grotius, who had also attributed the tragedy to Gregory. Following this suggestion, Russell M. Hillier presents notable parallels between the relation of Samson's death in *Samson Agonistes* and that of Christ's crucifixion in Grotius's *Christus Patiens*.[47]

Such parallels may prove ironic. Whereas Grotius's tragedy enacts his belief in the triumphant supersession of Hebraic belief and polity, the characters of *Samson* resist being reinscribed into a universalizing Christian schema. Manoa, Samson, and the Chorus do not demonstrate a deep knowledge of the Hebrew scriptures, but they cherish their cultural memory. The Chorus recalls Samson's predecessors Gideon and Jephtha, and Samson exclaims, "Of such examples add me to the roll" (*SA* 290). Exemplarity governs much of the characters' concerns about past and future. At the end of the poem Manoa plans to make a monument of Samson, where "valiant youth" will "from his memory inflame their breasts / To matchless valour" (lines 1738–40). In death, Samson will be remembered as a hero befitting his legacy; Samson's valor will be like that of "matchless Gideon" (line 280). Exemplarity contrasts sharply with typology, whereby the future fills in the shadowy outlines of the past. The description of both Gideon and Samson as matchless reveals a paradox about exemplarity: both the latter-day hero and the emulated predecessor must remain unique, and their relationship can be one neither of superiority nor of equality.

Exemplarity arrests temporal development as much as it fosters it. Christian typology demands that Jesus overcome this dilemma. If the original Joshua cannot prove himself equal to or better than the matchless Moses, the second Joshua must. The roll call of faith in the eleventh chapter of the epistle to the Hebrews conscripts Gideon, Samson, and Jephthah into this pattern, claiming that they operated through a faith in "some better thing" that God had in store—namely, Christ (Heb. 11:32, 40). Wittreich has detailed the tradition of interpreting Samson typologically to show the difficulties that Samson presents to this mode of exegesis. Luther, for example, approvingly cites Samson as a hero and as a type of Christ. Yet faced with a war of peasants unleashed in part by his ideas, Luther renounces Samson as a model of political violence, declaring that miracles (not to mention types) are not the same as practical examples.[48]

Whereas typological readings would orient Samson's story toward Christ, the Jewish characters of *Samson Agonistes* reject a future-oriented narrative that would relegate their hero to relative obsolescence. Their desires are, in other words, idolatrous, based on the singular memory of a hero who should serve as a signifier of the ultimate referent, the Son of God.[49] In a provocative political reading of *Samson Agonistes*, Julia

Reinhard Lupton concludes, "Milton's Samson is finally not typological (a figure of Christ), or even typological in a terminally suspended way ('exil'd from light'), but *anti-typological*, arresting the recuperative movement of typology in the sheer violence of his act."[50] Samson may thus come to resemble the idol Dagon; Lupton punningly refers to Milton's protagonist as Samson Dagonistes. Samson sacrifices himself for the sake of iconoclasm, but *Samson Agonistes* raises the possibility that his superfluous actions bring glory to his own memory and not to God.[51] Early on, Samson declares his hope that the strife between God and Dagon, between Israel and the Philistine, "with me hath end" (line 461). The phrase seems to foreshadow Samson tearing down Dagon's temple, but in context it expresses the wish of a vanquished hero that God settle his own affairs: "all the contest is now / 'Twixt God and Dagon" (lines 461–62). God will indeed go on to defeat Dagon through the unmediated presence of his archive, the ark that will topple the idol without the aid of any human hands (1 Sam. 5). Later in the poem, when confronted by Harapha, Samson proclaims that his strength derives from "the power of Israel's God" (line 1150). Yet the eventual fulfillment of Samson's initial desire—that God act for himself—suggests that Samson's monument may testify to his own heroism rather than to God's victory over Dagon (let alone to Christ's victory on the cross). "Samson hath quit himself / Like Samson," Manoa memorably declares (lines 1709–10). The tautology expresses a desire to preserve his son's uniqueness, and Manoa envisions a family archive that brings honor to itself.

The Semichorus likens Samson to "that self-begotten bird / In the Arabian woods embossed, / That no second knows or third" (lines 1699–1701). The comparison may initially sound felicitous to the Christian reader, who understands that both pagan myth and Hebraic hero serve as types of Christ. Yet self-begetting is a satanic impulse that rejects one's creaturely standing before divine preexistence. At stake is a relationship not just to the past but to the future, expressed through a basic and intractable problem within typological thinking. Samson—or, more precisely, Samson like the phoenix—will have enduring fame but "no second knows or third." The formula makes it unclear whether the phoenix has been imported into Samson's Hebraic archive or the other way around. Samson may have been the true Atlas, but he can only be likened to the phoenix, which admits no successors. Bird and judge are both shadowy types, but they idolatrously resist the future imprint of truth.[52] Christ may be like unto Samson and the phoenix and supersede them, but Manoa and the Chorus want Samson to remain like Samson alone.

Hebraic idolatry assumes a pervasive role in *Samson Agonistes* through its pattern of borrowings and deviations from its scriptural source. As Northrop Frye has pointed out, in Judges, Samson's story is followed by a story of the Danites' idolatry.[53] The episode begins with Micah restoring eleven hundred shekels that he had stolen from his mother. This sum recalls the "eleven hundred pieces of silver" that the Philistine lords offer to Delilah in exchange for the secret of Samson's strength (Judg. 16:5). With two hundred of the restored shekels, Micah's mother makes idols, and Micah eventually enlists a Levite to be his household priest. Micah's story becomes not just associated with Samson's but a continuation of it when Danites arrive at Micah's house. These Danites are "from Zorah, and from Eshtaol" and are sent to spy out land for their tribe (Judg. 18:2); Samson's story begins with "a certain man of Zorah, of the family of the Danites, whose name was Manoah" and concludes with Samson being buried "between Zorah and Esthaol in the burying place of Manoah his father" (Judg. 13:2, 16:31). These Danites initially consult Micah's priest, but they eventually steal both him and his idol away from Micah. The founding of the city of Dan is thus ominously tainted with idolatry. "And the children of Dan set up the graven image," the conclusion of the Micah story tells us, "and they set them up Micah's graven image" (Judg. 18.30–31).

Micah's story provides a relevant example of how the transition from a familial, maternal realm to a public one can be marked by idolatrous formations. *Samson Agonistes* excises the most explicit connection between Micah's and Samson's stories. When Milton's Samson accuses Dalila of betraying him for money, he refers not to eleven hundred pieces of silver but to "Philistian gold" (line 831). In Judges, the repeated element of eleven hundred pieces of silver suggests how, within the structure of patriarchal tribal lineage, the relationship between son and new wife echoes that of son and mother. Both are fraught with peril. In *Samson Agonistes*, Milton conspicuously reworks this narrative. Whereas *Paradise Regained* tells the Hamletesque story of Jesus's connection to the maternal body troubling the transmission of his Father's knowledge, *Samson Agonistes* adopts the *Lear*-like strategy of excising the hero's mother, who figures prominently in the scriptural source.[54]

Yet the power that Milton divests from Samson's mother he confers upon Dalila.[55] If Milton removes a possible allusion to the account of Micah's idolatry when he replaces eleven hundred pieces of silver with Philistian gold, he nonetheless uses gold as a way of examining the fraught interplay between intergenerational relations, marriage, and cultural memory. Even before Dalila appears before him, Samson describes how she, having been "vitiated with gold / Though offered only, by the scent conceived / Her spurious first-born; treason against me" (lines 389–91). Samson imagines Dalila having been impregnated by gold with a bastard who would oppose him. Editors have long noted the possibility of an allusion to Danaë.[56] Such an allusion would multiply the threat that Dalila poses to Samson's sense of self in relation to family and God. Samson may be in a position analogous to that of Acrisius, the father of Danaë, who locks her up in a tower out of the fear of being killed by his own grandson. (Just as Samson abstains from wine, Acrisius refuses the worship of Bacchus.)[57] Dalila's treason, described as a dangerous bastard offspring, must logically be akin to that of Perseus. Yet as a son of Jove denied his divine heritage by Acrisius, Perseus also anticipates the role of Samson, once Heaven's nursling but fallen from grace. Samson will be, in fact, his own bastardly betrayer, playing Perseus to his own Acrisius. Facets of Samson would then seem to confront one another in the parallel pagan narrative. The first of Perseus's deeds narrated by Ovid is the petrification of Atlas with Medusa's head.[58] As we have already seen, Samson describes himself as having been the true Atlas, "like whom the Gentiles feign to bear up heaven." In Ovid, the story of Atlas's defeat is the story of how Atlas became Atlas as we know him—that is, as the Titan who, as a giant mountain, bears up Heaven. On the one hand, Dalila may serve as the Medusa's head by which Samson defeats himself and thereby becomes like Samson. On the other hand, Samson ascribes agency not to Dalila herself but to the Philistian gold that impregnates her. The implied association of Philistine gold with the pagan god Jove suggests that idolatry, and not mere greed, is the matter at hand. Yet finally, the accusation that Dalila was "vitiated with gold" may rebound onto the accuser if a golden god recalls the Israelites' own idolatry, which begins with the worship of a golden calf.[59]

Samson's accusations about Dalila's lust for gold thus serve as a kind of shorthand for the complex threat—erotic, familial, intratribal, and religious—that Dalila bears within her. I argued in chapter 3 that the conjugal narrative of *Paradise Lost* articulates vexing questions about cultural politics that appeals to international law raise but cannot fully answer. In the central confrontation of *Samson Agonistes*, Dalila shifts the terms of marital conflict toward legal matters. She insists that she was swayed not by gold but by the religious and civic leaders of her nation, because "to the public good / Private respects must yield" (lines 867–68). Samson responds that women forsake their parents and their country when they marry; thus the pleas of the Philistines who sought Dalila's aid were against "the law of nature, law of nations" (line 890). To contextualize Samson's and Dalila's respective claims, Victoria Kahn describes how contractual marriage and gender subordination serve as tropes for seventeenth-century theorists of sovereignty.[60] Theorists like Grotius appeal to marriage as a simultaneously natural and voluntary form of subordination. Thus Grotius makes his brand of absolutism more palatable in part by comparing subordination to a sovereign not just to slavery but to marriage. Yet such an analogy renders absolutism vulnerable to appeals to voluntarism and to natural rights preceding the sovereign's authority.

The similarities and differences between Milton and Grotius prove relevant again. Milton, as a defender both of divorce (but only when instigated by the husband) and of the people's rights to replace their ruler when deemed unfit, seems to have a more consistently voluntarist ideology of marriage and political power. Yet this context shows the seriousness of Dalila's challenge in *Samson Agonistes*. Samson not only appeals to husbandly superiority but also delegitimizes the Philistines as an "impious crew"; he can thus argue that his nationalism is compatible with an international, natural, and rational law. When Dalila argues back, however, she articulates "something like cultural relativism" and underscores "the antinomy of nationalism, its simultaneous dependence on and resistance to the law of nations."[61] With brutal concision, Milton turns a domestic conflict into an illustration of a fundamental dilemma: the ecumenical impulse toward shared reason and law is articulated within a defensively nation-bound matrix.

Dalila's threat runs even deeper than that of cultural relativism. Her speech culminates in an appeal to future knowledge and in a Philistine challenge to the Hebraic archive. Her last words reveal the archontic violence that the Hebraic archive must necessarily both preserve and forget.

Before leaving Samson, Dalila proclaims that she will be commemorated in her own country, "not less renowned than in Mount Ephraim / Jael, who with inhospitable guile / Smote Sisera" (lines 988–90). The problem, from Samson's perspective, is not merely that Dalila's people have a legacy of their own, or even that Dalila can enroll her knowledge of Jewish history in Philistine consciousness. More fundamentally, Dalila mocks the desire to uphold the patriarchal Hebraic archive as a unified cultural memory. Jael's killing of Sisera is celebrated in the Song of Deborah, which appears in the fifth chapter of Judges. Dalila reminds the reader that perhaps the oldest piece of Hebrew poetry recorded in all scripture is sung by a woman in praise of a woman. Jael may not be an Israelite, but she becomes an Israelite hero by defying the express wishes of her husband, Heber the Kenite, "which was of the children of Hobab the father in law of Moses" (Judg. 4:11).

The chain linking the biblical figures of Delilah, Jael, Heber, and Hobab to Moses may seem tenuous, yet it matters in the context of Dalila's challenge to the Hebraic archive. If Abraham is the first patriarch of the Israelites, Moses is the first archivist. Freud channeled both his psychoanalytic thought and his vexed relationship to Judaism in *Moses and Monotheism*, a text to which Yosef Yerushalmi and Derrida turn as they theorize Jewishness and the Jewish archive. Freud famously hypothesizes—as a claim about the genuinely "historical" rather than merely "material" past—that Moses was an Egyptian whom the Israelites murdered and then, as guilty parricides, obeyed. For Derrida, this means that even as the archive preserves memory and opens onto the future, it "must also import there, *in the same stroke*, the death drive, the violence of forgetting, *superrepression* (suppression and repression) . . . in short, the possibility of putting to death the very thing . . . which *carries the law in its tradition*."[62] This explains, according to Derrida, how the Freudian archive cannot simply distinguish between the past and the future, between the Jewish and the non-Jewish. James Nohrnberg presents a more hopeful alternative to Freud's oedipal reading of the Hebraic canon. Moses is not simply the father to be toppled and obeyed belatedly but is himself the heir of a number of biblical figures and their narratives: Joseph, Abraham, Noah, and, by way of marriage to a Kenite, Cain and Abel. Moses becomes the grand patriarch only by becoming a husband and a son-in-law to a Midianite priest (Jethro, who seems to be the same person as Hobab). Moses's marriage "is not intratribal, it is 'political,' between persons each of whom is foreign to the other. . . . The marriage is therefore between persons with a possible religious difference and implies a new ideological commitment on the part of a previously 'unchurched' or uncircumcised party."[63] Nohrnberg's reading makes the narrative of Israelite exceptionalism a capacious one. God is as much adoptive father as he is sovereign, and the Israelite-Egyptian binary admits a third term, the benevolent Midianite father-in-law.

In *Samson Agonistes*, Dalila's reference to Sisera reminds both the Jewish characters and the Christian reader that the Hebraic archive is the product of archontic violence, of recording and suppressing the unclean syncretism that gives rise to a sacred corpus. Dalila's erotic and political threat comes to strike at the level of sacred text; her defiant speech reveals the patterns of disavowal and usurpation within the archive that Christ must claim for his own. Dalila does, however, present a more harmonious vision of incorporation between Jew and Philistine. She offers— perhaps sincerely, or perhaps as yet another temptation—the resumption of marriage with Samson. What began as an political marriage may end in happy personal reunion. Yet such possibilities have always been foreclosed in *Samson Agonistes*. The characters within the tragedy wonder if Samson's two marriages have been sanctioned by God. Manoa, who does not approve of his son's marriages, recalls Samson's claim that "divine impulsion" guided his choices. "I state not that," Manoa remarks, at once evading direct confrontation and voicing his skepticism (lines 422–24). What is clear, however, is that Samson's marriages have been in bad faith with respect to his wives. His motivation has been not mutual incorporation but jealous violence.

Milton clears space for Samson's masculine heroism by removing his mother from his narrative; Samson himself must shoulder the responsibility of rejecting Dalila's offer of a renewed marriage. Samson memorably describes Dalila's former victory over his weakness as an act of emasculating penetration: "What boots it at one gate to make defence, / And at another to let in the foe / Effeminately vanquished?" (lines 560–62). By casting Dalila away, Samson affirms his link to his father as the only valid personal and cultural bond. He thus paves the way for his eventual return to his father's house. An exclusively patriarchal economy is also a culturally pure one, free from the entanglements Dalila embodies. As the Chorus recognizes, Manoa must fulfill maternal and paternal roles:

> Fathers are wont to lay up for their sons,
> Thou for thy son art bent to lay out all;
> Sons wont to nurse their parents in old age,
> Thou in old age car'st how to nurse thy son,
> Made older than thy age through eyesight lost.

(lines 1485–89)

Rachel Trubowitz argues that Samson's curious status as God's and Manoa's nursling rather than his mother's marks a transition from Hebraic exclusion toward a universalizing Christian model. According to her reading, "Milton implies that while the paternal and maternal belong to opposing categories, they are actually not all that different. Thus, by extension, rather than acting as opposite, enemy nations, Israel and Philistia are, in fact, locked in a deadly embrace."[64] Weaning Samson from the physical body of his mother toward the feminized body of God and father accommodates a progressive rather than an abrupt "translation from carnal to spiritual purity."[65]

Trubowitz provides a reading sensitive to Milton's nuanced thought about the relationship between Judaism and Christianity. Yet *Samson Agonistes* gestures toward the problems that beset the transition from one to the other. Manoa describes his maternal status in a voice analogous to Mary's in *Paradise Regained*. Distressed, Manoa recalls the initial annunciation of his heroic son and bemoans the possibility of an abject miscarriage: "What windy joy this day had I conceived / Hopeful of his delivery, which now proves / Abortive as the first-born bloom of spring / Nipped with the lagging rear of winter's frost" (lines 1574–77). Later the Messenger's narration of Samson's death suggests that his final state may be one of abominable mixture: "Samson with these immixed, inevitably / Pulled down the same destruction on himself" (lines 1657–58). Just as God would not allow his Son to suffer corruption in the grave, Manoa will recuperate Samson's integrity by retrieving his body, cleansing it of "clotted gore" and Philistian blood, and turning the body into a site of memory (line 1728).

That Manoa does this as a single parent affirms the possibility of a familial archive established exclusively between father and son.

Manoa resists the greater truth that will overshadow his son's heroism. As a father, Manoa does not affirm his son's self-sacrifice for the sake of Israel but rather tries to redeem his son in the literal sense by purchasing him from the Philistine lords: "For his redemption all my patrimony / If need be, I am ready to forgo / And quit" (lines 1482–84). The varied meanings of "patrimony" convey the movement of archival knowledge from familial to public realms: the word can refer to inheritance of property, a figurative inheritance, or the property of an institution, class, or, especially, a church. Manoa's willingness to forgo his patrimony for his son turns into a desire to see his own house become a place of civic devotion. After Samson's death, Manoa imagines his house as the site of repeated public pilgrimages. Yet if such a desire for a patriarchive turns idolatrous, Manoa's maternal status may align him with Micah's mother, who commissions for her son household idols that come to be the Danites' false gods. In Judges, the Danites remain the tribe of Israel who cannot settle in their territory, even after Samson's defeat of the Philistines. Regardless of his intentions, Milton's Manoa may, like Micah's mother, establish a household idol that hinders the public good.

In *Paradise Regained*, in language that echoes Manoa's description of Samson's monument, Jesus describes how "victorious deeds / Flamed in [his] heart, heroic acts; one while / To rescue Israel from Roman yoke" (1.215–17). Yet Jesus has come to reject such models of heroism in favor of humane and heavenly persuasion. From Milton's Christian perspective, Jesus should have every right both to reinterpret Hebraic stories and to reclaim them as having always been part his own archive. Even if Samson and Manoa resist such reinscription, Jesus has the right to subdue the stubborn. Such an exercise of archontic dominion would be neither unjustified nor undeserved. Yet the addition of *Samson Agonistes* to *Paradise Regained* presents, in the form of Samson's riddle, a temporal riddle about Christ's typological supervenience.

As the Chorus of *Samson Agonistes* describes the approach of Harapha the giant, Samson replies, "Be less abstruse, my riddling days are past," (line 1064). When the Chorus responds, "Look now for no enchanting voice, nor fear / The bait of honeyed words" (lines 1065–66), they refer simultaneously to Dalila's tempting speech and to Samson's original riddle:

"Out of the eater, something to eat; out of the strong, something sweet" (Judg. 14:14). This association is fitting. In Judges, the story of Samson eating honey out of a lion's carcass coincides meaningfully with his first marriage to a Philistine. Samson's parents object to their son's desire for the woman of Timnah, but they "knew not that it was from the LORD, that he sought an occasion against the Philistines" (Judg. 14:4). On the road to Timnah, Samson confronts a young lion and kills it with God-given strength. Curiously, the text specifies that Samson was traveling with his parents, and yet his parents do not know what has transpired, for "he told not his father or his mother what he had done" (Judg. 14:6). Samson's secret multiplies when, on his way to marry his bride, he sees bees and honey in the carcass of the same lion. He eats the honey and gives some of it to his parents without telling them its source. After his marriage, Samson turns his experience into a riddle for the Philistines. When the Philistines obtain the answer ("What is sweeter than honey? And what is stronger than a lion?" [Judg. 14:18]) through Samson's bride, Samson responds violently. In another display of God-given strength, he strikes down thirty Philistines and strips them of their belongings at Ashkelon. Samson's marriage is annulled, and he returns to his father's house.

For Harapha, such behavior makes Samson a "murderer, a revolter, and a robber" (line 1180). The scriptural account clearly suggests that, as distasteful as Samson's actions may seem, he carries them out with the power of divine inspiration. Yet Samson has his own reasons for wishing to put his riddling days behind him. The episode represents an unhappy and unsuccessful attempt at personal, heroic, and sexual maturation. Hebrew scriptures often describe honey on the lips and tongue as images of sexual contact and of erotically charged speech. In the Song of Solomon, for example, the bride has honey in her lips and under her tongue, and the bridegroom partakes of honey in his garden (Song 4:11, 5:1). In the book of Proverbs, "the lips of the strange woman drop as an honeycomb" (Prov. 5:3).[66] For Samson, tasting honey is closely related to the first experience of marriage. Yet if in marriage "shall a man leave his father and his mother, and shall cleave unto his wife," as Genesis teaches (Gen. 2:24), Samson transgressively shares the honey with his parents, who remain ignorant of its significance. The meaning should remain Samson's private secret, one that gives him mastery over his parents, but when the Philistines uncover his knowledge, Samson responds with the fury of sexual humiliation.

After routing the Philistines, Samson must return to his parents' house in the wake of a failed marriage.

Milton's Samson wants to put the riddle of gender relations behind him rather than genuinely solving it. He will return once and for all to his father's house as a dead hero. Yet his fate suggests that even this conclusion does not free his identity from its riddle. In a reading of Judges, Mieke Bal argues that the dissymmetry of knowledge posed by the riddle genre is eroticized and gendered. Taking an interpretive path of which Milton's Dalila would approve, Bal argues that Sisera's comment to Jael before she kills him constitutes a kind of riddle, one that Jael solves through her violent act. Before retiring, Sisera commands Jael, "Stand in the door of the tent, and it shall be, when any man doth come and inquire of thee, and say, Is there any man here? that thou shalt say, No" (Judg. 4:20). By killing Sisera, Jael turns him into a no man indeed. "This can be read," Bal argues, "as a response to Samson's riddle: How can a strong lion/woman yield pleasure? Answer: As a dead lion/woman."[67] Yet in *Samson Agonistes* as in the story of Jael and Sisera, it is the man and not the woman who must die. Early in the poem, Milton's Chorus recalls Samson's ability to kill the lion, and then goes on to identify Samson with the lion: "The bold Ascalonite / Fled from his lion ramp" (lines 138–39). Samson will become the answer to and the victim of his own riddle. He will be the strong but dead body out of which sweetness emerges—not honey but, according to Manoa, the "sweet lyric song" shared by his future admirers (line 1737).

Upon Samson's riddle converge the various motifs that I have been tracing across Milton's 1671 poems: bodily purity, gendered and sexual identity, familial versus public knowledge, and the way all these factors beset the typological settlement of Hebraic past and Christian future. Whereas Milton's Samson alludes to his riddle begrudgingly because it represents the perils of erotic knowledge, the author makes central use of the riddle while skirting the matter of honey because of the paradox it presents. Eating honey out of an unclean animal's carcass violates not only the laws of kashrut but also the terms of Samson's purity as a Nazirite.[68] Even before the cutting of his hair, Samson should already have compromised his source of strength, yet the narrative in Judges suggests God's relative indifference to the violation. Francis Quarles's 1631 *Historie of Samson* investigates this problem thoroughly. The angel announces to Samson's mother that her child "*shall be a holy* Nazirite, *from the wombe*"; she must thus avoid the pollution of "*Law-forbidden meates*" such as camel, coney, hare, swine, goshawk, eagle, pye, kite, raven, snail, cuckoo, osprey, cormorant, pelican, crow, stork, and vulture.[69] After the passage narrating Samson's eating honey from the lion, Quarles's ninth meditation begins with an *o altitudo* about the "unscrutable" and "obscure" ways of God. According to God's secret plan, "Samson *must downe to* Timnah; *In the way / Must meete a* Lyon," and from "*The Lyo'ns putrid* Carkas" there must arise a riddle to be read. Quarles presents a typological answer to the riddle of Samson's seemingly unclean act. The meditation calls upon Jesus not only as the "*Lambe* of Sion" but also as "*that wounded* Lyon: / O, in thy dying body, we have found / A world of hony.*"[70] This interpretation presents the human reader with a glimpse of the divine view of history, whereby even a seemingly transgressive act conveys the highest spiritual truth. Such a typological reading of Samson's honey was commonplace. In the preface to *Grace Abounding to the Chief of Sinners*, Bunyan tells his reader, "*I have sent you here enclosed a drop of that honey, that I have taken out of the Carcase of a* Lyon (Judg. 14. 5, 6, 7, 8).*"[71]

Unlike both the Royalist Quarles and the Nonconformist Bunyan, however, Milton seems unable to apply any straightforward typological solution to Samson's riddle. In the context of the 1671 poems, such a solution would raise as many problems as it answers. As I have argued, Jesus's dream of Elijah in *Paradise Regained* suggests the difficulty of his calling by requiring a simultaneous identification with the hungry prophet, the food that sustains him, and the unclean ravens that bear this food to him. Samson's riddle poses similar problems: Jesus must identify with but also surpass Samson, who is his type, but he must also play the role of the honey that sustains him and the "*putrit* Carkas" from which this honey emerges.

Samson's problem of purity is Jesus's problem of temporality. Bound by strict codes of behavior, Samson nonetheless receives mysterious dispensations from God. Typological interpretations suggest that God's foreknowledge of Christ legitimizes otherwise dubious acts. Within Milton's 1671 poems, however, this means that Samson enjoys something like Christian liberty, whereas Jesus must insist on his purity, simultaneously proving himself fit to be the messiah while making his Christly mission difficult to fulfill. By abrogating the Law, Jesus allows for the emergence of a subject who internalizes abjection, whose mouth does not resist external defilement but rather confesses the sin within. In *Samson Agonistes*, Milton transforms unclean honey into the bait of honeyed words. In the gospels, John the Baptist announces the new messiah wearing camel's fur and eating locusts and honey. In Revelation, the apostle John eats a book as sweet as honey in his mouth but bitter in his belly. His mission will be to prophesy the message he has digested "before many peoples, and nations, and tongues, and kings" (Rev. 10:11). Yet if the typological reading of Samson's riddle demands that Jesus be both the honey and the lion's carcass, Jesus cannot taste the sweetness of his own liberating truth.

After death, Paul teaches, a man can be free from the Law. As Jael's response to Sisera's riddle would suggest, Jesus must become a dead man— no man at all—in order to fulfill his mission. Jesus does not effect archontic violence but becomes its victim. Others will thus have to perform the work of establishing the Christian archive by remembering Jesus in his absence. The final verse of John's gospel surmises that this archival work may never end and that the expanding archive might fill the entire world, thereby sanctioning writers like Milton to narrate Jesus's life anew. Yet even after death and resurrection, the Word of God is faced with Samson's riddle in an archive that looks both backward and forward and mediates between ideational content and the embodied life of memory. Jesus must remain pure in order to become the carcass that has already fed the Hebraic heroes of the past and will feed the Gentile Christians to come.

The Vulgar Remains

In the introduction to this book, I acknowledged that the historicist inquiry of the ensuing chapters would be motivated by my sense that Milton's crisis continues to locate us in our present-day moment. I conclude by suggesting briefly how Milton's 1671 poems speak to our present-day crises and, specifically, to the recent appeals to a Pauline subject liberated from the divisions of culture, nation, class, and gender.[72] Milton teaches us the limitations of Pauline universalism. Even while imparting faith in the future, his writings remind us of the intractable divisions that persist in a world full of undeserved dominion. *Paradise Regained* and *Samson Agonistes* reveal lived experience as the medium of cultural knowledge. Milton archives Jesus's life in language that conveys both its spiritual meaning and its bodily intensity. Yet such a medium hinders the transcendence of cultural boundaries in the name of universality. Milton's 1671 poems warn us about the precariousness of any appeal to universalism as a mode of embodied life. Such an appeal might call us to live in freedom by forgetting the claims of a cultural legacy that lays claim upon us, body and mind. Jesus cannot do this. Universalism may also appeal to a future perfection that we cannot actually know unless the future were as legible as the past. Samson does this in an act of mysterious ignorance, but he resists the future that must justify and subsume him.

These lessons serve as a powerful corrective to recent post-secular thought. Alain Badiou, for example, champions Paul as a thinker who bequeaths to Western thought a lasting notion of universality. For Badiou, the Pauline subject receives freedom from a messiah whose actual life seems unimportant while looking forward to secular universalism, which occupies the place of eschatological fulfillment. Paul, as Badiou emphasizes, seems almost wholly uninterested in Jesus's life or teachings; Badiou follows suit.[73] The difference between thinkers like Badiou and Milton is not merely one of nonbelief versus belief in Jesus. Rather, this indifference to the actual life of the messiah who underwrites the Pauline subject leaves room for the persistence of a problematic dualism. Badiou points out that centuries of Platonic and Neoplatonic thought make it difficult to read the opposition between *pneuma* and *sarx* as anything but that between spirit and flesh. Badiou counters that these two modes present "thoughts" or subjective stances.[74] Yet this argument simply reinscribes dualism by idealizing both *pneuma* and *sarx*. As a result, Badiou's theory of Pauline universalism ignores the significance of bodily markers of cultural difference (circumcision being a privileged example, though certainly not the only one), of suffering, or even of death. Badiou simply does not wish to address experiences like abjection—the politically charged sense of revulsion and attraction in the face of elements at once foreign and uncannily familiar. His appeal to universalism must remain at the level of an idealized subjective stance.

Giorgio Agamben has rightly qualified Badiou's optimistic turn to Paul with a more refined understanding of the apostle's ostensible dualism. According to Agamben's reading, Paul does not simply abolish the Jew/non-Jew distinction but rather creates internal divisions within these categories. Thus Jews can be divided into Jews according to spirit (*pneuma*) and Jews according to the flesh (*sarx*). The same division applies to non-Jews. The result is "a remnant on either side, which cannot be defined either as a Jew, or as a non-Jew."[75] Agamben argues that Paul's universalism lies not in an abolition of differences but in "the impossibility of the Jews and *goyim* to coincide with themselves; they are something like a remnant between every people and itself, between every identity and itself."[76] Both Jewish and Christian followers of the messiah become, in this account, "non-non-Jews." The only transcendence made available by Paul involves the lived experience of a tension and a noncoincidence within every identity.

By attending to the experience of messianic time, Agamben gives a much fuller account than does Badiou of the potentially universal Pauline subject. In his focus on the epistle to the Romans, however, Agamben largely disregards a central feature of the Pauline "division of divisions." Paul's rejection of (physical) circumcision as devoid of spiritual value must struggle to deny the fact that not all non-non-Jews are alike. The Jew who lives in messianic time is neither a non-Jew according to *sarx* nor a non-Jew according to *pneuma*. The debate over the relative status of Jewish and Gentile Christians, culminating in the so-called incident at Antioch, is internal to the origins of Christianity and to the New Testament itself. Paul's universalizing impulse arises partly as a strategic rejection of the spiritual value of physical circumcision. This context reveals, *pace* Badiou, that the dualism ascribed to his works is more than a mere byproduct of the syncretism between Christian and Platonic thought. Questions persist about the messianic subject for whom bodily and cultural difference should have been rendered indifferent.

In Milton's monist universe, agonistic creation invariably leaves behind material dregs; as a result, the ascent from flesh to spirit and the passage from particularity to universality are always imperiled. The consequences manifest themselves upon the body, where the prohibition against abjection polices cultural and interpersonal boundaries. Such a lesson certainly casts a shadow on Badiou's Pauline rallying cry. Milton's writings also warn us of the theological, political, and philosophical problems that challenge Agamben's more sophisticated account. Like Milton before him, however, Agamben meditates on how the problems besetting *sarx* and *pneuma* become the grounds for a refined mode of being. For Agamben, what must be overcome in messianic subjectivity is not just bodily or cultural difference but temporality itself. According to his reading, the exact same division

of divisions that leads to "a remnant between every people and itself" applies to the temporal experience of the Pauline subject. This subject lives
in human, earthly time and yet in such a liberated way as to render time
inoperative. Paul uses the verb *katargein* to describe the messianic function of deactivating secular time. Agamben traces the enormously conse-
quential afterlife of Pauline *katargesis*, which "does not merely abolish" but
"preserves and brings to fulfillment." Luther translates *katargein* as *Aufhe-
ben*, thus providing Hegel with a theological foundation for his account of
dialectical sublation.[77] Agamben thus offers an intellectual genealogy that
shows how the remnants of history have been not only redeemed but also
mobilized as a new dialectical movement toward universal plenitude.

This movement occurs through a mode of being that is at once a mode of
knowing and of remembering. Agamben introduces the term "exigency"
as "a messianic modality" that may perhaps "coincide with the possibility
of philosophy itself."[78] Exigency is that which must remain unforgettable
even though nobody remembers it. At the level of historical memory, the
dregs of time become recuperated in a dialectical process; what seems to be
lost proves to be the foundations of archival knowledge. "The exigency of
the lost does not entail being remembered and commemorated," Agamben
writes; "rather, it entails remaining in us and with us as forgotten, and
in this way and only in this way, remaining unforgettable."[79] Agamben
argues that the messianic subject is saved by occupying the place of exigency—nullified and preserved, canceled in its sin but awaiting sanctifica-
tion into eternal life. Creation itself may have fallen into futility and decay,
but it groans and awaits redemption from this position of loss.

In Agamben's philosophical genealogy, the movement toward "all in
all" comes to incorporate within it those elements that universal plenitude seems to have discarded. If, however, an unaccountable remnant—
the division of the division between proper and improper—allows for
katargesis, this second-order division continues to leave behind an abject
residue. Milton's writings insist on the sobering awareness that this residue clogs the dialectical machinery of history rather than allowing it to
operate. The end of *Samson Agonistes* provides a vivid reminder that not
all that is exigent can be redeemed or remembered. Some forms of the
exigent (etymologically, "driven out") will not find a home even in the
many rooms of the messianic archive. In "Ad Joannem Rousium," a
younger Milton had sought to shelter his work from "lingua procax vulgi."

In *Samson Agonistes*, the mature Milton acknowledges that those excluded from knowledge are not merely impudent tongues but human lives. The Hebraic Messenger who relates Samson's triumphant death ends his account with the remark, "The vulgar only scaped who stood without" (line 1659). This addition to Judges has led to optimistic interpretations, according to which Milton allows those without political agency to escape divine wrath.[80] At the same time, however, these vulgar quite literally have no place to go; bereft of their "lords, ladies, captains, counselors, or priests, / Their choice nobility and flower," they will leave behind no history (lines 1653–54). By contrast, death "immixes" these Philistine lords and ladies with Samson, and even though Manoa imagines cleansing Samson of their "clotted gore" with purifying herbs, their physical remains become remnants of knowledge, at once suppressed and preserved, in the Hebraic archive. From the vulgar Milton withholds even the decency of a memorable death. The description of the vulgar must be fleeting, the barest hint that an undistinguished multitude will leave behind no memory.

In the first chapter I argued that the Eastern Tartars occupied in the early modern European imagination a place analogous to the dregs of chaos in Milton's cosmology. Plans to convert the Tartars and the fanciful theory that the Tartars are the Lost Tribes of Israel leave hope that the barbarians must be redeemed. Milton does not share such optimism. The vulgar throng of the Philistines in *Samson Agonistes* similarly represent living human beings who become the dregs of divine history. Marked by differences of bodily purity, social status, and education, these vulgar and uncircumcised bodies cannot be recuperated by a division of divisions. Even though Jesus will redeem the Gentiles through the place of exigency, not all will be saved. Once again, an abject fate threatens closer to home. The New Testament suggests that even Samson's people may be excised from the divine archive. Revelation 7 conspicuously omits Dan from the list of tribes that receive the divine seal on their foreheads; the Danites may very well be among those who were "not found written in the book of life" and thus "cast into the lake of fire" (Rev. 20:15). The loss of human dregs—both Gentile and Jew—haunt the possibility of the all in all that transcends all earthly divisions.

Milton's writings may aspire to universality, but they emerge from an impasse that precludes any path to universalism. Their ultimate value cannot lie in prescriptions but rests in acts of reading that bind spiritual and political impulses together through a poetic medium that affects both mind and body. Such a lesson should not be surprising to post-secular thinkers who look to a messianic subjectivity as a way to confront our present-day dilemmas. Theorists such as Agamben have inherited an archival mode of thought from Walter Benjamin's signal essay "Theses on the Philosophy of History" and the posthumous collection, *Illuminations*, in which this essay has been handed down to us. For Benjamin, the advent of messianic time would achieve a radiant synthesis of knowledge and action, of reading and politics. I conclude this chapter by briefly pairing the archival thinking performed by the published volumes of Milton's and Benjamin's works. In a book primarily historicist in its outlook, this late discussion of Milton and post-secular thought can only amount to a postscript. As Benjamin teaches us, however, the genre of the postscript captures something of the shifting, open-ended relationship between past, present, and future. After one has traced the contours of a contradiction besetting all creation, the only closure to be offered is a fleeting consummation of deceased author and living reader in the anticipation of an elusive future perfection.

Milton's 1671 poems first entered the world through the hands of another J.M. whose identity continues to prove somewhat uncertain. Months before Milton's death, Brabazon Aylmer printed Milton's familiar letters, thereby continuing the archival transformation of private matters into a public resource.[81] Yet Aylmer's plans to print Milton's state letters were thwarted, forcing him instead to reach back to Milton's juvenilia and to publish his academic prolusions. This late episode merely confirms what Milton already knew well: his painstaking self-presentation could not fully banish other hands and contingencies from his archive.

Far direr circumstances gave rise to Benjamin's *Illuminations*. Fleeing Nazi persecution and soon to commit suicide, Benjamin surrendered control of his late writings. Yet he found in Hannah Arendt a thoughtful caretaker of his writings. To the editor belongs the power of consignation, and Arendt foregrounds archival concerns as she compiles and orders Benjamin's essays. The collection begins with "Unpacking My Library: A Talk about Book Collecting," a deceptively lighthearted piece that voices an intense longing to maintain control over a personal and familial archive. "Of all the ways of acquiring books, writing them oneself is regarded as the most praiseworthy method," Benjamin quips. Later he declares that "inheritance is the soundest way of acquiring a collection."[82] Yet *habent sua fata libelli*; Benjamin acknowledges that books have their own destiny while omitting the agency of the reader in the original Latin expression. Perhaps the omission is as apt as it is wry, as the destiny of a writer's books may depend as much on editors, printers, and booksellers as on *captu lectoris*.

Yet the mortal author longs to be a part of his book's uncertain destiny. In "The Storyteller," Benjamin exhibits a nostalgia for the "full corporeality" of embodied narration as social communication. The novel represents literature at its furthest remove from the storyteller, born of a solitary individual and existing only through the printing press. Epic, however, mediates between story and novel. Whereas the novel exists in books, "memory is the epic faculty *par excellence*."[83] The epic poet both sings and publishes the contents of his memory, a storehouse long of private and public things. The author of epic can embed his social and corporeal being in his narration. Throughout this book I have largely avoided questions of Milton's biography, preferring to focus on what Benjamin calls the life and afterlife of artwork rather than the life of its creator. Yet the archive always bears the imprints of lived experience, and this is especially true for an epic poet who strove toward the monistic fusion of body and spiritual truth. Reading Milton's 1671 poems as a miniature archive necessarily implies a vision of Milton himself. *Dominion Undeserved* has told the story of a conflicted Milton caught between the desire for all-encompassing unity on the one hand and the impulse to maintain integrity through force on the other. If Milton's writings continue to impart meaning, they do so by compelling readers to confront the renewed forms of abjection that hinder any movement toward an ecumenical spirit. The affective, intellectual, and spiritual force within Milton's archive continues to imprint on us the difficult lessons of his own lived experience. The effects—at once aesthetically and politically charged—must be open-ended, transforming the meanings that bind reader and author together.

By placing "Theses on the Philosophy of History" at the end of *Illuminations*, Arendt makes emphatic the way Benjamin's excursus on messianic time strives to bind past and present textually, to restore to books the social corporealities of their composition and of their eventual consumption. To an essay of twenty-eight numbered sections, Benjamin adds two lettered codas. Having finished but still continuing, Benjamin adds in the first coda: "Historicism contents itself with establishing a causal connection between various moments in history. But no fact that is a cause is for that very reason historical. It became historical posthumously, as it were, through events that may be separated from it by thousands of years."[84] Messianic time allows the vital connection of past and present, but Benjamin's second coda concludes by suggesting the open-ended contingency of the messiah's arrival: "For every second of time was the strait gate through which the Messiah might enter."[85] Toward the end of his career Milton arrives at a similar nonconclusion. Milton looks back to the gospels to narrate the life of the messiah anew, yet he leaves this most familiar of stories incomplete. In *Paradise Regained*, the young messiah finds himself in the position of waiting for himself to emerge fully.

In the introduction to *Illuminations*, Arendt likens Benjamin to "a pearl diver who descends to the bottom of the sea, not to excavate the bottom and bring it to light but to pry loose the rich and the strange, the pearls and the coral in the depths," to excavate the remnants of the past that have undergone a sea change and "survive in new crystallized forms and shapes that remain immune to the elements."[86] I have attempted to read Milton in a genuinely historical way—that is, to look back at the products of an impasse that still confronts us urgently after four centuries. My time reading Milton was not spent in the hope that the author himself might enter through the strait gate, nor do I await the arrival or the return of a messiah. Yet I have read and written in the conviction that Milton may still teach us how to think of the past to write the present, and to await—impatiently but not faithlessly—a future that will confer a genuine universalism over and above undeserved dominion and all of its invidious consequences.

EPILOGUE

Before, during, and after Milton's quadricentennial in 2009, Milton scholars asked why Milton matters. In a brief essay on the topic, Stanley Fish took to task critics who fail to connect their historicist research to genuinely literary questions of form and genre (which, for Fish, largely equate to questions of authorial intention). Fish identifies a desire on the part of many critics to align Milton's views with their own political convictions as both source and symptom of misguided scholarship. Fish is right that some historicist scholarship loses sight of the fact that Milton's literary influence outweighs his contributions to political theory or to historiography. Yet Fish provokes excessively by omitting selectively. He begins by adding to the question of why Milton matters the questions "Matter to whom? And matter as what?"[1] Fish omits equally essential questions: How has Milton mattered in the past? How has this history set the terms for Milton's present and future relevance?

I conclude this book by briefly turning to the way one writer, Olaudah Equiano, would adapt Milton's writings for purposes at once literary and political. Equiano's late-eighteenth-century autobiography traces the author's journey not only from freedom, enslavement, to liberation, and from paganism to Christianity, but also from illiteracy to authorship. This last trajectory culminates in a 112-line autobiographical and devotional poem by Equiano; the reader is prepared for the appearance of this poem by the frequency of poetical allusions throughout Equiano's account. In a particularly dramatic and condensed stretch of *The Interesting Narrative*, Equiano quotes from the first two books of *Paradise Lost* three times. (After the Bible, Milton's is the work quoted most frequently.) Equiano places himself and his fellow West Indies slaves in the position of Milton's devils despairing in Hell. Equiano quotes lines from book 1 to describe his first sight of Montserrat:

and soon after I beheld those

> Regions of sorrow, doleful shades, where peace
> And rest can rarely dwell. Hope never comes
> That comes to all, but torture without end
> Still urges.

At the sight of this land of bondage, a fresh horror ran through all my frame, and chilled me to the heart.[2]

It is unclear whether the alterations to the lines from *Paradise Lost* are deliberate or the result of quoting from memory. Regardless, the change from the original "rest can never dwell" to "rest can rarely dwell" is fitting, suggesting that the abject conditions of slavery in the West Indies are less absolutely hellish than what the devils face. Yet perhaps only slightly so, for Equiano goes on to detail some of the brutal treatment that the slaves endure, and he remarks,

Is it surprising that usage like this should drive the poor creatures to despair, and make them seek a refuge in death from those evils which render their lives intolerable—while,

> With shudd'ring horror pale, and eyes aghast,
> They view their lamentable lot, and find
> No rest!

This they frequently do.[3]

Here, the alteration from Milton's past-tense "found" to the present-tense "find" suggests the shift from the mythic world of Milton's Hell to the urgent, real-world conditions of slavery. Milton's devils explore Hell and find "a universe of death, which God by curse / Created evil, for evil only good / Where all life dies, death lives" (2.622–24). The slaves in Equiano's narrative "seek a refuge in death from those evils" and attempt suicide.

These first two quotations of *Paradise Lost* anticipate the third, which is the longest and the most remarkable. In a moment of rhetorical fervor, Equiano declares that the deplorable treatment of slaves in the West Indies can only lead to rebellion. He concludes his ominous plea by quoting Milton:

Are you not hourly in dread of an insurrection? Nor would it be surprising: for when

—No peace is given
To us enslav'd, but custody severe;
And stripes and arbitrary punishment
Inflicted—What peace can we return?
But to our power, hostility and hate;
Untam'd reluctance, and revenge, though slow.
Yet ever plotting how the conqueror least
May reap his conquest, and may least rejoice
In doing what we most in suffering feel.

But by changing your conduct, and treating your slaves as men, every cause of fear would be banished.[4]

Equiano seamlessly incorporates Beelzebub's argument into his own rhetoric; what *Paradise Lost* deems "devilish counsel" Equiano uses as evidence for his claim that the maltreatment of slaves can only lead to uprising (2.379). A few years before William Blake would memorably declare that Milton was unwittingly of the devil's party, Equiano speaks through the perspective of Milton's fiends in order to describe his experience of slavery.

Equiano appropriates Milton for his own archive, an autobiography with a pointed political aim. In so doing, Equiano also inserts himself into Milton's archive, activating new possibilities for reading *Paradise Lost*. Equiano, to use a term elaborated by Srinivas Aravamudan, tropicalizes Milton, reshaping the meaning of his writing by applying it to the evolving political geography of the Western hemisphere. As Aravamudan observes, Equiano wrote during a time when literary canon formation played a part in the consolidation of British nationalism: Equiano thus "looks backward in 1789 and implicitly recognizes preceding literary production as rationalizing the nation."[5] In Milton, however, Equiano finds a national poet who already offers an internally divided view of all nations and empires. Although Equiano consistently situates his narrative within a providentialist, *felix culpa* schema of religious conversion, his comparison of black slaves to Milton's devils cannot be explained as the result of an internalized disdain for his own race or pagan past.[6] On the contrary, Equiano quotes passages from *Paradise Lost* to evoke sympathy for the slaves-as-devils, the "poor creatures." Equiano's slaves are devilish not because they are intrinsically sinful, but because they have been forced into the hellish conditions of England's transatlantic slave trade. If Equiano's Hell is a psychological state of despair, it is one caused by geopolitical and economic trends in dire need of redress. Equiano consistently imparts a theological, devotional significance to his political account, and he does so in part by establishing new grounds for the political significance of Milton's biblical epic.

Just as understanding Milton's fractured view of political order helps us understand Equiano's project, Equiano's deployment of *Paradise Lost* compels us to return to Milton's epic with renewed attention to potential racial currents in the narrative. Kim Hall has argued that the schema of black as evil and white as good or beautiful "relies on an idea of African difference"—not only in writings about other nations and peoples but also in such literary forms as the Petrarchan sonnet.[7] Black and white, light and dark are primary to Milton's poetic palette; we recall the verbal chiaroscuro of his descriptions of both Heaven and Hell. Whether or not Milton had in mind—consciously or subconsciously—African bodies when he describes fallen angels as "sons of darkness" (6.715) remains at the level of speculation. What is certain is the way Milton's depiction of Hell speaks to Equiano's lived experience as a black slave. Equiano compels us to attend to the importance of the slave trade for the narrative of *Paradise Lost*. Christopher Kendrick notes, in his influential Marxist reading of Milton's writings, how the concept of slavery informs the sense of fate in the Virgilian epic.[8] Maureen Quilligan responds that such a reading does not ask "what part *actual* slavery might have had to play in the mercantilist developments of the economy of Cromwell's Commonwealth."[9] She goes on to trace how both classical and early modern forms of slavery bear upon Milton's writings. Returning to Milton's description of Satan as a merchant explorer in book 2 of *Paradise Lost*, we see the prominence of Africa in his Eastern voyage:

> As when far off at sea a fleet descried
> Hangs in the clouds, by equinoctial winds
> Close sailing from Bengala, or the isles
> Of Ternate and Tidore, whence merchants bring
> Their spicy drugs; they on the trading flood
> Through the wide Ethiopian to the Cape
> Ply stemming nightly toward the pole.

(2.636–42)

Milton's ironic allusion to *The Lusiads* reminds us that Vasco da Gama's voyage takes him to Africa before he arrives at his Indian destination. (Even in Camões's laudatory narrative, we witness Gama's dubious and even underhanded dealings with the peoples of Mombassa and Malindi.) Equiano's allusions to *Paradise Lost*, in turn, remind us that Gama's voyage paved the way not only for Portugal's trade with India but also for its prominence in the African slave trade. Equiano's *Narrative* suggests how the transatlantic ventures encoded within the early modern epic eventually result in a Hell on earth.

Yet Equiano quotes Milton also to testify to his patriotism as he appeals to English readers. At the end of the narrative, Equiano continues to seek opportunities for African evangelism, and he expresses the kind of national messianism that had once informed Milton's prose: "May Heaven make the British senators the dispersers of light, liberty, and science, to the uttermost parts of the earth: then will be glory to God on the highest, on earth peace, and good-will to men."[10] This religious fervor goes hand in hand with—or even gives way to—a strategic calculation of the economic benefits of abolitionism: "A commercial intercourse with Africa opens an inexhaustible source of wealth to the manufacturing interests of Great Britain, and to all which the slave trade is an objection." Equiano predicts that abolitionism will prevail "from motives of interest as well as justice and humanity."[11] The larger rhetorical patterns of *The Interesting Narrative* reveal the complex reasons why Equiano engages with *Paradise Lost* selectively, in ways that echo, amplify, or twist Milton's meanings as part of their historical evolution.

When a Miltonist asks why Milton matters, the underlying and anxious question is how Milton's writings may continue to be culturally relevant. The greatness of Milton's poetry is the most satisfying answer, but only if our definition of greatness includes the impressions both of history and of the future. Milton's literary legacy has been preserved and altered by the work of John Dryden, Daniel Defoe, Alexander Pope, Phillis Wheatley, William Blake, Mary Shelley, Nathaniel Hawthorne, Thomas Hardy, T. S. Eliot, C. S. Lewis, Peter Ackroyd, and Philip Pullman, to name only a few examples. These writers returned to Milton with interests ranging from theological heterodoxy to versification, republicanism, and the history of companionate marriage. Milton's importance has ebbed and flowed for reasons at once artistic and ideological. As the example of Equiano's *Narrative* suggests, great works such as *Paradise Lost* are inextricably tied to a history of alliances and disavowals—a robust afterlife that continues to evolve whenever literary critics, historians, casual readers, musicians, theologians, poets, painters, novelists, and filmmakers grapple with Milton's writings and their myriad manifestations.

NOTES

Introduction

1. Louis L. Martz, in *Milton: Poet of Exile*, 2nd ed. (New Haven: Yale University Press, 1986), has described Milton as a poet who disrupts the celebratory goals of Virgilian epic with patterns of change and instability that link him to the great Roman poet of exile, Ovid. Christopher D'Addario, *Exile and Journey in Seventeenth-Century Literature* (Cambridge: Cambridge University Press, 2007), 87–123, situates Milton in the experience of exile that conjoins seventeenth-century English subjects with bitterly opposed convictions. For Milton and his contemporaries, exilic spirituality exists alongside "an ongoing interest in the public affairs of the homeland that had gone astray" (94).

2. John Milton, *The Complete Prose Works of John Milton*, ed. Don M. Wolfe et al., 8 vols. (New Haven: Yale University Press, 1953–1982), 8:4. Unless otherwise noted, all quotations from Milton's prose are from this edition and are cited parenthetically by volume and page with the abbreviation *CPW*. For a discussion of Milton's letter to Heimbach, see David Loewenstein and Paul Stevens, "Introduction: Milton's Nationalism; Challenges and Questions," in *Early Modern Nationalism and Milton's England*, ed. David Loewenstein and Paul Stevens (Toronto: University of Toronto Press, 2008), 3–4.

3. All quotations from *Paradise Lost* are taken from John Milton, *Paradise Lost*, ed. Alastair Fowler, 2nd ed. (Harlow: Longman, 1998) and are cited parenthetically by book and line numbers with the abbreviation *PL*.

4. See Gordon Teskey, *Delirious Milton: The Fate of the Poet in Modernity* (Cambridge: Harvard University Press, 2006).

5. Stanley Fish, *How Milton Works* (Cambridge: Harvard University Press, 2001).

6. David Ainsworth, *Milton and the Spiritual Reader: Reading and Religion in Seventeenth-Century England* (New York: Routledge, 2008), 34.

7. I borrow the distinction between totalizing and exhaustive interpretations from Stanley Cavell's influential reading of *King Lear* in *Disowning Knowledge in Six Plays of Shakespeare* (Cambridge: Cambridge University Press, 1987), 83.

8. See, for example, J. Martin Evans's statement, in *Milton's Imperial Epic:* Paradise Lost *and the Discourse of Colonialism* (Ithaca: Cornell University Press, 1996), 147, concerning Milton's political commentary: "In and of itself, colonialism was neither good nor bad. Everything depended on the identity of the colonizer, the nature of the colonized, and the purpose of the colony. And so it is in *Paradise Lost.*" Such a reading would turn Milton into a precursor of J. A. Hobson, the classical theorist of empire who argued for a distinction between "colonialism," which promotes a healthy internationalism, and cutthroat imperialism. Even Hobson admits, however, that the former is rare in history. See J. A. Hobson, *Imperialism: A Study*, 4th ed. (London: George Allen & Unwin, 1948).

9. Joanna Picciotto, in *Labors of Innocence in Early Modern England* (Cambridge: Harvard University Press, 2010), 462, demonstrates how "Milton puts himself and his reader to work to make uncertainty productive, and therefore redemptive." For Picciotto (and *pace* Fish's influential reading in *Surprised by Sin*), the strenuous intellectual labor of interpretation allows Milton's fallen reader to approach perfected knowledge that reclaims something of paradise.

10. The force of this temptation is manifested in Michael Bryson's argument, in *The Tyranny of Heaven: Milton's Rejection of God as King* (Newark: University of Delaware Press, 2004), that Milton's theodicy is ironic, and that the poet deliberately creates a loathsome God in order to make a strong claim against monarchical tyranny. Such a reading does lead to moments of insight, but only by refusing the artful ambivalence of Milton's writings. Bryson expands on the more restrained claims made by Stevie Davies in *Images of Kingship in* Paradise Lost: *Milton's Politics and Christian Liberty* (Columbia: University of Missouri Press, 1983).

11. For a study of Miltonic uncertainty, see Peter C. Herman, *Destabilizing Milton:* Paradise Lost *and the Poetics of Incertitude* (Basingstoke: Palgrave Macmillan, 2005), in which Herman calls for a new Milton criticism that breaks with orthodoxies about Milton's supposedly stable thought. As Marshall Grossman argues, however, in his review of *Destabilizing Milton*, *Modern Philology* 104 (2006): 263–68, Herman's rhetoric of a paradigm shift within Milton criticism may amount to a misapplication of Kuhnian terms. If Milton criticism is something like a normative science, its norms already allow for analysis of Miltonic uncertainty.

12. Marshall Grossman, "The Genders of God and the Redemption of the Flesh in *Paradise Lost*," in *Milton and Gender*, ed. Catherine Gimelli Martin (Cambridge: Cambridge University Press, 2004), 95–114, provides a provocative meditation about the gender of chaos. Grossman argues that Milton aligns the feminine with non-being and the masculine with being; procreation in both divine and human forms represents a way to conjoin plenitude and lack. In my reading, the feminine represents not a lack but an abundance of matter, teeming with both productive potential and a threat to order.

13. Regina M. Schwartz, *Remembering and Repeating: On Milton's Theology and Poetics*, 2nd ed. (Chicago: University of Chicago Press, 1993), 28.

14. See John P. Rumrich, *Milton Unbound: Controversy and Reinterpretation* (Cambridge: Cambridge University Press, 1996), 118–46. For other important arguments about a morally neutral chaos, see Michael Lieb, *The Dialectics of Creation: Patterns of Birth and Regeneration in* Paradise Lost (Amherst: University of Massachusetts Press, 1970); and Catherine Gimelli Martin, "Fire, Ice, and Epic Entropy: The Physics and Metaphysics of Milton's Reformed Chaos," *Milton Studies* 35 (1997): 73–113.

15. Kristeva expounds her theory in Julia Kristeva, *Powers of Horror: An Essay on Abjection*, trans. Leon S. Roudiez (New York: Columbia University Press, 1982), 4.

16. Ibid., 90–112.

17. Unless otherwise noted, all biblical quotations are taken from the Authorized Version.

18. Ibid., 128.

19. Rumrich, *Milton Unbound*, 70–93.

20. Judith Butler, *Gender Trouble: Feminism and the Subversion of Identity* (New York: Routledge, 1990), 79–93, levels a withering critique at Kristeva's theories as unfit for contemporary feminism. For Butler, Kristeva's ideas are self-defeating because they accept not only the alignment of matter as feminine and maternal, but also the primacy of the masculine, symbolic order.

21. I allude here to Janet Adelman, *Suffocating Mothers: Fantasies of Maternal Origins in Shakespeare's Plays,* Hamlet *to* The Tempest (New York: Routledge, 1992), which makes a compelling argument for the simultaneous desire for and fear of the maternal body in Shakespearean drama. Especially relevant is Adelman's reading of *King Lear*, in which *"one* and *twain . . .* specify what needs redeeming," leading to Lear's desire for a paradisal union with the wholesome maternal body (122). In *Lear*, the threatening power of the maternal body can be writ large in the storm; in *Paradise Lost*, this menace can loom even larger as primordial chaos.

22. Kristeva, *Powers*, 67.

23. Self-creation is a satanic fantasy in *Paradise Lost* (5.853–963). Despite a preponderance of maternal imagery, however, a rejection of maternal origins is ubiquitous in the epic. Milton consistently describes the primacy and the agency of the masculine in creation. W. B. C Watkins, in *An Anatomy of Milton's Verse* (Baton Rouge: Louisiana State University Press, 1955), 38, therefore speaks of "a masculine theogony" in which "God Himself loves Christ as the reflection of His own glory and perfection," thus "enabling God to know Himself by creating Logos, the Son, leaving the Holy Ghost an ambiguous role and variably attributed sex." Of course, such a suppression is always uneven. As Watkins later comments (in a quip that may or may not be intentional), "Milton has already admitted through the back door at the very beginning the [feminine] animating principle" (59).

24. See Kristeva, *Powers*, 101–2: "The subject then gives birth to himself by fantasizing his own bowels as the precious fetus of which he is to be delivered; and yet it is an abject fetus, for even if he calls them his own he has no other idea of the bowels than one of abomination, which links him to the ab-ject, to that non-introjected mother who is incorporated as devouring, and intolerable."

25. Milton does not simply deem anthropomorphic thinking with regard to deity inappropriate. In *Tetrachordon* he describes the "prime institution of Matrimony, wherein [man's] native pre-eminence ought most to shine" (*CPW* 2:587). The tract goes on to compare the "peculiar comfort in the maried besides the genial bed" with God's "own recreations before the world was built; *I was* saith the eternall wisdome, *dayly his delight, playing always before him*" (2:596–97). Book 3 of *Paradise Lost* refers to God's Son as his wisdom. The proem to book 7, however, describes how the heavenly muse Urania and her sister Wisdom play before God. In the divorce tract, God's playful interaction with Wisdom justifies the husband's God-given need for a wife. In *Paradise Lost*, the ambiguous status of wisdom—variously identified with the Son and with a female personification—calls into question God's claims for his autonomous happiness. God, like the man created in his image, may very well desire someone like himself, but it is unclear if he finds full satisfaction in his Son or if he requires a female counterpart. By personifying wisdom, Milton externalizes a trait that belongs to God and thus hints at the possibility of lonely self-estrangement within the godhead. Perhaps even God needs to recreate with a fragment of himself.

26. David Quint, *Epic and Empire: Politics and Generic Form from Virgil to Milton* (Princeton: Princeton University Press, 1993), 300.

27. Rumrich, *Milton Unbound*, 130.

28. See Quint, *Epic and Empire*, 42–45.

29. David Norbrook, *Writing the English Republic: Poetry, Rhetoric and Politics, 1627–1660* (Cambridge: Cambridge University Press, 1998), 470–73.

30. For a fuller account of the significance of the Nimrod episode, see chapter 3.

31. Andrew Escobedo wryly remarks that a scholar examining early modern nationhood "starts off with few friends," yet his work and the work of other historically minded critics have cleared a path for productive inquiry; see Andrew Escobedo, *Nationalism and Historical Loss in Renaissance England* (Ithaca: Cornell University Press, 2004), 10. Escobedo responds to influential theorists including Benedict Anderson, John Brueilly, Ernest Gellner, and Eric Hobsbawm, who argue that the nation is a distinctly modern phenomenon that cannot be applied to the early modern period. Medievalists, however, may also contend that national consciousness arises before the early modern period. Escobedo argues that a nebulous, often contradictory, but nonetheless significant English national consciousness "emerges at a point in history *before* the English had constructed a narrative of progress to accommodate the nation's seeming novelty." G. R. Elton, *The Tudor Revolution in Government: Administrative Changes in the Reign of Henry VIII* (Cambridge: Cambridge University Press, 1953), offers an early and influential argument that the modern nation-state develops in sixteenth-century England; this position has been maintained more recently by Liah Greenfeld in *Nationalism: Five Roads to Modernity* (Cambridge: Harvard University Press, 1992). See also Claire McEachern, *The Poetics of English Nationhood, 1590–1612* (Cambridge: Cambridge University Press, 1996); and David J. Baker, *Between Nations: Shakespeare, Spenser, Marvell, and the Question of Britain* (Stanford: Stanford University Press, 1997).

32. Richard Helgerson, *Forms of Nationhood: The Elizabethan Writing of England* (Chicago: University of Chicago Press, 1992), 22.

33. Norbrook, *Writing the English Republic*, 439.

34. Benedict Anderson, *Imagined Communities: Reflections on the Origin and Spread of Nationalism*, rev. ed. (London: Verso, 1991), 93.

35. As Linda Gregerson observes in "Colonials Write the Nation: Spenser, Milton, and England on the Margins," in *Milton and the Imperial Vision*, ed. Balachandra Rajan and Elizabeth Sauer (Pittsburgh: Duquesne University Press, 1999), 169–90, Milton's *History of Britain* reveals "the modern nation as a back-formation, part of the retroactive logic of empire" (170). In "Body Politics in *Paradise Lost*," *PMLA* 121 (2006): 390, Rachel J. Trubowitz observes, "[Benedict] Anderson argues that nation and empire are opposing concepts . . . ; in early modern England, however, they are mutually constitutive ideas."

36. See Paul Stevens, "Milton's Janus-Faced Nationalism: Soliloquy, Subject, and the Modern Nation State,"*Journal of English and Germanic Philology* 100 (2001): 247–68.

37. Tom Nairn, *The Break-Up of Britain: Crisis and Neo-nationalism*, 2nd ed. (London: Verso, 1981), 14–20.

38. Partha Chatterjee, in *The Nation and Its Fragment: Colonial and Postcolonial Histories* (Princeton: Princeton University Press, 1993), 13, responds to Benedict Anderson's influential argument about the nation as imagined community by asking, "Whose imagined community?" This question allows Chatterjee to trace "the numerous fragmented resistances" to the "hegemonic project of nationalist modernity." Homi Bhabha, in *The Location of Culture* (London: Routledge, 1994), 142, describes the "ambivalent temporalities of the nation-space" in order to show that the "language of culture and community is poised on the fissures of the present becoming the rhetorical figures of a national past."

39. Barbara Fuchs, "Imperium Studies: Theorizing Early Modern Expansion," in *Postcolonial Moves: Medieval through Modern*, ed. Patricia Clare Ingham and Michelle R. Warren (New York: Palgrave Macmillan), 71–90.

40. Nigel Smith, *Is Milton Better Than Shakespeare?* (Cambridge: Harvard University Press, 2008), 7.

41. For some important examples, see J. Martin Evans, *Milton's Imperial Epic: Paradise Lost and the Discourse of Colonialism* (Ithaca: Cornell University Press, 1996); Rajan and Sauer, *Milton and the Imperial Vision*; and Stevens, "Milton's Janus-Faced Nationalism."

42. Ken Hiltner, in *Milton and Ecology* (Cambridge: Cambridge University Press, 2003), 30, argues that Milton's monism generates a *"Christianity rooted in the Earth,"* thus contributing simultaneously to theology, concern for the environment, and philosophical thinking that anticipates Heideggerean *Destruktion* and deconstruction. See also Mary C. Fenton, *Milton's Places of Hope: Spiritual and Political Connections of Hope with Land* (Aldershot: Ashgate, 2006); and Diane Kelsey McColley, ed., *Poetry and Ecology in the Age of Milton and Marvell* (Aldershot: Ashgate, 2007). After the events of September 11, 2001, John Carey sparked debate about Milton and terrorism in "A Work in Praise of Terrorism? September 11 and *Samson Agonistes*," *Times Literary Supplement,* September 6, 2002, 15–16. Much of the ensuing conversation circled around the propriety of applying a present-day understanding of religious violence to Milton's works. The most lucid verdict is provided by Feisal G. Mohamed, "Confronting Religious Violence: Milton's *Samson Agonistes*," *PMLA* 120 (2005): 327–40.

1. The Strange Fire of the Tartars

1. John Rogers, *The Matter of Revolution: Science, Poetry, and Politics in the Age of Milton* (Ithaca: Cornell University Press, 1996), 133.

2. For the connection between Tartarus and the Tartars in Paris's work, see "Relations touching the Tartars, taken out of the Historie of R. Wendover and Mat. Paris," in R. Wendover and Mat[thew] Paris, *Hakluytus Posthumus, or Purchas His Pilgrimes*, 20 vols., ed. Samuel Purchas (Glasgow: James MacLehose and Sons, 1905), 11:173–74.

3. Anne McClintock, *Imperial Leather: Race, Gender, and Sexuality in the Colonial Contest* (New York: Routledge, 1995), 72.

4. Yves of Narbonne, "Part of an Epistle written by one Yvo of Narbona . . . Recorded by Mathew Paris," in *The Principal Navigations Voyages Traffiques & Discoveries of the English Nation*, 12 vols., ed. Richard Hakluyt (Glasgow: James MacLehose and Sons, 1903), 1:50. All quotations from *The Principal Navigations* are hereafter cited parenthetically in the text by volume and page number with the abbreviation *PN*.

5. "Concilium Lugdunese I (First Council of Lyons)—1245," in *Decrees of the Ecumenical Councils*, ed. Norman P. Tanner, S.J., 2 vols. (London and Washington, DC: Sheed & Ward and Georgetown University Press, 1990), 1:297.

6. Claude Cahen, "The Mongols and the Near East," in *The Later Crusades, 1189–1311*, ed. Robert Lee Wolff and Harry W. Hazard, vol. 2 of *A History of the Crusades*, ed. Kenneth M. Setton (Madison: University of Wisconsin Press, 1969–1989), 720–21. For more extensive accounts of Mongol history, see J. J. Saunders, *The History of the Mongol Conquests* (London: Routledge and Kegan Paul, 1971); David Morgan, *The Mongols*, 2nd ed. (Malden, MA: Blackwell, 2007).

7. See Lev. 11:39–40. For a provocative discussion of the cultural function of Levitical codes of purity in encounters with the New World, see Paul Stevens, "Milton and the New World: Custom, Relativism, and the Discipline of Shame," in *Milton and the Imperial Vision*, ed. Balachandra Rajan and Elizabeth Sauer (Pittsburgh: Duquesne University Press, 1999), 90–111.

8. *The Travels of Marco Polo*, trans. and ed. Aldo Ricci (London: George Routledge and Sons, 1931), 85–6.

9. Ibid., 85.

10. Richard W. Cogley, "'The Most Vile and Barbarous Nation of All the World': Giles Fletcher the Elder's *The Tartars Or, Ten Tribes* (ca. 1610)," *Renaissance Quarterly* 58 (2005): 784.

11. Edward Said, *Orientalism*, 25th anniversary ed. (New York: Vintage, 1994), 39. Although Said is primarily concerned with representations of Near Eastern Islamic peoples from the late eighteenth century on, his work has been influential in accounts of earlier relations between Europe and eastern Asia. Said suggests that the difference between older and modern forms of Orientalist discourse is one of degree rather than of kind, noting that "the range of representation expanded enormously in the later period" (34). Said's theoretical contributions continue to be debated, however, especially with regard to earlier historical epochs. Current analysis seeks to show how the concept of Orientalism can shed light on early European writings about eastern Asia, especially when Said's primarily spatial or geographical focus is supplemented by a temporal and historical one.

12. On Fletcher's motivations for writing about Russia, see Daryl W. Palmer, *Writing Russia in the Age of Shakespeare* (Aldershot: Ashgate, 2004), 129–54.

13. One of Fletcher's few qualifications about the Tartars' savageness comes at the expense of the Russians' honesty; the "Cheremessen" Tartars are "said to be just and true in their dealings: and for that cause they hate the Russe people, whom they account to be double, false in al their dealing" (*PN* 3:400).

14. Giles Fletcher, *Israel Redux: Or the Restauration of Israel* (London, 1677), 21.

15. Alvaro Semedo, *The History of That Great and Renowned Monarchy of China. . . . To which is added the History of the late Invasion, and Conquest of that flourishing Kingdom by the Tartars* (London, 1655), 255.

16. Ibid., 260.

17. Ibid., 297.

18. Ibid., 306.

19. *A Continuation of the Former Newes. Three great Invasions already attempted* (London: for Thomas Archer and Benjamin Fisher, 1624), 3.

20. *A Declaration, or Letters Patent of this present King of Poland John the Third . . . Now faithfully translated from the Latin Copy. by John Milton* (London, 1674), 6.

21. Ibid., 9–10.

22. See Robert Markley, *The Far East and the English Imagination, 1600–1730* (Cambridge: Cambridge University Press, 2006), 70–103.

23. John Michael Archer, *Old Worlds: Egypt, Southwest Asia, India, and Russia in Early Modern English Writing* (Stanford: Stanford University Press, 2001), 102.

24. Andrew Escobedo, *Nationalism and Historical Loss in Renaissance England* (Ithaca: Cornell University Press, 2004), 194, has shown that Milton's prose takes part in a larger pattern of constructing a national identity out of an irretrievable past; his *History of Britain* thus stages an "awkward conflict between history and fiction."

25. R. D. Bedford, "Milton's Journey North: *A Brief History of Moscovia* and *Paradise Lost*," *Renaissance Studies* 7 (1993): 72.

26. Edmund Spenser, *A View of the State of Ireland*, ed. Andrew Hadfield and Willy Maley (Oxford: Blackwell, 1997), 63. On the significance of this description of drinking blood, see Richard McCabe, *Spenser's Monstrous Regiment: Elizabethan Ireland and the Poetics of Difference* (Oxford: Oxford University Press, 2002), 59–61. Maley has discussed how Milton's political thought was influenced by Spenser's *View*. See Willy Maley, "How Milton and Some Contemporaries Read Spenser's *View*," in *Representing Ireland: Literature and the Origins of Conflict, 1534–1660*, ed. Brendan Bradshaw, Andrew Hadfield, and Willy Maley (Cambridge: Cambridge University Press, 1993), 191–208.

27. See Kathleen Wilson, "Empire, Gender, and Modernity in the Eighteenth Century," in *Gender and Empire*, ed. Philippa Levine (Oxford: Oxford University Press, 2004), 24.

28. Thomas Morton, *New English Canaan* (London, 1632), 19.

29. J. Martin Evans, *Milton's Imperial Epic:* Paradise Lost *and the Discourse of Colonialism* (Ithaca: Cornell University Press, 1996), 108.

30. *PL* 3.431–41n.

31. All quotations from poems by Milton other than *Paradise Lost* are taken from John Milton, *Complete Shorter Poems*, ed. John Carey, 2nd rev. ed. (Harlow: Longman, 2007) and are cited parenthetically by line numbers.

32. Evans, *Milton's Imperial Epic,* 108.

33. For more about Milton's involvement in these affairs, see Leo Miller, *John Milton and the Oldenburg Safeguard: New Light on Milton and His Friends in the Commonwealth from the Diaries and Letters of Hermann Mylius* (New York: Loewenthal Press, 1985), and *John Milton's Writings in the Anglo-Dutch Negotiations, 1651–1654* (Pittsburgh: Duquesne University Press, 1992); and Robert T. Fallon, *Milton in Government* (University Park: Pennsylvania State University Press, 1993).

34. David Quint, *Epic and Empire: Politics and Generic Form from Virgil to Milton* (Princeton: Princeton University Press, 1993), 253–56.

35. Luís Vaz de Camões, *The Lusiad*, trans. Richard Fanshawe (London: for Humphrey Moseley, 1655), canto 7, stanza 62.

36. The *OED* cites examples of "Tartarian" in reference to the Tartars dating back to the fourteenth-century *Travels of Sir John Mandeville.*

37. See, for instance, Stevie Davies, *Images of Kingship in* Paradise Lost: *Milton's Politics and Christian Liberty* (Columbia: University of Missouri Press, 1983), 51–88.

38. See "In Proditionem Bombardican," in John Milton, *Complete Shorter Poems*, ed. John Carey, 2nd rev. ed. (Harlow: Longman, 2007), 34. David Quint, in *Epic and Empire,* 268–81, has shown how the Gunpowder Plot would leave a lasting impression on Milton's poetic career.

39. Quint, *Epic and Empire,* 27–31.

40. Cogley, "The Most Vile and Barbarous Nation," 800–805.

41. Jeffrey Shoulson, *Milton and the Rabbis: Hebraism, Hellenism, and Christianity* (New York: Columbia University Press, 2001), 51.

42. For arguments that Milton's writings implicitly support the Restorationist position, see N. I. Matar, "Milton and the Idea of the Restoration of the Jews," *SEL* 27 (1987): 109–24; Douglas Brooks, "'Ill-Matching Words and Deeds Long Past': Englished Hebrew and 'the Readmission of the Jews' in *Paradise Lost*," *Philological Quarterly* 81 (2002): 53–80.

43. In writings such as *Animadversions* (1641), Milton deploys typological thinking and anti-Judaic rhetoric almost in the same breath to describe England's condition. Against Bishop Hall's claim that tradition and custom support episcopacy, Milton declares, "This was the plea of *Judaisme*, and Idolatry against *Christ* and his *Apostles*, of *Papacie* against Reformation" (*CPW* 1:703). Yet this same response concludes in a prayer that likens deliverance from idolatry to Israel's redemption from Egypt (*CPW* 1:706).

44. Achsah Guibbory, "England, Israel, and the Jews in Milton's Prose, 1649–1660," in *Milton and the Jews,* ed. Douglas Brooks (Cambridge: Cambridge University Press, 2008), 34. See also Guibbory, "Israel and English Protestant Nationalism: 'Fast Sermons' during the English Revolution," in *Early Modern Nationalism and Milton's England*, ed. David Loewenstein and Paul Stevens (Toronto: University of Toronto Press, 2008), 115–38.

45. All quotations from *Paradise Regained* are from Milton, *Complete Shorter Poems*, and are cited parenthetically by book and line numbers with the abbreviation *PR.*

46. Quint, *Epic and Empire,* 325–26.

47. For a literary account of this trait of the Tartars, see Edmund Spenser, *The Faerie Queene*, ed. A. C. Hamilton et al., 2nd ed. (Harlow: Longman, 2006), 2.11.26. All quotations from *The Faerie Queene* are from this edition and are hereafter cited parenthetically by book, canto, and stanza with the abbreviation *FQ.*

48. *PL* 54.

49. Richard Helgerson, *Forms of Nationhood: The Elizabethan Writing of England* (Chicago: University of Chicago Press, 1992), 59.

50. Ibid., 61.

51. Roger Ascham, *The Scholemaster*, in *English Works*, ed. William Aldis Wright (Cambridge: Cambridge University Press, 1904), 289.

52. Ibid., 224–5.

53. Ibid., 290.

54. John S. Diekhoff, "Rhyme in Paradise Lost," *PMLA* 49 (1934): 539–43; J.M. Purcell, "Rime in *Paradise Lost*," *Modern Language Notes* 59 (1944): 171–72. More recently, Lawrence H. McCauley, "Milton's Missing Rhymes," *Style* 28 (1994): 242–59, has expanded the discussion of rhyme in *Paradise Lost* to include slant rhyme, internal rhyme, and a number of rhyme-like devices.

55. On the effects of rhyme in *Samson Agonistes*, see Robert Beum, "The Rhyme in *Samson Agonistes*," *Texas Studies in Language and Literature* 4 (1962): 177–82; Michael Cohen, "Rhyme in *Samson Agonistes*," *Milton Quarterly* 8 (1974): 4–6; and Keith Hull, "Rhyme and Disorder in *Samson Agonistes*," *Milton Studies* 30 (1993): 163–81.

56. Homi K. Bhabha, *The Location of Culture* (London: Routledge, 1994), 62. In light of the concerns about cultural purity that pervade *Paradise Lost*, Milton's note on verse functions ironically as, in Bhabha's words, a "reminder to the postimperial West, of the hybridity of its mother tongue, and the heterogeneity of its national space" (60).

57. W. M. Clarke, "Intentional Rhyme in Vergil and Ovid," *Transactions and Proceedings of the American Philological Association* 103 (1972): 49–77. See also H. T. Johnstone, "Rhymes and Assonances in the *Aeneid*," *Classical Review* 10 (1890): 9–13. I thank Steve Fallon for bringing to my attention the relevance of rhyming in classical verse.

58. *PL* 55. Samuel Barrow's prefatory note, "In Paradisum Amissam," declares Milton superior not only to moderns but also to Homer and Virgil—who, in comparison to Milton's universal Christian vision, sang only of frogs and gnats. See *PL* 52–53.

59. Andrew Marvell's prefatory poem to the 1674 edition of *Paradise Lost* alludes to Dryden's composition. Although Marvell praises Milton for scorning his "readers to allure / With tinkling rhyme," Marvell's own verse aligns him with the rhyming "town-Bayes." In a gesture that is equal parts humble and arch, Marvell concludes his commendatory poem with a couplet that declares that Milton's sublime theme does not need rhyme. See A.M., "On *Paradise Lost*," in *PL* 53–54.

60. Angelica Duran, "Milton among Hispanics: Jorge Luis Borges and Milton's 'Condemnation of Rhyme,'" *Prose Studies* 28.2 (2006): 234–44.

61. Ibid., 240.

2. Eden, the Country House, and the Indies (East and West)

1. J. Martin Evans, *Milton's Imperial Epic: Paradise Lost and the Discourse of Colonialism* (Ithaca: Cornell University Press, 1996), 4. Evans argues, "Nowhere is the colonial theme in *Paradise Lost* more evident than in Milton's treatment of the garden of Eden" (43).

2. Anthony Pagden, *European Encounters with the New World* (New Haven: Yale University Press, 1993), 10.

3. For a meditation on this simile, see Balachandra Rajan, "Banyan Trees and Fig Leaves: Some Thoughts on Milton's India," in *Of Poetry and Politics: New Essays on Milton and His World*, ed. P. G. Stanwood (Binghamton, NY: Medieval & Renaissance Texts and Studies, 1995), 213–28.

4. Barbara K. Lewalski, *Paradise Lost and the Rhetoric of Literary Forms* (Princeton: Princeton University Press, 1985), 181. See also Donald Friedman's description of Adam and Eve's

"rural seat" as the seat of "regnal authority" over a country estate in "The Lady in the Garden: On the Literary Genetics of Milton's Eve," *Milton Studies* 35 (1997): 114–33.

5. See D. M. Rosenberg, "Milton's *Paradise Lost* and the Country Estate Poem," *Clio* 18 (1989): 123–34; Christopher Wortham, "'A happy rural seat': Milton's *Paradise Lost* and the English Country House Poem," *Parergon* 9.1 (1991): 137–50.

6. Ben Jonson, "To Penshurst," lines 1, 30, and 37, in *Ben Jonson: The Complete Poems*, ed. George Parfitt (New Haven: Yale University Press, 1982), 95. All quotations of Jonson's poetry are from this volume and are hereafter cited parenthetically in the text.

7. Thomas Carew, "To Saxham," lines 43–44, in *The Poems of Thomas Carew with His Masque* Coelum Britannicum, ed. Rhodes Dunlap (Oxford: Clarendon, 1949), 28. All quotations from Carew's poetry are taken from this source and are cited parenthetically in the text.

8. See Don E. Wayne, *Penshurst: The Semiotics of Place and the Poetics of History* (Madison: University of Wisconsin Press, 1984); and Hugh Jenkins, *Feigned Commonwealths: The Country-House Poem and the Fashioning of the Ideal Community* (Pittsburgh: Duquesne University Press, 1998), especially 1–33. For other studies of the country house genre, see G. R. Hibbard, "The Country House Poem of the Seventeenth Century," *Journal of the Warburg and Courtauld Institutes* 19 (1956): 159–74; Charles Molesworth, "Property and Virtue: The Genre of the Country House Poem in the Seventeenth Century," *Genre* 1 (1968): 141–57; and William A. McClung, *The Country House in English Renaissance Poetry* (Berkeley: University of California Press, 1977).

9. Leah Marcus, *The Politics of Mirth: Jonson, Herrick, Milton, Marvell, and the Defense of Old Holiday Pastimes* (1986; rpt. Chicago: University of Chicago Press, 1989), 19.

10. Heather DuBrow, "The Country-House Poem: A Study in Generic Development," *Genre* 12 (1979): 161.

11. As Hugh Jenkins points out, recent scholarship has complicated the dichotomy of court and country, yet this basic split seems unavoidable in a discussion of the genre. See Jenkins, *Feigned Commonwealths*, 34–38.

12. Rosenberg, "Milton's *Paradise Lost* and the Country Estate Poem," 131.

13. Michael Bryson, *The Tyranny of Heaven: Milton's Rejection of God as King* (Newark: University of Delaware Press, 2004), 49–50, argues, "The earliest portions of the Hebrew Bible . . . reveal that the roots of heavenly kingship are no less 'oriental'—and therefore . . . no more 'despotic'—than are the roots of the Satanic monarchy so vividly realized in *Paradise Lost*."

14. Homi K. Bhabha, *The Location of Culture* (London: Routledge, 1994), 86–87.

15. Wortham, "A happy rural seat," 143.

16. Stephen M. Fallon, *Milton among the Philosophers: Poetry and Materialism in Seventeenth-Century England* (Ithaca: Cornell University Press, 1991), 195.

17. Robert Herrick, "The Country Life," lines 7 and 10, in *The Poetical Works of Robert Herrick*, ed. L. C. Martin (Oxford University Press, 1956), 229.

18. John Michael Archer, *Old Worlds: Egypt, Southwest Asia, India, and Russia in Early Modern English Writing* (Stanford: Stanford University Press, 2001), 87.

19. *See Georgics*, 2.461–66 in *Virgil*, vol. 1, *Eclogues, Georgics, Aeneid I–VI*, ed. and trans. H. Rushton Fairclough, rev. G. R. Gould, Loeb Classical Library (Cambridge: Harvard University Press, 1999).

20. Stella P. Revard, "Vergil's *Georgics* and *Paradise Lost*: Nature and Human Nature in a Landscape," in *Vergil at 2000: Commemorative Essays on the Poet and His Influence*, ed. John D. Bernard (New York: AMS Press, 1986), 278.

21. See stanza 50, in which the laborers "Massacre the Grass" and inadvertently kill a rail, a bird associated with Charles I. Stanza 57 explicitly mentions the Levellers, reminding the reader that Thomas Fairfax had suppressed a Leveller uprising in 1649. Derek Hirst and Steve Zwicker, in "High Summer at Nun Appleton, 1651: Andrew Marvell and Lord Fairfax's Occasions,"

Historical Journal 36 (1993): 247–69, argue that such politically charged allusions do not merely refer to the events of the 1640s but also point to immediate concerns. They note that Leveller leaders were organizing riots near Fairfax's estate in the summer of 1651. All quotations of Marvell's poetry are from *The Poems and Letters of Andrew Marvell*, ed. H. M. Margoliouth, rev. Pierre Legouis and E. E. Duncan-Jones, 3rd ed., 2 vols. (Oxford: Oxford University Press, 1971), and are hereafter cited parenthetically in the text.

22. Rosalie L. Colie, "Marvell's 'Bermudas' and the Puritan Paradise," *Renaissance News* 10 (1957): 75. Colie was the first to suggest the similarities between "Bermudas" and Lewis Hughes's *Plaine and True Relation of the Goodness of God towards the Somer Islands* (1621). Readers have also noted Marvell's personal connection to John Oxenbridge, a Puritan minister who had traveled to the Bermudas. See Pierre Legouis, *Andrew Marvell: Poet, Puritan, Patriot*, 2nd ed. (Oxford: Oxford University Press, 1968), 94–96.

23. Annabel Patterson, "*Bermudas* and *The Coronet*: Marvell's Protestant Poetics," *ELH* 44 (1977): 490.

24. Tay Fizdale, in "Irony in Marvell's 'Bermudas,'" *ELH* 42 (1975): 203–13, has argued that Marvell undermines any straightforward celebration of a Puritan paradise. Marvell articulates a critique that is subtle enough that it never lapses into a "scathing denunciation" (211).

25. For a discussion of the widespread use of the Norman Yoke rhetoric, see Christopher Hill, *Puritanism and Revolution: Studies in Interpretation of the English Revolution of the Seventeenth Century* (New York: Schocken, 1964), 50–122.

26. Quoted in Evans, *Milton's Imperial Epic*, 33.

27. Bruce McLeod, *The Geography of Empire in English Literature, 1580–1745* (Cambridge: Cambridge University Press, 1999), 80.

28. Raymond Williams, *The Country and the City* (New York: Oxford University Press, 1973), 32.

29. Wortham, "A happy rural seat," 149.

30. Eden does have indigenous residents. God grants Adam and Eve dominion over Eden "and all things that therein live, / Or live in sea, or air, beast, fish and fowl" (8.340–341). Nevertheless, there is no violence done to these animals by the vegetarian Adam and Eve, nor does the original couple yoke any creatures into labor. If Adam and Eve subjugate the animals, surely theirs is a nonexploitive colonialism that would never occur in postlapsarian history.

31. William Empson, in *Milton's God*, rev. ed. (Cambridge: Cambridge University Press, 1981), 97, argues that God's apparent joke about the warring angels' threat to his omnipotence in book 5 is "appallingly malignant" because "God has a second purpose in remaining passive; to give the rebels false evidence that he is a usurper, and thus drive them into real evil." In book 3, the light of God's inability to detect Satan's presence may seem to the fallen reader like a cruel joke at the expense of humankind. There are other clues that God's neglectful administration might explain the Fall. In book 2, the reader wonders why God has left the duty of guarding the gates of Hell to Sin, whose essence is transgression. Later, when Satan is admonished by Gabriel for escaping from Hell, his response is as cogent as it is defiant: "Let him surer bar / His iron gates, if he intends our stay / In that dark durance" (4.897–99). Gabriel has no satisfying response.

32. John Rogers, *The Matter of Revolution: Science, Poetry, and Politics in the Age of Milton* (Ithaca: Cornell University Press, 1996), 109.

33. James Grantham Turner, *The Politics of Landscape: Rural Scenery and Society in English Poetry, 1630–1660* (Oxford: Basil Blackwell, 1979), 38.

34. See Pagden, *European Encounters with the New World*, 51–87, for an account of "the autoptic imagination" in early modern descriptions of the New World. For the role of the eye in colonialist writings, see also Stephen Greenblatt, *Marvelous Possessions: The Wonder of the New World* (University of Chicago Press, 1991), especially 119–51.

35. Ralph Hamor, *A True Discourse of the Present Estate of Virginia* (London, 1615), sig. B1.

36. Shannon Miller, *Engendering the Fall: John Milton and Seventeenth-Century Women Writers* (Philadelphia: University of Pennsylvania Press, 2008), 59. We do not know with certainty whether or not Milton read Lanyer's poetry. Nevertheless, Kari Boyd McBride and John C. Ulreich, in "Answerable Styles: Biblical Poetics and Biblical Politics in the Poetry of Lanyer and Milton," *Journal of English and Germanic Philology* 100.3 (2001): 333–54, have described meaningful connections between the two poets' modes of biblical interpretation and the political implications of their respective hermeneutics.

37. Aemilia Lanyer, "The Description of Cooke-ham," lines 57, 67–70. All quotations of Lanyer's poetry are from *The Poems of Aemilia Lanyer: Salve Deus Rex Judaeorum*, ed. Susanne Woods (New York: Oxford University Press, 1993), and are hereafter cited parenthetically in the text.

38. McLeod, *Geography of Empire,* 137 and 140.

39. Regina M. Schwartz, "Through the Optic Glass: Voyeurism and *Paradise Lost*," in *Desire in the Renaissance: Psychoanalysis and Literature*, ed. Valeria Finucci and Regina Schwartz (Princeton: Princeton University Press, 1994), 156.

40. Peter C. Herman, *Destabilizing Milton:* Paradise Lost *and the Poetics of Incertitude* (New York: Palgrave Macmillan, 2005), 117–19, describes how Milton's ostensibly omniscient Muse ("for heaven hides nothing from thy view" [*PL* 1.27]) proves a questionable source of knowledge and judgment.

41. Evans, *Milton's Imperial Epic,* 123.

42. John P. Rumrich, *Milton Unbound: Controversy and Reinterpretation* (New York: Cambridge University Press, 1996), 130.

43. In a different but relevant reading of *Paradise Lost*'s conjugal politics, John Rogers argues that the "inflexible aristocratic hierarchy" of marital relations conflicts with Eden's otherwise egalitarian nature: "The situation, in other words, is untenable; the contradictory social formation of paradise, inherently unstable." See John Rogers, "Transported Touch: The Fruit of Marriage in *Paradise Lost*," in *Milton and Gender*, ed. Catherine Gimelli Martin (Cambridge: Cambridge University Press, 2004), 125.

44. Upon his death in 1605, George Clifford excluded his only surviving heir, Anne, from most of his inheritance, bequeathing his estates instead to his brother Francis Clifford. Lady Margaret began a series of legal litigation to restore her daughter's claim. Although Margaret successfully argued her case before the court in 1607, Francis Clifford would continue to occupy many of the family estates. "Cooke-ham" and the family crises to which it refers reveal the tenuous position that the country house lady occupied. Barbara Lewalski has argued influentially that Lanyer attempts to imagine an ideal female community, especially by refashioning the patronage system. See, for example, Barbara Lewalski, *Writing Women in Jacobean England* (Cambridge: Harvard University Press, 1993), 213–41. Other critics have stressed the importance of class dynamics in Lanyer's writings. See, for example, Ann Baynes Coiro, "Writing in Service: Sexual Politics and Class Position in the Poetry of Aemilia Lanyer and Ben Jonson," *Criticism* 35 (1993): 357–76; Mary Ellen Lamb, "Patronage and Class in Aemilia Lanyer's *Salve Deus Rex Judaeorum*," in *Women, Writing, and the Reproduction of Culture in Tudor and Stuart Britain*, ed. Mary E. Burke et al. (Syracuse University Press, 2000), 38–57; and Su Fang Ng, "Aemilia Lanyer and the Politics of Praise," *ELH* 67 (2000): 433–51.

45. For a discussion of virginity as a political principle during the seventeenth century, see John Rogers, "The Enclosure of Virginity: The Poetics of Sexual Abstinence in the English Revolution," in *Enclosure Acts: Sexuality, Property, and Culture in Early Modern England*, ed. Richard Burt and John Michael Archer (Ithaca: Cornell University Press, 1994), 229–50.

46. Fallon, *Milton among the Philosophers,* 201.

47. See ibid., 203–6, for an account of the devils' Cartesianism.

48. Ibid., 80.

49. Adam's maternal fantasy recalls some of his earliest experiences: when he first falls asleep on "a green shady bank profuse of flowers," he thinks that he will dissolve into his former state of nonexistence (8.286). The second time he experiences dazzling sleep, it is so he can witness the emergence of Eve out of his side; when he awakes and cannot find her, he becomes as close to suicidal as an unfallen man can be.

50. Rachel J. Trubowitz, "Body Politics in *Paradise Lost*," *PMLA* 121 (2006): 399.

51. For a discussion of Milton's critical attitude toward primogeniture, see Su Fang Ng, *Literature and the Politics of Family in Seventeenth-Century England* (Cambridge: Cambridge University Press, 2007), 49–75. See also Richard C. McCoy's discussion of Milton's attack on the sacred bases of kingship in *Alterations of State: Sacred Kingship in the English Reformation* (New York: Columbia University Press, 2002), 87–122.

52. To what extent Milton leads his reader to extend egalitarianism to gender politics and to what extent he affirms patriarchal values has been the focus of long-standing debate. Mary Nyquist, in "The Genesis of Gendered Subjectivity in the Divorce Tracts and in *Paradise Lost*," in *Re-membering Milton*, ed. Mary Nyquist and Margaret W. Ferguson (New York: Methuen, 1988), 165–93, argues powerfully that any meaningful sense of subjectivity that accrues to Eve ultimately serves Adam's sense of a need for another self. For important readings of Milton as less misogynistic and more egalitarian than his predecessors and contemporaries in depicting Eve, see Diane Kelsey McColley, *Milton's Eve* (Urbana: University of Illinois Press, 1983); and Joseph Wittreich, *Feminist Milton* (Ithaca: Cornell University Press, 1987), which turns to the responses of female readers in the eighteenth century to argue that Milton was of Eve's party. Shannon Miller, in *Engendering the Fall*, has put Milton in dialogue with a number of women writers both before and after him; for Miller, such a conversation highlights both traditional and antipatriarchal strains of Milton's thinking and provides a multifaceted reading of *Paradise Lost*.

53. In addition to Filmer's influential *Patriarcha, Or the Natural Power of Kings* (1680), see his comments linking the acceptance of patriarchal reproductive politics and of political sovereignty in Sir Robert Filmer, *Observations Concerning the Original of Government*, in *Patriarcha and Other Writings*, ed. J. P. Sommerville (Cambridge: Cambridge University Press, 1991), 192: "But we know that God at creation gave the sovereignty to the man over the woman, as being the nobler and principal agent in generation. As to the objection that 'it is not known who is the father to the son but by the discovery of the mother', . . . if the mother be not in the possession of a husband, the child is not reckoned to have any father at all. . . . No child naturally and infallibly knows who are his true parents, yet he must obey."

54. Rogers, *Matter of Revolution*, 148–49.

55. Paul Stevens, "'Leviticus Thinking' and the Rhetoric of Early Modern Colonialism," *Criticism* 35 (1993): 449.

56. Milton, as Stevens points out, does so when he denounces the Irish in texts such as *Eikonoklastes* and *Observations upon the Articles of Peace* (both 1649). Yet *Eikonoklastes* also articulates the narrow limits of England's supposed ascendancy, which is contingent on a commitment to liberty and religious zeal. Milton's later disillusionment with the citizenry and politics of his country is well known. Fredric Jameson has claimed that the inward, spiritual focus of Milton's later works marks a retreat from politics. See Fredric Jameson, "Religion and Ideology: A Political Reading of *Paradise Lost*," in *1642: Literature and Power in the Seventeenth Century*, ed. Francis Barker et al. (Colchester: University of Essex Press, 1981), 315–36. As David Quint reminds us, however, in *Epic and Empire: Politics and Generic Form from Virgil to Milton* (Princeton: Princeton University Press, 1993), 268, "Critics as different as Northrop Frye and Christopher Hill warn us not to confuse this attitude with a mere quietism."

57. C. S. Lewis, *A Preface to* Paradise Lost (London: Oxford University Press, 1942), 47.

58. Christopher Columbus, *Select Documents Illustrating the Four Voyages of Columbus*, trans. and ed. Cecil Jane, 2 vols. (London: Hakluyt Society, 1930), 2:30.

59. Anne McClintock, *Imperial Leather: Race, Gender, and Sexuality in the Colonial Contest* (New York: Routledge, 1995), 22 and 24.

60. For an argument that Milton published the piece ironically, as a veiled act of protest against Cromwell, see Martin Dzelzainis, "Milton and the Protectorate in 1658," in *Milton and Republicanism*, ed. David Armitage et al. (Cambridge: Cambridge University Press, 1995), 181–205. In "Milton's 'Renunciation' of Cromwell," *Modern Philology* 98 (2001): 363–92, Paul Stevens argues that Milton's admiration for Cromwell and Raleigh was genuine.

61. The quotation describes marital customs within the context of missionary work in Africa: Raleigh observes that the Christian condemnation of polygamy ultimately leads the natives of "the kingdom of Congo" to reject conversion. See *CPW* 1:411.

62. Louis Adrian Montrose, "The Work of Gender in the Discourse of Discovery," *Representations* 33 (1991): 25. In *Tough Love: Amazon Encounters in the English Renaissance* (Durham: Duke University Press, 2000), Kathryn Schwarz provides an extensive analysis of the figure of the Amazon in early modern English writings; see especially 50–78.

63. Albert C. Labriola, "Milton's Eve and the Cult of Elizabeth I," *Journal of English and Germanic Philology* 95 (1996): 38–51.

3. *Paradise Lost* and the Question of Ireland

1. William Kerrigan and Gordon Braden, *The Idea of the Renaissance* (Baltimore: Johns Hopkins University Press, 1989), 201.

2. *Metamorphoses* 3.434–36, quoted from Ovid, *Metamorphoses*, trans. Frank Justus Miller, rev. G. P. Goold, 2 vols., Loeb Classical Library (Cambridge: Harvard University Press, 1984).

3. Jacques Lacan, *The Four Fundamental Concepts of Psychoanalysis*, trans. Alan Sheridan, ed. Jacques-Alain Miller (New York: Norton, 1981), 140–42, destabilizes the Cartesian *cogito* by pointing to this split that inheres in language.

4. In book 3 of the *Metamorphoses*, Narcissus's reflecting pool harkens back to Gargaphie, a wondrous place wrought by nature and not by the work of art ("arte laboratum nulla"); see Ovid, *Metamorphoses* 3.158. Ovid, however, wittily elevates art with the suggestion that by creating Gargaphie, nature has imitated art. The fact that he can describe the perfection of this place without distortion suggests the power of verbal art. See also Philostratus's and Callistratus's uses of the Narcissus myth, as documented by Louise Vinge, *The Narcissus Theme in Western European Literature up to the Early Nineteenth Century*, trans. Robert Dewsnap and Nigel Reeves (Lund: Gleerups, 1967), 29–33. Philostratus and Callistratus describe, respectively, a painting and a statue of Narcissus that may not ever have existed. They do so in part to suggest the capacity to describe forms of mimesis that cannot actually be achieved. Painters, however, would use the Narcissus story to describe the merits of their medium. See, for example, Leon Battista Alberti's acceptance, in *On Painting*, trans. John R. Spencer (New Haven: Yale University Press, 1966), 64, of the poets' claim that Narcissus is the first painter and his affirmation that the painter can indeed embrace the surface of the pool.

5. As C. S. Lewis puts it in *A Preface to* Paradise Lost (London: Oxford University Press, 1942), 122: "She who thought it beneath her dignity to bow to Adam or to God, now worships a vegetable. She has at last become 'primitive' in the popular sense." Lewis describes how Eve "does 'low Reverence' before it 'as to the power that dwelt within,' and thus completes the parallel between her fall and Satan's." It is possible that Lewis's comparison between Eve and Satan suggests that "within" refers not only to the tree's insides but to Eve's as well: after all, the condition of Satan's interiority is the greatest marker of his fallenness. Yet Lewis largely avoids the suggestion

that Eve's adoration of the tree might be a return to her original narcissism, for the possibility of a predisposition to sin would complicate Milton's theodicy.

6. Benedict Anderson, in *Imagined Communities: Reflections on the Origin and Spread of Nationalism*, rev. ed. (London: Verso, 1991), 24, borrows a phrase from Walter Benjamin to argue that national consciousness can arise only in a modern sense of "homogenous, empty time." Homi K. Bhabha, in *The Location of Culture* (London: Routledge, 1994), 160–61, observes that this "empty time" is linked to a notion of the arbitrary sign that accommodates the imagined community of the nation. Bhabha responds to Anderson by reminding us of the internal temporal cleavages within the ostensibly linear narrative on which the modern nation grounds itself discursively.

7. Linda Gregerson, "Colonials Write the Nation: Spenser, Milton, and England on the Margins," in *Milton and the Imperial Vision*, ed. Balachandra Rajan and Elizabeth Sauer (Pittsburgh: Duquesne University Press, 1999), 170.

8. In what has become an oft-quoted passage, the *Observations upon the Articles of Peace* imputes to the Irish "a disposition not onely sottish but indocible and averse from all Civility and amendment," describing them as a people "rejecting the ingenuity of all other Nations to improve and waxe more civill by a civilizing Conquest" (*CPW* 3:304). Yet even official documents like the *Observations* register awareness of the dangerous motility of labels such as barbarism and rebellion. As Jim Daems argues in "Dividing Conjunctions: Milton's *Observations Upon the Articles of Peace*," *Milton Quarterly* 33.2 (1999): 51–55, Milton's sense of his own country's propensity for backsliding informs the *Observations*, so that Ireland is "the antithesis of the English" but also "England's mirror image" (53).

9. For Milton's reading of the *View*, see Willy Maley, "How Milton and Some Contemporaries Read Spenser's *View*," in *Representing Ireland: Literature and the Origins of Conflict, 1534–1660*, ed. Brendan Bradshaw, Andrew Hadfield, and Willy Maley (Cambridge: Cambridge University Press, 1993), 191–208.

10. Walter S. H. Lim, in *The Arts of Empire: The Poetics of Colonialism from Raleigh to Milton* (Newark: University of Delaware Press, 1998), 142–93, argues that *Paradise Lost* registers "Milton's sense . . . that England has lost its cultural mandate" (196)—including its claim to legitimate power over Ireland.

11. Milton did republish the first *Defense*, which contains anti-Irish rhetoric, in 1658. Mary C. Fenton comments that Milton "actively revised" the *Defense* up to its republication date in "Milton's View of Ireland," *Milton Studies* 44 (2005): 221. Paul Stevens, in an essay that contests Milton's supposed renunciation of Cromwell, notes in passing that the piece was "published in October 1658 but revised for publication well before that date." See Paul Stevens, "Milton's 'Renunciation' of Cromwell," *Modern Philology* 98.3 (2001): 367. The question of why Milton republished the *Defense* plays an important role in the long-standing debate about Milton's views on Cromwell and the Protectorate.

12. Roger Boyle, Earl of Orrery, *The Answer of a Person of Quality to a Scandalous Letter* (Dublin, 1662), 41.

13. Orrery's personal history renders deeply ironic such arguments as "'Tis not the fighting, but the *ground* and *end* of the fighting, which proves which is the good Subject" (ibid., 48).

14. Arthur Capel, *Letters Written by His Excellency Arthur Capel, Earl of Essex, Lord Lieutenant of Ireland, in the Year 1675* (Dublin, 1770), 2, quoted in T. C. Barnard, "Crises of Identity among Irish Protestants 1641–1685," *Past and Present* 127 (1990): 55. Barnard contextualizes the occasion of Temple's *History* and its republication in subsequent decades.

15. Deana Rankin, *Between Spenser and Swift: English Writing in Seventeenth-Century Ireland* (Cambridge: Cambridge University Press, 2005), 185. See also John Kerrigan, "Orrery's Ireland and the British Problem, 1641–1679," in *British Identities and English Renaissance Literature*, ed. David J. Baker and Willy Maley (Cambridge: Cambridge University Press, 2002), 197–225.

16. For the connection between Milton and the Boyle family—especially through his friendship with Katherine Boyle, Lady Ranelagh—see Christopher Hill, *Milton and the English Revolution* (New York: Viking, 1978), 133–35; and William Riley Parker, *Milton: A Biography*, 2 vols. (Oxford: Clarendon, 1968–69), 922–24.

17. Edmund Spenser, *A View of the State of Ireland*, ed. Andrew Hadfield and Willy Maley (Oxford: Blackwell, 1997), 59.

18. See chapter 1 for the link between the Irish and the barbarous Tartars in the English imagination.

19. Barnabe Rich, *The Irish Hubbub, or, The English Hue and Crie* (London, 1619), 1.

20. David J. Baker, *Between Nations: Shakespeare, Spenser, Marvell, and the Question of Britain* (Stanford: Stanford University Press, 1997), 66–123. See also Richard McCabe, "Translated States: Spenser and Linguistic Colonialism," in *Edmund Spenser: Essays on Culture and Allegory*, ed. Jennifer Klein Morrison and Matthew Greenfield (Aldershot: Ashgate, 2000), 67–88.

21. Patricia Palmer, in *Language and Conquest in Early Modern Ireland: English Renaissance Literature and Elizabethan Imperial Expansion* (Cambridge: Cambridge University Press 2001), 110, details how this project proved "less an achievement than an aspiration."

22. Rich, *Hubbub*, sig. A2.

23. Ibid., 51.

24. Bitumen was long associated with biblical lands; see definition 1 of "bitumen" in the *OED* as well as Thomas Newton's comments along this line in John Milton, *Paradise Lost. A Poem in Twelve Books. The Author John Milton*, ed. Thomas Newton, 2 vols. (London, 1749). Given the association of Nimrod and Ireland, the image of black turf being made from Irish bogs might be of some relevance. In chap. 20 of *Irelands Naturall History* (London, 1657), 154–62, Gerard Boate (part of the Hartlib circle) describes how the Irish make both turf and bricks.

25. Edmund Campion, *Historie of Ireland*, in *The Historie of Ireland, Collected by Three Learned Authors* (Dublin, 1633), 11.

26. Ibid., 22.

27. Ibid., 23.

28. Meredith Hanmer, *The Chronicle of Ireland*, in *The Historie of Ireland*, 2.

29. Geoffrey Keating, *The History of Ireland*, ed. and trans. David Comyn and Patrick S. Dineen, 4 vols. (London: Irish Texts Society, 1908), 2:3. Fenius Farsa's association with Babel dates back at least to the twelfth-century *Book of the Taking of Ireland* (*Lebor Gabála Érenn*).

30. See Richard F. Hardin, "Milton's Nimrod," *Milton Quarterly* 22.2 (1988): 38–44; Stevie Davies, *Images of Kingship in Paradise Lost: Milton's Politics and Christian Liberty* (Columbia: University of Missouri Press, 1983), 10.

31. Elizabeth Sauer, *Barbarous Dissonance and Images of Voice in Milton's Epics* (Montreal: McGill-Queen's University Press, 1996), 14–34.

32. William Covell, *Polimanteia* (Cambridge, 1595), sig. C5–C6.

33. Walter Raleigh, *The Historie of the World in Five Books* (London, 1628), 158.

34. Ibid.

35. Ibid, 159.

36. Annabel Patterson, *Reading between the Lines* (Madison: University of Wisconsin Press, 1993), 256. Her reading relies partly on J. G. A. Pocock's analysis of Nimrod's significance in early modern political theory. Republican theorists such as James Harrington seek to challenge or qualify the sense conveyed by absolutist versions of the Nimrod story that *jus conquestus* forms a kernel of *jus gentium*. See John Greville Agard Pocock, *The Ancient Constitution and the Feudal Law: A Study of English Historical Thought in the Seventeenth Century*, rpt. ed. (Cambridge: Cambridge University Press, 1987), 283–34.

37. For a discussion of the appeal to natural law along these lines, see Armand Himy, *"Paradise Lost* as a 'Tractatus Theologico-Politicus,'" in *Milton and Republicanism*, ed. David Armitage et al. (Cambridge: Cambridge University Press, 1995), 118–34.

38. Tho[mas] Shipman, *Carolina, or, Loyal Poems* (London, 1683), 57.

39. Milton, *Paradise Lost. A Poem in Twelve Books*, ed. Thomas Newton, 4th ed., 2 vols. (London: 1757), 2:397n.

40. David Loewenstein, *Representing Revolution in Milton and His Contemporaries* (Cambridge: Cambridge University Press, 2001), 43.

41. Henry Fletcher (?), *The Perfect Politician: Or, a Full View of the Life and Actions (Military and Civil) of O. Cromwell* (London, 1660), 252–53.

42. Elizabeth Sauer, "Milton's *Of True Religion*, Protestant Nationhood, and the Negotiation of Liberty," *Milton Quarterly* 40.1 (2006): 9–10.

43. William Cobbett, *The Parliamentary History of England*, 36 vols. (London, 1808), 4:517.

44. Ibid, 4:523.

45. An Act for Encouraging Protestant-Strangers and Others (Dublin, 1662), 4.

46. Jews, in fact, began settling in Ireland in the mid-seventeenth century without the kind of official readmission policies proposed in England. For a brief discussion outlining historical questions about this topic, see Gordon M. Weiner, "Irish Jewry in the Seventeenth and Eighteenth Centuries," in *From Strangers to Citizens: The Integration of Immigrant Communities in Britain, Ireland, and Colonial America, 1550–1750*, ed. Randolph Vigne and Charles Littleton (Sussex: Sussex Academic Press, 2002), 276–82.

47. *OED*, definition 2. The Scottish brother/Irish denizen distinction has been discussed by Fenton, "Milton's View," 206–7.

48. For some representative works in this debate, see Karl Bottigheimer, "Kingdom and Colony: Ireland in the Westward Enterprise, 1536–1660," in *The Westward Enterprise: English Activities in Ireland, the Atlantic, and America, 1480–1650*, ed. Kenneth R. Andrews et al. (Detroit: Wayne State University Press, 1979), 45–64; Steven G. Ellis, *Tudor Ireland: Crown, Community and the Conflict of Cultures, 1470–1603* (London: Longman, 1985); Nicholas Canny, "Identity Formation in Ireland: The Emergence of the Anglo-Irish," in *Colonial Identity in the Atlantic World, 1500–1800*, ed. Nicholas P. Canny and Anthony Pagden (Princeton: Princeton University Press, 1987), 159–212.

49. Spenser, *View*, 105.

50. Spenser's writings labor against the challenges that the Irish populations pose for England's sense of the law. In *A Power to Do Justice: Jurisdiction, English Literature, and the Rise of Common Law, 1509–1625* (Chicago: University of Chicago Press, 2007), 133–76, Bradin Cormack discusses how Irish cultural practices resisted the spread of English common law, which was based on a system of precedent but had to deny the legitimacy of Irish customs. Faced with contested and unstable sovereignty, New English colonization needed to resort ultimately to reconquest. Book 6 of *The Faerie Queene* articulates Spenser's justification of this agenda in part by refuting as a false pastoral vision a golden age, communal landscape without private ownership. Instead, Spenser upholds the legitimacy of inheritance and dominion. Milton's representation of the postdiluvian world in book 12 of *Paradise Lost* responds indirectly to such literary ideologies. The almost complete communalism of Eden cannot reemerge in a fallen world, and familial possession does exist even in the relatively blissful conditions immediately after the Flood. Yet if full-fledged political authority must be, it comes to be established by Nimrod, whom Spenser himself places in Ate's hall.

51. William Molyneux, *The Case of Ireland's Being Bound by Acts of Parliament in England* (Dublin, 1698), 148.

52. As Martin Dzelzainis has pointed out in "Milton's Classical Republicanism," in *Milton and Republicanism*, ed. David Armitage et al. (Cambridge: Cambridge University Press, 1995), 16–17,

Milton uses the metaphor of the body politic as he applies the Aristotelian precept of *autonomia* to his developing republicanism.

53. Hill, *Milton and the English Revolution*, 375. See also 117–45 for an argument that Milton's views on marriage and sexuality align him with seventeenth-century radicalism.

54. Richard Halpern, "Puritanism and Maenadism in *A Mask*," in *Rewriting the Renaissance: The Discourses of Sexual Difference in Early Modern Europe*, ed. Margaret W. Ferguson, Maureen Quilligan, and Nancy J. Vickers (Chicago: University of Chicago Press, 1986), 98 and 105. See also Cedric C. Brown, "Presidential Travels and Instructive Augury in Milton's Ludlow Masque," *Milton Quarterly* 21.4 (1987): 1–12; and Michael Wilding, "Milton's *A Masque Presented at Ludlow Castle, 1634*: Theatre and Politics on the Border," *Milton Quarterly* 21.4 (1987): 35–51.

55. Philip Schwyzer, "Purity and Danger on the West Bank of the Severn: The Cultural Geography of *A Masque Presented at Ludlow Castle, 1634*," *Representations* 60 (1997): 35.

56. Stephen Greenblatt, in *Renaissance Self-Fashioning: From More to Shakespeare* (Chicago: University of Chicago Press, 1983), 179, links Guyon's violent destruction of the bower to "the European response to the native cultures of the New World, the English colonial struggle in Ireland, and the Reformation attack on images." Jeffrey Knapp, in *An Empire Nowhere: England, America, and Literature From* Utopia *To* The Tempest (Berkeley: University of California Press, 1992), 16, disagrees, arguing that Spenser's epic "derives . . . from the 'savadge soyle' only of Ireland, not the New World." Writing almost a century after Spenser, Milton incorporates overlapping images of the New World, of Ireland, and of idolatrous barbarity in his narrative of the Fall.

57. Bede, *Bede's Ecclesiastical History of the English People*, ed. and trans. Bertram Colgrave and R. A. B. Mynors (Oxford: Oxford University Press, 1969), 21.

58. See Giraldus Cambrensis, *Topographia Hibernica et Expugnatio Hibernica*, in *Giraldus Cambrensis Opera*, ed. James F. Dimock, vol. 5, *Rerum Britannicarum Medii Aevi Scriptores, or Chronicles and Memorials of Great Britain and Ireland during the Middle Ages* (London: Longmans, Green, Reader, and Dyer, 1867), 62.

59. See Richard McCabe, *Spenser's Monstrous Regiment: Elizabethan Ireland and the Poetics of Difference* (Oxford: Oxford University Press, 2002), 57–61.

60. B.B. [Robert Rochford], *The Life of the Glorious Bishop S. Patricke . . . with the Lives of the Holy Virgin S. Bridgit and of the Glorious Abbot Saint Columbe* (St. Omer, 1625), xi.

61. G.S., *A Briefe Declaration of the Barbarous and inhumane dealings of the Northern Irish Rebels* (London, 1641), 1.

62. Boate, *Irelands Naturall History,* sig. A4.

63. Spenser, *View*, 71.

64. Barnabe Rich, *A New Description of Ireland: Wherein is described the disposition of the Irish* (London, 1610), 31.

65. *The Barbarous & Inhumane Proceedings Against the Professors of the Reformed Religion* (London, 1655), 6–7.

66. William Petty, *The Political Anatomy of Ireland* (1672; London, 1691), 30.

67. For a discussion on this subject, see Wendy Beth Hyman, "Seizing Flowers in Spenser's Bower and Garden," *English Literary Renaissance* 37 (May 2007): 193–214.

68. Sigmund Freud, "The Uncanny," in *The Standard Edition of the Complete Psychological Works of Sigmund Freud*, vol. 17, trans. Alix Strachey, ed. James Strachey (London: Hogarth, 1955), 235.

69. Ibid., 243.

70. Bhabha, *Location of Culture,* 9.

71. Ibid., 145.

72. Paul Stevens, "Milton and the New World: Custom, Relativism, and the Discipline of Shame," in Rajan and Sauer, *Milton and the Imperial Vision*, 93.

73. As Patricia Palmer puts it, "for a remarkable number of Ralegh's closest associates in the New World, Ireland had been 'their earlier America' "; see Palmer, *Language and Conquest,* 149. One of the many damning connections between the New World and Ireland was cannibalism. Robert Viking O'Brien has argued, in "Cannibalism in Edmund Spenser's *Faerie Queene,* Ireland, and the Americas," in *Eating Their Words: Cannibalism and the Boundaries of Cultural Identity,* ed. Kristen Guest (Albany: State University of New York Press, 2001), 35–56, that *The Faerie Queene* is influenced by accounts of cannibalism in Ireland and in the New World, particularly among the Caribs. See also Nicholas Canny, *Kingdom and Colony: Ireland in the Atlantic World, 1560–1800* (Baltimore: Johns Hopkins University Press, 1988), 1–29.

74. Elizabeth Sauer, "Toleration and Nationhood in the 1650s," in *Milton and Toleration,* ed. Sharon Achinstein and Elizabeth Sauer (Oxford: Oxford University Press, 2007), 216–17.

75. [Peter Walsh], *The Irish Colours Folded, or The Irish Roman Catholicks Reply* (London, 1662), 9.

76. Bede's *Ecclesiastical History* suggests that England had been colonized by the more civilized Irish; such ideas have continued to prove powerful in the popular imagination, as demonstrated by Thomas Cahill, *How the Irish Saved Civilization* (New York: Nan A. Talese, 1995). Unsurprisingly, Cahill cites Bede to suggest that Ireland was a haven for learning and civility (158).

77. B.B., *Life of S. Patricke,* vi.

78. McCabe, "Translated States," 87.

79. Clair Wills, "Language Politics, Narrative, Political Violence," *Oxford Literary Review* 13 (1991): 21.

80. See chap. 3 of John Calvin, *Commentaries on the First Book of Moses Called Genesis,* trans. John King, 2 vols. (Edinburgh: Calvin Translation Society, 1847–1850), hereafter cited as Calvin's commentary.

81. In order to make this latter case, Calvin argues against allegorical interpretations of the serpent's punishment as really being an account of Satan's. Instead, Calvin reads this passage anagogically, drawing a link between the literal serpent and the devil that possessed the beast. Book 10 of *Paradise Lost* graphically splits the difference between allegorical and anagogical interpretations by transforming Satan and his minions into beasts and describing how this transformation would occur on a cyclical basis. The episode serves in part as a fable of biblical interpretation.

82. Joan S. Bennett, "God, Satan, and King Charles: Milton's Royal Portraits," *PMLA* 92 (1977): 441–57. Catherine Canino, in "The Discourse of Hell: Paradise Lost and the Irish Rebellion," *Milton Quarterly* 32.1 (1998): 15–23, has read Satan and the devils as echoing Jesuit casuists in their defense of the 1641 uprising.

83. See Calvin's commentary on Genesis 3.

84. J.L., *An Alarum to Warre. . .* (London, 1642).

85. An Act for the better Execution of his Majesties Gracious Declaration (Dublin, 1662), 26.

86. Ibid., 1.

87. Petty, *Political Anatomy of Ireland,* 7.

88. Edmund Borlase, *Brief Reflections on the Earl of Castlehaven's Memoirs* (London, 1682), 15. This pamphlet exchange between Borlase and Castlehaven took part in a larger series of debates ultimately between Arthur Annesley, first Earl of Anglesey, and the Duke of Ormond. Anglesey encouraged Borlase to publish his *Brief Reflections,* and had himself attacked Castlehaven in print, taking this occasion to criticize Ormond's management of Irish affairs.

89. J. Martin Evans, *Milton's Imperial Epic: Paradise Lost and the Discourse of Colonialism* (Ithaca: Cornell University Press, 1996), 53.

90. F[rancis] S[ynge], *A Panegyrick On the Most Auspicious and long-wish'd-for Return of the Great Example of the Greatest Virtue* (Dublin, 1661), 4.

91. These passages rely on the addressee's understanding of shifting identities: despite his education in England, ardent Protestantism, and campaigns against the Irish Confederates, Ormond would remain susceptible to accusations of being an Irish "rebel" because he was born to a Catholic Old English family. Milton certainly understood this about Ormond. Thomas Corns reminds us that "throughout *Observations*, the word 'rebel' [is] reserved for the Irish Catholics," but that Milton expands his usage of the word when he attacks the Protestant Duke of Ormond, the Royalist Lord Lieutenant. See Thomas N. Corns, "Milton's *Observations upon the Articles of Peace:* Ireland under English Eyes," in *Politics, Poetics, and Hermeneutics in Milton's Prose*, ed. David Loewenstein and James Grantham Turner (Cambridge: Cambridge University Press, 1990), 123–34.

92. Roderic O'Flaherty, *Ogygia, or, A Chronological Account of Irish Events*, trans. James Hely (Dublin, 1793), xiii.

93. Ibid., xiii–iv. On this, see Andrew Hadfield and Willy Maley, "Introduction: Irish Representations and English Alternatives," in Bradshaw, Hadfield, and Maley, *Representing Ireland*, 5.

94. The original reads, "Iam iam nulla mora est; sequor et qua ducitis adsum." See Virgil, *Aeneid*, in *Virgil*, ed. and trans. H. Rushton Fairclough, rev. G.R. Gould, 2 vols. (Cambridge: Harvard University Press, 1999–2000), 2.701.

95. For an eloquent meditation on this topic, see Julia Kristeva, "Stabat Mater," in *Tales of Love*, trans. Leon S. Roudiez (New York: Columbia University Press, 1987), 234–63.

4. *Gemelle Liber:* Milton's 1671 Archive

1. I use "Delilah" to refer to the biblical personage and "Dalila" to refer to Milton's literary character, thereby preserving his idiosyncratic spelling.

2. Against Samuel Johnson's well-known critique of *Samson* as a tragedy lacking "a middle, since nothing passes between the first act and the last, that either hastens or delays the death of Sampson," recent readers have tended to see the exchange with Dalila as a decisive turning point. See Samuel Johnson, *The Rambler*, vols. 3–4 of *The Yale Edition of the Works of Samuel Johnson*, ed. W.J. Bate and Albrecht B. Strauss (New Haven: Yale University Press, 1969), 4:376.

3. It is thus no accident that some readings of the dramatic poem turn misogynistic in their accounts of Dalila. In *Toward* Samson Agonistes: *The Growth of Milton's Mind* (Princeton: Princeton University Press, 1978), 38–39, Mary Ann Radzinowicz aligns Samson with the mind and Dalila with the body and contrasts Samson's "inner logic and consistency" with Dalila's "psychopathic personality." We should remember that it is Samson who warns his wife not to touch him, "lest fierce remembrance wake / My sudden rage to tear thee joint by joint" (lines 952–53). The terrible desire to dismember one's wife is a common early modern motif (most familiar from Shakespearean drama), and it is generally a sign of a mind vitiated by passion.

4. In "Things and Actions Indifferent: The Temptation of Plot in *Paradise Regained*," *Milton Studies* 17 (1983): 163–86," Stanley Fish has argued that little happens in the way of plot in *Paradise Regained* because heroic epic action is a temptation that Jesus must resist.

5. For an extended overview of the orthodox and revisionist readings, see Derek N.C. Wood, *"Exiled from Light": Divine Law, Morality, and Violence in* Samson Agonistes (Toronto: University of Toronto Press, 2002), 1–26.

6. On J.M. as John Macocke, see John Milton, *The Complete Poetical Works Reproduced in Photographic Facsimile*, ed. Harris Francis Fletcher, 4 vols. (Urbana: University of Illinois Press, 1944–1948), 4:12, editor's note.

7. Tobias Gregory, "The Political Messages of *Samson Agonistes*," *SEL* 50 (2010): 191.

8. See, for example, John T. Shawcross, "The Genres of *Paradise Regain'd* and *Samson Agonistes*: The Wisdom of Their Joint Publication," *Milton Studies* 17 (1983): 225–48; Ashraf H.A. Rushdy, *The Empty Garden: The Subject of Late Milton* (Pittsburgh: University of Pittsburgh Press, 1992), 277–344; Anne K. Krook, "The Hermeneutics of Opposition in *Paradise Regained*

and *Samson Agonistes*," *SEL* 36 (1996): 129–47; and Stephen B. Dobranski, "Text and Context for *Paradise Regain'd* and *Samson Agonistes*," in *Altering Eyes: New Perspectives on* Samson Agonistes, ed. Mark R. Kelley and Joseph Anthony Wittreich (Newark: University of Delaware Press, 2002), 30–53.

9. Balachandra Rajan, "'To Which Is Added *Samson Agonistes*—,'" in *The Prison and the Pinnacle*, ed. Balachandra Rajan (Toronto: University of Toronto Press, 1973), 98.

10. Stephen B. Dobranski, *Milton, Authorship, and the Book Trade* (Cambridge: Cambridge University Press, 1999), 2. See 41–62 for Dobranski's illuminating discussion of the sequence of error and correction preserved in the *Omissa* of the 1671 edition of *Samson*.

11. For Milton's wily self-representation in this poem, see ibid., 102–3. My thoughts about this poem have also been influenced by two unpublished works. The first is a talk by Richard DuRocher, titled "Hermes's Blessed Retreats: Rival Views of Learning in *Paradise Regained*," delivered at the 2009 Conference on John Milton, Murfreesboro, TN; the second is an essay by Thomas Ward, "The Song That Failed," presented to the University of Pennsylvania Medieval-Renaissance Seminar, March 3, 2010.

12. Annabel Patterson, *Milton's Words* (Oxford: Oxford University Press, 2009), 117.

13. *CPW* 6:587–88, quoted ibid., 120.

14. Jacques Derrida, *Archive Fever: A Freudian Impression*, trans. Eric Prenowitz (Chicago: University of Chicago Press, 1996), 3.

15. The composition of *Paradise Regained* may attest to the transformation of a domestic space into the site of public significance. Thomas Ellwood's famous claim that his question "But what hast thou to say of *Paradise Found?*" motivated Milton to write his second epic strikes readers as apocryphal. This account, however, is prefaced by the much more credible claim that Ellwood secured "a pretty Box for [Milton] in *Giles-Chalfont*." For Ellwood, inspiring new poetry goes hand in hand with brokering a new dwelling for the poet. See Thomas Ellwood, *The History of the Life of Thomas Ellwood*, 2nd ed. (London, 1714), 246.

16. See, for example, Matt. 11:11. When Herod hears of Jesus's ministry, he utters, "It is John, whom I beheaded: he is risen from the dead" (Mark 6:16). Herod is not alone; Jesus's first followers distinguish themselves from those who do not understand Jesus's identity and think him to be John the Baptist or Elijah (Matt. 16:13–17). In the Acts of the Apostles, Paul must convert followers of John the Baptist (Acts 18:24–19:7).

17. On the notion of divine narcissism as it relates to Milton's poetry, see Maggie Kilgour, "'Thy perfect image viewing': Poetic Creation and Ovid's Narcissus in *Paradise Lost*," *Studies in Philology* 102 (2005): 307–39.

18. Derrida's theory of the archive follows Yosef Yerushalmi's study of Freud in *Judaism Terminable and Interminable*, in which Yerushalmi attempts to claim psychoanalysis and the Freudian archive for Judaism. Such an attempt must remain open-ended, but the key piece of historical evidence for Yerushalmi is a Bible, re-bound by Freud's father and presented to him as a gift, inscribed with a record of Sigmund's birth and circumcision. The new skin of this Bible points to the inscription of cultural memory on Freud's body; the book suggests how Freud's archive acts in deferred obedience to his father's legacy. But if Freud—who often seemed to deny his Jewish heritage in the name of secularism—plays the role of Oedipus, his daughter Anna is analogous to Antigone. Anna Freud had spoken on behalf of her father's legacy by writing publicly that the notion of psychoanalysis as a Jewish science could serve as a title of honor. Yet Yerushalmi's "monologue with Freud" ends by asking if Anna had actually spoken in her father's name. Sigmund Freud almost inevitably acts in deferred obedience to his father, but whether Anna Freud can legitimately speak in her father's name remains in doubt. See Derrida, *Archive Fever*, 43–44.

19. William Kerrigan, *The Sacred Complex: On the Psychogenesis of* Paradise Lost (Cambridge: Harvard University Press, 1983), 10. For an attempt (daring and imaginative in the face of limited

evidence) to recuperate the importance of Milton's mother in the poet's archive, see John P. Rumrich, *Milton Unbound: Controversy and Reinterpretation* (New York: Cambridge University Press, 1996), 70–93.

20. See also Louis Schwartz, *Milton and Maternal Mortality* (Cambridge: Cambridge University Press, 2009), 166–69.

21. Jesus is thus akin to Jeremiah, to whom God declares, "Before I formed thee in the belly I knew thee; and before thou camest forth out of the womb I sanctified thee, and I ordained thee a prophet unto the nations" (Jer. 1:5). In book 3 of *Paradise Regained*, Satan tells Jesus that King David is "by mother's side thy father" (3.154). In a certain sense, Satan does Jesus a favor by being imprecise: the gospels of Luke and of Matthew trace Jesus's Davidic lineage through Joseph, but Joseph is not Jesus's father.

22. Quoted from *The Bible: That Is, the Holy Scriptures . . . With most profitable Annotations* (London, 1595).

23. Hugo Grotius, *Hugo Grotius's Defence of Christian Religion*, trans. C.B. (London,1678), 45 (sig. D2r).

24. Ibid., 32–34 (sig. C4).

25. Hugo Grotius, *Of the Law of Warre and Peace* (London, 1655), "The Preface of the Author."

26. Hugo Grotius, *Christs Passion. A Tragedie. With Annotations*, trans. George Sandys (London, 1640), 57.

27. Sandys's annotations to act 3 suggest that the Jewish women who lament Jesus's death believe in Pythagorean teachings about the transmigration of souls; Sandys emphasizes that Grotius associates Jewish beliefs with outmoded pagan ones. See ibid., 102–3 n. 238.

28. A long-standing body of criticism deals with Milton's engagement with Judaism. For some relevant examples, see F. Michael Krause, *Milton's Samson and the Christian Tradition* (Princeton: Princeton University Press, 1949); H. R. MacCallum, "Milton and Figurative Interpretation of the Bible," *University of Toronto Quarterly* 31 (1962): 397–415; Barbara Lewalski, *Milton's Brief Epic: The Genre, Meaning, and Art of* Paradise Regained (Providence: Brown University Press, 1966); Regina Schwartz, "From Shadowy Types to Shadowy Types: The Unendings of Paradise Lost," *Milton Studies* 24 (1988): 123–39; Achsah Guibbory, *Christian Identity, Jews, and Israel in Seventeenth-Century England* (Oxford: Oxford University Press, 2010), 252–94.

29. Jeffrey Shoulson, *Milton and the Rabbis: Hebraism, Hellenism, and Christianity* (New York: Columbia University Press, 2001), 76.

30. Jason Rosenblatt, in *Torah and Law in* Paradise Lost (Princeton: Princeton University Press, 1994), 12–70, argues that Milton's depiction of Eden is nontypological, and that it presents the Law not merely as an impossible obligation that drives humanity to await its supersession, but as a covenant that makes ample room for obedience, human growth, and love.

31. See John C. Ulreich, "Typological Symbolism in Milton's Sonnet XXIII," *Milton Quarterly* 8.1 (1974): 7–10.

32. See, for example, Stanley Fish, "Inaction and Silence: The Reader in *Paradise Regained*," in *Calm of Mind: Tercentenary Essays on* Paradise Regained *and* Samson Agonistes *in Honor of John S. Diekhoff*, ed. J. A. Wittreich Jr. (Cleveland: Case Western Reserve University Press, 1971), 43–44.

33. Ovid, *Metamorphoses*, trans. Frank Justus Miller, rev. G. P. Goold, 2 vols., Loeb Classical Library (Cambridge: Harvard University Press, 1984), 9.264–65. On this topic, see Kathleen M. Swaim, "Hercules, Antaeus, and Prometheus: A Study of the Climactic Epic Similes in *Paradise Regained*," *SEL* 18 (1978): 145.

34. On the difficulty of this idea within Milton's theology, see John C. Ulreich, "Substantially Express'd: Milton's Doctrine of the Incarnation," *Milton Studies* 39 (2001): 101–28; and John

Rumrich, "Milton's *Theanthropos*: The Body of Christ in *Paradise Regained*," *Milton Studies* 42 (2003): 50–67.

35. See Lewalski, *Brief Epic*, 133–63. Lewalski influentially suggests the relevance of a Socinian view of Jesus's human identity. To what extent Milton's Jesus is human or divine is part of the long-standing question of Milton's Trinitarianism or heterodoxy. Among more recent arguments, I find compelling Rumrich's alignment of Milton's views with Arianism; see John P. Rumrich, "Milton's Arianism: Why It Matters," in *Milton and Heresy*, ed. Stephen B. Dobranski and John P. Rumrich (Cambridge: Cambridge University Press, 1998), 75–92. John Rogers, in "*Paradise Regained* and the Memory of *Paradise Lost*," in *The Oxford Handbook of Milton*, ed. Nicholas McDowell and Nigel Smith (Oxford: Oxford University Press, 2009), 589–612, has provided a lucid and comprehensive account of Milton's Christology in *Paradise Regained* and of the critical debates surrounding the topic.

36. See Lewalski, *Brief Epic*, 195–204.

37. Ibid., 192.

38. For an extended discussion of *Comus*'s sexual temptation, see Kerrigan, *Sacred Complex*, 22–72. Rumrich, "Milton's Arianism," 70–93, responds by attempting to restore the mother—and specifically Milton's mother, Sara—as much more than the negated object of desire that the oedipal model suggests.

39. The original 1671 publication of *Paradise Regained* contains a fortuitous error. Satan urges Jesus to eat by reminding him that "that Prophet / Native of *Thebes* wandring here was fed" (2.312–13). The errata sheet instructs us to replace Thebes with Thebez, but the slip connects Elijah with Tiresias (and perhaps Oedipus) and eating with dangerous erotic knowledge.

40. For an extended analysis of this moment, see Kerrigan, *Sacred Complex*, 82–89, and "The Riddle of *Paradise Regained*," in *Poetic Prophecy in Western Literature*, ed. Jan Wojcik and Raymond-Jean Fontain (Rutherford: Fairleigh Dickinson University Press, 1984), 64–80.

41. James Nohrnberg, "*Paradise Regained* by One Greater Man: Milton's Wisdom Epic as a 'Fable of Identity,'" in *Centre and Labyrinth: Essays in Honor of Northrop Frye*, ed. Eleanor Cook (Toronto: University of Toronto Press, 1985), 85.

42. Yosef Hayim Yerushalmi, *Zakhor: Jewish History and Jewish Memory* (Seattle: University of Washington Press, 1996), 9, quoted in Derrida, *Archive Fever*, 76.

43. Derrida, *Archive Fever*, 78–79.

44. Line 150. All quotations from *Samson Agonistes* are from John Milton, *Complete Shorter Poems*, ed. John Carey, 2nd rev. ed. (Harlow: Longman, 2007) and are cited parenthetically by book and line numbers with the abbreviation *SA*.

45. William Riley Parker, *Milton's Debt to Greek Tragedy in* Samson Agonistes (Baltimore: Johns Hopkins University Press, 1937), remains perhaps the most influential work about *Samson Agonistes* and Greek tragedy.

46. William Riley Parker, "The Date of *Samson Agonistes*," *Philological Quarterly* 28 (1949): 145–66. Parker uses this connection to argue that *Samson* was composed in the late 1640s.

47. See Joseph Wittreich, "Still Nearly Anonymous: *Christos Paschon*," *Milton Quarterly* 36.3 (2002): 193–98; Russell M. Hillier, "Grotius's *Christus Patiens* and Milton's *Samson Agonistes*," *Explicator* 65 (2006): 9–13.

48. Joseph Wittreich, *Interpreting* Samson Agonistes (Princeton: Princeton University Press, 1986), 28–35.

49. Achsah Guibbory has shown how typological thinking about the Judaic past and the Christian present inform seventeenth-century controversy over the idolatrous nature of human art. Milton was a committed iconoclast, but his later writings reveal "the costs of iconoclasm" and admit idolatry as "an ineradicable part of human experience." See Achsah Guibbory, *Ceremony and Community from Herbert to Milton: Literature, Religion, and Cultural Conflict in Seventeenth-Century England* (Cambridge: Cambridge University Press, 1998), 28–34 and 147–227.

50. Julia Reinhard Lupton, *Citizen-Saints: Shakespeare and Political Theology* (Chicago: University of Chicago Press, 2005), 202. Lupton responds here in part to Derek N. C. Wood's revisionist reading of Milton's Samson as merely a shadowy type of Christ who remains subject to the Law and cannot be fully regenerated; see Wood, *"Exiled from Light."*

51. The question of why and to what end humans should act at all in a world governed by an omnipotent God pervades virtually all of Milton's writings. For a provocative argument that the classical (humanist) impulses in Milton's thought prevail over the Christian demand for humility before divine omnipotence, see Richard Strier, "Milton against Humility," in *Religion and Culture in Renaissance England*, ed. Claire McEachern and Debora Shuger (Cambridge: Cambridge University Press, 2006), 258–86.

52. Joseph Wittreich, in *Shifting Contexts: Reinterpreting* Samson Agonistes (Pittsburgh: Duquesne University Press, 2002), 263, argues that the pagan symbol of the phoenix works against a typological interpretation, dividing "the slayer of men and their savior into two very different traditions of heroism." For a counterargument, see Sanford Budick, "Milton's Joban Phoenix in *Samson Agonistes*," *Early Modern Literary Studies* 11.2 (September 2005): 5.1–15.

53. Northrop Frye, *Spiritus Mundi: Essays on Literature, Myth, and Society* (Bloomington: Indiana University Press, 1976), 222.

54. On the connection between *Samson Agonistes* and *King Lear*, see Wittreich, *Interpreting* Samson Agonistes, 55–56 and 242–44; see also Joseph Wittreich, *"Image of that Horror": History, Prophecy, and Apocalypse in* King Lear (San Marino, CA: Huntington Library, 1984), 14–46.

55. On the connection between Samson's mother and Delilah, see Mieke Bal, *Death and Symmetry: The Politics of Coherence in the Book of Judges* (Chicago: University of Chicago Press, 1988), 217–29.

56. See Stephen B. Dobranski, *A Variorum Commentary on the Poems of John Milton*, vol. 3, *Samson Agonistes* (Pittsburgh: Duquesne University Press, 2009), 196–97 n. 389 and 390.

57. See Ovid, *Metamorphoses*, 3.528–71.

58. Ibid., 4.604–62.

59. This act of idolatry, committed while Moses covenants with God, bears upon Jesus's story. Whereas all Israelites were to be God's priests, this act of idolatry leads to the exclusive priesthood of the Levites. As a result, non-Levite Israelites must redeem their firstborn through the *pidyon ha'ben*. That Jesus is not a Levite means that he is tribally unfit to assume one of his three roles of prophet, priest, and king. The epistle to the Hebrews circumvents this problem by appealing to the more ancient priesthood of Melchizedek rather than to Aaronic priesthood.

60. Victoria Kahn, "Disappointed Nationalism: Milton in the Context of Seventeenth-Century Debates about the Nation-State," in *Early Modern Nationalism and Milton's England*, ed. David Loewenstein and Paul Stevens (Toronto: University of Toronto Press, 2008), 249–72. See also Catherine Gimelli Martin, "Dalila, Misogyny, and Milton's Christian Liberty of Divorce," in *Milton and Gender*, ed. Catherine Gimelli Martin (Cambridge: Cambridge University Press, 2004), 53–74.

61. Kahn, "Disappointed Nationalism," 263.

62. Derrida, *Archive Fever,* 79.

63. James Nohrnberg, *Like unto Moses: The Constituting of an Interruption* (Bloomington: Indiana University Press, 1995), 154.

64. Rachel Trubowitz, "'I was his nursling once': Nation, Lactation, and the Hebraic in *Samson Agonistes*," in Martin, *Milton and Gender*, 174.

65. Ibid., 176.

66. On these passages and their relationship to the Samson narrative in Judges, see Claudia V. Camp, *Wise, Strange and Holy: The Strange Woman and the Making of the Bible* (Sheffield: Sheffield Academic Press, 2000), 130–38.

67. Bal, *Death and Symmetry,* 144.

68. The corpse of a lion is unclean, and as a Nazirite, Samson has a special responsibility to avoid dead bodies. Honey itself is kosher, but explaining why a product of insects should be acceptable food has required careful explanation. See, for example, Moses Maimonides, *The Code of Maimonides*, bk. 5, trans. Louis I. Rabinowitz and Philip Grossman, Yale Judaica Series (New Haven, Yale University Press, 1965), 164.

69. Francis Quarles, *The History of Samson* (London, 1631), sect. 4.

70. Ibid., meditat. 9.

71. John Bunyan, *Grace Abounding to the Chief of Sinners*, ed. Roger Sharrock (Oxford: Clarendon, 1962), 1. The significance of this passage in particular and of Bunyan's identification with Samson more generally has been discussed by Sharon Achinstein in *Literature and Dissent in Milton's England* (Cambridge: Cambridge University Press, 2003), 84–114.

72. For a much fuller account of Milton and present-day political thought, see Feisal G. Mohamed, *Milton and the Post-secular Present: Ethics, Politics, and Terrorism* (Stanford: Stanford University Press, 2011).

73. Alain Badiou, *Saint Paul: The Foundation of Universalism*, trans. Ray Brassier (Stanford: Stanford University Press, 2003), 32–33.

74. Ibid., 55–56.

75. Giorgio Agamben, *The Time That Remains: A Commentary on the Letter to the Romans*, trans. Patricia Dailey (Stanford: Stanford University Press, 2005), 51.

76. Ibid., 52.

77. Ibid., 99–108.

78. Ibid., 39.

79. Ibid., 40.

80. See, for example, Christopher Hill, *The Experience of Defeat: Milton and Some Contemporaries* (London: Faber and Faber, 1984), 306.

81. Dobranski, in *Milton, Authorship, and the Book Trade*, 179, notes that Aylmer, appropriately enough, may have served as one of Milton's pallbearers.

82. Walter Benjamin, "Unpacking My Library: A Talk about Book Collecting," in *Illuminations*, ed. Hannah Arendt, trans. Harry Zohn (New York: Schocken, 1968), 61 and 66.

83. Walter Benjamin, "The Storyteller," ibid., 97.

84. Walter Benjamin, "Theses on the Philosophy of History," ibid., 263.

85. Ibid., 264.

86. Hannah Arendt, "Introduction," ibid., 50–51.

Epilogue

1. Stanley Fish, "Why Milton Matters; Or, Against Historicism," *Milton Studies* 44 (2005): 1.

2. Olaudah Equiano, *The Interesting Narrative of the Life of Olaudah Equiano*, 2nd ed., 2 vols. (London: 1789), 1:189–90.

3. Ibid., 1:213–14.

4. Ibid., 1:227.

5. Srinivas Aravamudan, *Tropicopolitans: Colonialism and Agency, 1688–1804* (Durham: Duke University Press, 1999), 235.

6. Equiano's *felix culpa* narrative is self-consciously literary. He fuses classical golden age rhetoric with imagery from the Hebrew Bible to describe his African homeland, where "as we are unacquainted with idleness, we have no beggars." Equiano cites and supports contemporary theories that connect Africans and ancient Jews. He thus compares "the customs of my countrymen and those of the Jews, before they reached that Land of Promise, and particularly the patriarchs while they were yet in that pastoral state which is described in Genesis." Equiano, *Interesting Narrative*, 1:21–44.

7. Kim F. Hall, *Things of Darkness: Economies of Race and Gender in Early Modern England* (Ithaca: Cornell University Press, 1995), 7.

8. Christopher Kendrick, *Milton: A Study in Ideology and Form* (New York: Methuen, 1986), 106–9.

9. Maureen Quilligan, "Freedom, Service and the Trade in Slaves: The Problem of Labor and *Paradise Lost*," in *Subject and Object in Renaissance Culture*, ed. Margreta de Grazia, Maureen Quilligan, and Peter Stallybrass (Cambridge: Cambridge University Press, 1996), 215.

10. Equiano, *Interesting Narrative,* 2:260–61.

11. Ibid., 2:263–65.

Bibliography

Primary Sources

An Act for the better Execution of his Majesties Gracious Declaration. Dublin, 1662.

An Act for Encouraging Protestant-Strangers and Others. Dublin, 1662.

Alberti, Leon Battista. *On Painting*. Translated by John R. Spencer. New Haven: Yale University Press, 1966.

Aristotle. *The Poetics*. In *Aristotle: In Twenty-three Volumes*. Translated by W. Hamilton Fyfe. Rev. ed. Vol. 23. Loeb Classical Library. Cambridge: Harvard University Press, 1932.

Ascham, Roger. *The Scholemaster*. In *English Works of Roger Ascham*. Edited by William Aldis Wright, 171–302. Cambridge: Cambridge University Press, 1904.

The Barbarous & Inhumane Proceedings Against the Professors of the Reformed Religion. London, 1655.

B.B. [Rochford, Robert]. *The Life of the Glorious Bishop St. Patricke . . . with the Lives of the Holy Virgin S. Bridgit and of the Glorious Abbot Saint Columbe*. St. Omers, 1625.

Bede. *Bede's Ecclesiastical History of the English People*. Edited and translated by Bertram Colgrave and R. A. B. Mynors. Oxford: Oxford University Press, 1969.

The Bible: That Is, the Holy Scriptures . . . With most profitable Annotations. London, 1595.

Boate, Gerard. *Irelands Naturall History*. London, 1657.

Borlase, Edmund. *Brief Reflections on the Earl of Castlehaven's Memoirs*. London, 1682.

Boyle, Roger, Earl of Orrery. *The Answer of a Person of Quality to a Scandalous Letter*. Dublin, 1662.

———. *A Treatise on the Art of War*. London, 1677.

Bunyan, John. *Grace Abounding to the Chief of Sinners*. Edited by Roger Sharrock. Oxford: Clarendon, 1962.

Calvin, John. *Commentaries on the First Book of Moses Called Genesis*. Translated by John King. 2 vols. Edinburgh: Calvin Translation Society, 1847–1850.

de Camões, Luís Vaz. *The Lusiad*. Translated by Richard Fanshawe. London, 1655.

Campion, Edmund. *Historie of Ireland*. In *The Historie of Ireland, Collected by Three Learned Authors*. Dublin, 1633.

Capel, Arthur. *Letters Written by His Excellency Arthur Capel, Earl of Essex, Lord Lieutenant of Ireland, in the Year 1675*. Dublin, 1770.

Carew, Thomas. *The Poems of Thomas Carew with His Masque* Coelum Britannicum. Edited by Rhodes Dunlap. Oxford: Clarendon, 1949.

Cobbett, William. *The Parliamentary History of England*. 36 vols. London, 1808.

Columbus, Christopher. *Select Documents Illustrating the Four Voyages of Columbus*. Translated and edited by Cecil Jane. 2 vols. London: Hakluyt Society, 1930.

A Continuation of the Former Newes. Three great Invasions already attempted. London, 1624.

Covell, William. *Polimanteia*. Cambridge, 1595.

A Declaration, or Letters Patent of this present King of Poland John the Third . . . Now faithfully translated from the Latin Copy. by John Milton. London, 1674.

Ellwood, Thomas. *The History of the Life of Thomas Ellwood*. 2nd ed. London, 1714.

Equiano, Olaudah. *The Interesting Narrative of the Life of Olaudah Equiano*. 2nd ed. 2 vols. London, 1789.

Filmer, Sir Robert. *Patriarcha and Other Writings*. Edited by J.P. Sommerville. Cambridge: Cambridge University Press, 1991.

Fletcher, Giles. "The Ambassage of M. Giles Fletcher." In Hakluyt, 3:353–412.

———. *Israel Redux:Orthe Restauration of Israel*. London, 1677.

Fletcher, Henry (?). *The Perfect Politician: Or, a Full View of the Life and Actions (Military and Civil) of O. Cromwell*. London, 1660.

Giraldus Cambrensis. *Topographia Hibernica et Expugnatio Hibernica*. In *Giraldus Cambrensis Opera*. Vol. 5. *Rerum Britannicarum Medii Aevi Scriptores, or Chronicles and Memorials of Great Britain and Ireland during the Middle Ages*. Edited by James F. Dimock. London: Longmans, Green, Reader, and Dyer, 1867.

Grotius, Hugo. *Christs Passion. A Tragedie. With Annotations*. Translated and annotated by George Sandys. London, 1640.

———. *Hugo Grotius's Defence of Christian Religion*. Translated by C.B. London, 1678.

———. *Of the Law of Warre and Peace*. London, 1655.

G.S. *A Brief Declaration of the Barbarous and inhumane dealings of the Northern Irish Rebels*. London, 1641.

Hakluyt, Richard. *The Principal Navigations Voyages Traffiques & Discoveries of the English Nation*. 12 vols. Glasgow: James MacLehose and Sons, 1903–1905.

Hamor, Ralph. *A True Discourse of the Present Estate of Virginia*. London, 1615.

Hanmer, Meredith. *The Chronicle of Ireland*. In *The Historie of Ireland, Collected by Three Learned Authors*. Dublin, 1633.

Herrick, Robert. *The Poetical Works of Robert Herrick*. Edited by L. C. Martin. Oxford: Clarendon, 1956.

Hughes, Lewis. *A Plaine and True Relation of the Goodness of God towards the Somer-Islands*. London, 1621.

J.L. *An Alarum to Warre . . . To Subjugate Savage cruelties, and inhumane Massacres Acted by the Nocent Papists*. London, 1642.

Jonson, Ben. *Ben Jonson: The Complete Poems*. Edited by George Parfitt. New Haven: Yale University Press, 1982.

Keating, Geoffrey. *The History of Ireland*. Edited and translated by David Comyn and Patrick S. Dineen. 4 vols. London: Irish Texts Society, 1902–1914.

Lanyer, Aemilia. *The Poems of Aemilia Lanyer: Salve Deus Rex Judaeorum*. Edited by Susanne Woods. New York: Oxford University Press, 1993.

Maimonides, Moses. *The Code of Maimonides*. Book 5. Translated by Louis I. Rabinowitz and Philip Grossman. Yale Judaica Series. New Haven: Yale University Press, 1965.

Mandeville, Sir John. *The Adventures of Sir John Mandeville*. Translated by C. W. R. D. Moseley. London: Penguin, 1983.

Marvell, Andrew. *The Poems and Letters of Andrew Marvell*. 2 vols. Edited by H. M. Margoliouth. Revised by Pierre Legouis and E. E. Duncan-Jones. 3rd ed. Oxford: Clarendon, 1971.

Milton, John. *The Complete Poetical Works Reproduced in Photographic Facsimile*. Edited by Harris Francis Fletcher. 4 vols. Urbana: University of Illinois Press, 1944–1948.

——. *The Complete Prose Works of John Milton*. Edited by Don M. Wolfe et al. 8 vols. New Haven: Yale University Press, 1953–1982.

——. *Complete Shorter Poems*. Edited by John Carey. 2nd rev. ed. Harlow: Longman, 2007.

——, trans. *A Declaration, or Letters Patent of this present King of Poland John the Third*. 2 vols. London, 1674.

——. *Paradise Lost*. Edited by Alastair Fowler. 2nd ed. Harlow: Longman, 1998.

——. *Paradise Lost. A Poem in Twelve Books. The Author John Milton*. Edited by Thomas Newton. 4th ed. 2 vols. London, 1757.

Molyneux, William. *The Case of Ireland's Being Bound by Acts of Parliament in England*. Dublin, 1698.

Morton, Thomas. *New English Canaan*. London, 1632.

O'Flaherty, Roderic. *Ogygia, or, A Chronological Account of Irish Events*. Translated by James Hely. Dublin, 1793.

Ovid. *Metamorphoses*. Translated by Frank Justus Miller. Revised by G. P. Goold. 2 vols. Loeb Classical Library. Cambridge: Harvard University Press, 1984.

Petty, William. *The Political Anatomy of Ireland*. London, 1691.

Polo, Marco. *The Travels of Marco Polo*. Translated and edited by Aldo Ricci. London: George Routledge and Sons, 1931.

Quarles, Francis. *The History of Samson*. London, 1631. Raleigh, Walter. *The discovery of the large, rich, and beautifull Empire of Guiana*. In Hakluyt, 10:338–431.

——. *The Historie of the World in Five Books*. London, 1628.

Rich, Barnabe. *The Irish Hubbub, or, The English Hue and Crie.* London, 1619.

———. *A New Description of Ireland: Wherein is described the disposition of the Irish.* London, 1610.

Semedo, Alvaro. *The History of that Great and Renowned Monarchy of China. . . . To which is added the History of the late Invasion, and Conquest of that flourishing Kingdom by the Tartars.* London, 1655.

Shipman, Tho[mas]. *Carolina, or, Loyal Poems.* London, 1683.

Sidney, Philip. *The Countesse of Pembrokes Arcadia.* 1590. In *The Prose Works of Sir Philip Sidney.* Edited by Albert Feuillerat. Vol. 1. Cambridge: Cambridge University Press, 1965.

Spenser, Edmund. *The Faerie Queene.* Edited by A.C. Hamilton et al. 2nd ed. Harlow: Longman, 2006.

———. *A View of the State of Ireland.* Edited by Andrew Hadfield and Willy Maley. Oxford: Blackwell, 1997.

S[ynge], F[rancis]. *A Panegyrick On the Most Auspicious and long-wish'd-for Return of the Great Example of the Greatest Virtue.* Dublin, 1661.

Tanner, Norman P., S.J., ed. *Decrees of the Ecumenical Councils.* 2 vols. London and Washington, DC: Sheed & Ward and Georgetown University Press, 1990.

Temple, John. *The Irish Rebellion.* London, 1646.

Virgil. *Aeneid.* In *Virgil.* Edited and translated by H. Rushton Fairclough. Revised by G.R. Gould. 2 vols. Loeb Classical Library. Cambridge: Harvard University Press, 1999–2000.

———. *Georgics.* In *Virgil,* vol. 1, *Eclogues, Georgics, Aeneid I–VI.* Edited and translated by H. Rushton Fairclough. Revised by G. R. Gould. Loeb Classical Library. Cambridge: Harvard University Press, 1999.

Waller, Edmund. *The Poems of Edmund Waller.* Edited by G. Thorn Drury. London: Routledge, 1900.

[Walsh, Peter]. *The Irish Colours Folded, or The Irish Roman-Catholick's Reply.* London, 1662.

Wendover, R. and Mat[thew] Paris. "Relations touching the Tartars, taken out of the Historie of R. Wendover and Matthew Paris." In *Hakluytus Posthumus or Purchas His Pilgrimes.* 20 vols. Edited by Samuel Purchas, 11:173–82. Glasgow: James MacLehose and Sons, 1905.

William of Rubruck. "The journal of frier William de Rubruiqus." In *Hakluyt,* 1:229–93.

Yves of Narbonne. "Part of an Epistle written by one Yvo of Narbona. . . . Recorded by Mathew Paris." In *Hakluyt,* 1:50–54.

Secondary Sources

Achinstein, Sharon. "Imperial Dialectic: Milton and Conquered Peoples." In Rajan and Sauer, 67–89.

———. *Literature and Dissent in Milton's England.* Cambridge: Cambridge University Press, 2003.

Adelman, Janet. *Suffocating Mothers: Fantasies of Maternal Origins in Shakespeare's Plays*, Hamlet *to* The Tempest. New York: Routledge, 1992.

Aers, David, and Bob Hodge. "'Rational Burning': Milton on Sex and Marriage." *Milton Studies* 13 (1979): 3–33.

Agamben, Giorgio. *The Time That Remains: A Commentary on the Letter to the Romans*. Translated by Patricia Dailey. Stanford: Stanford University Press, 2005.

Ainsworth, David. *Milton and the Spiritual Reader: Reading and Religion in Seventeenth-Century England*. New York: Routldge, 2008.

Anderson, Benedict. *Imagined Communities: Reflections on the Origin and Spread of Nationalism*. Rev. ed. London: Verso, 1991.

Aravamudan, Srinivas. *Tropicopolitans: Colonialism and Agency, 1688–1804*. Durham: Duke University Press, 1999.

Archer, John Michael. *Old Worlds: Egypt, Southwest Asia, India, and Russia in Early Modern English Writing*. Stanford: Stanford University Press, 2001.

Arendt, Hannah. Introduction. In Walter Benjamin. *Illuminations*. Edited by Hannah Arendt. Translated by Harry Zohn, 1–55. New York: Schocken, 1968.

Armitage, David. "John Milton: Poet against Empire." In Armitage et al., 206–25.

Armitage, David, et al., eds. *Milton and Republicanism*. Cambridge: Cambridge University Press, 1995.

Badiou, Alain. *Saint Paul: The Foundation of Universalism*. Translated by Ray Brassier. Stanford: Stanford University Press, 2003.

Baker, David J. *Between Nations: Shakespeare, Spenser, Marvell, and the Question of Britain*. Stanford: Stanford University Press, 1997.

Bal, Mieke. *Death and Symmetry: The Politics of Coherence in the Book of Judges*. Chicago: University of Chicago Press, 1988.

Barnard, T.C. "Crises of Identity among Irish Protestants, 1641–1685." *Past and Present* 127 (1990): 39–83.

Bateson, Gregory. *Steps to an Ecology of Mind*. Chicago: University of Chicago Press, 2000.

Bedford, R.D. "Milton's Journey North: *A Brief History of Moscovia* and *Paradise Lost*." *Renaissance Studies* 7 (1993): 71–85.

Benjamin, Walter. *Illuminations*. Edited by Hannah Arendt. Translated by Harry Zohn. New York: Schocken, 1968.

Bennett, Joan S. "God, Satan, and King Charles: Milton's Royal Portraits." *PMLA* 92 (1977): 441–57.

Beum, Robert, "The Rhyme in *Samson Agonistes*." *Texas Studies in Language and Literature* 4 (1962): 177–82.

Bhabha, Homi K. *The Location of Culture*. London: Routledge, 1994.

Bottigheimer, Karl. "Kingdom and Colony: Ireland in the Westward Enterprise, 1536–1660." In *The Westward Enterprise: English Activities in Ireland, the Atlantic, and America, 1480–1650*, edited by Kenneth R. Andrews et al., 45–63. Detroit: Wayne State University Press, 1979.

Breuilly, John. *Nationalism and the State*. 2nd ed. Chicago: University of Chicago Press, 1994.

Brooks, Douglas. "'Ill-Matching Words and Deeds Long Past': Englished Hebrew and 'the Readmission of the Jews' in *Paradise Lost*." *Philological Quarterly* 81 (2002): 53–80.

——, ed. *Milton and the Jews*. Cambridge: Cambridge University Press, 2008.

Brown, Cedric C. "Great Senates and Godly Education: Politics and Cultural Renewal in Some Pre- and Post-revolutionary Texts of Milton." In Armitage et al., 43–60.

——. "Presidential Travels and Instructive Augury in Milton's Ludlow Masque." *Milton Quarterly* 21.4 (1987): 1–12.

Bryson, Michael. *The Tyranny of Heaven: Milton's Rejection of God as King*. Newark: University of Delaware Press, 2004.

Budick, Sanford. "Milton's Joban Phoenix in *Samson Agonistes*." *Early Modern Literary Studies* 11.2 (September 2005): 5.1–15.

Butler, Judith. *Gender Trouble: Feminism and the Subversion of Identity*. New York: Routledge, 1990.

Cahen, Claude. "The Mongols and the Near East." In *The Later Crusades, 1189–1311*, edited by Robert Lee Wolff and Harry W. Hazard, 715–34. Vol. 2 of *A History of the Crusades*, edited by Kenneth M. Setton. 6 vols. Madison: University of Wisconsin Press, 1969–89.

Cahill, Thomas. *How the Irish Saved Civilization*. New York: Nan A. Talese, 1995.

Camp, Claudia V. *Wise, Strange and Holy: The Strange Woman and the Making of the Bible*. Sheffield: Sheffield Academic Press, 2000.

Canino, Catherine. "The Discourse of Hell: Paradise Lost and the Irish Rebellion." *Milton Quarterly* 32.1 (1998): 15–23.

Canny, Nicholas. "Identity Formation in Ireland: The Emergence of the Anglo-Irish." In *Colonial Identity in the Atlantic World, 1500–1800*, edited by Nicholas P. Canny and Anthony Pagden, 159–212. Princeton: Princeton University Press, 1987.

——. *Kingdom and Colony: Ireland in the Atlantic World, 1560–1800*. Baltimore: Johns Hopkins University Press, 1988.

Carey, John. "A Work in Praise of Terrorism? September 11, 2001, and *Samson Agonistes*." *Times Literary Supplement*, September 6, 2002, 15–16.

Cavell, Stanley. *Disowning Knowledge in Six Plays of Shakespeare*. Cambridge: Cambridge University Press, 1987.

Chatterjee, Partha. *The Nation and Its Fragment: Colonial and Postcolonial Histories*. Princeton: Princeton University Press, 1993.

Clarke, W. M. "Intentional Rhyme in Vergil and Ovid." *Transactions and Proceedings of the American Philological Association* 103 (1972): 49–77.

Cogley, Richard W. " 'The Most Vile and Barbarous Nation of All the World': Giles Fletcher the Elder's *The Tartars Or, Ten Tribes* (ca. 1610)." *Renaissance Quarterly* 58 (2005): 781–809.

Cohen, Michael. "Rhyme in *Samson Agonistes*." *Milton Quarterly* 8 (1974): 4–6.

Coiro, Ann Baynes. "Writing in Service: Sexual Politics and Class Position in the Poetry of Aemilia Lanyer and Ben Jonson." *Criticism* 35 (1993): 357–76.

Colie, Rosalie L. "Marvell's 'Bermudas' and the Puritan Paradise." *Renaissance News* 10 (1957): 75–79.

Cormack, Bradin. *A Power to Do Justice: Jurisdiction, English Literature, and the Rise of Common Law, 1509–1625*. Chicago: University of Chicago Press, 2007.

Corns, Thomas. "Milton's *Observations upon the Articles of Peace:* Ireland under English Eyes." In *Politics, Poetics, and Hermeneutics in Milton's Prose*, edited by

David Loewenstein and James Grantham Turner, 123–34. Cambridge: Cambridge University Press, 1990.

D'Addario, Christopher. *Exile and Journey in Seventeenth-Century Literature*. Cambridge: Cambridge University Press, 2007.

Daems, Jim. "Dividing Conjunctions: Milton's *Observations Upon the Articles of Peace*." *Milton Quarterly* 33 (1999): 51–55.

Davies, Stevie. *Images of Kingship in* Paradise Lost: *Milton's Politics and Christian Liberty*. Columbia: University of Missouri Press, 1983.

Derrida, Jacques. *Archive Fever: A Freudian Impression*. Translated by Eric Prenowitz. Chicago: University of Chicago Press, 1996.

Diekhoff, John S. "Rhyme in Paradise Lost." *PMLA* 49 (1934): 539–43.

Dobranski, Stephen B. *Milton, Authorship, and the Book Trade*. Cambridge: Cambridge University Press, 1999.

———. "Text and Context for *Paradise Regain'd* and *Samson Agonistes*." In *Altering Eyes: New Perspectives on* Samson Agonistes, edited by Mark R. Kelley and Joseph Anthony Wittreich, 30–53. Newark: University of Delaware Press, 2002.

———. *A Variorum Commentary on the Poems of John Milton*, Vol. 3. *Samson Agonistes*. Pittsburgh: Duquesne University Press, 2009.

DuBrow, Heather. "The Country-House Poem: A Study in Generic Development." *Genre* 12 (1979): 153–79.

Duran, Angelica. "Milton among Hispanics: Jorge Luis Borges and Milton's 'Condemnation of Rhyme.'" *Prose Studies* 28.2 (2006): 234–44.

Durham, Charles W., and Kristin A. Pruitt, eds. *"All in All": Unity, Diversity, and the Miltonic Perspective*. Selinsgrove: Susquehanna University Press, 1999.

Dzelzainis, Martin. "Milton and the Protectorate in 1658." In Armitage et al., 181–205.

———. "Milton's Classical Republicanism." In Armitage et al., 3–24.

Ellis, Steven G. *Tudor Ireland: Crown, Community and the Conflict of Cultures, 1470–1603*. London: Longman, 1985.

Elton, G. R. *The Tudor Revolution in Government: Administrative Changes in the Reign of Henry VIII*. Cambridge: Cambridge University Press, 1953.

Empson, William. *Milton's God*. Rev. ed. Cambridge: Cambridge University Press, 1981.

Escobedo, Andrew. *Nationalism and Historical Loss in Renaissance England*. Ithaca: Cornell University Press, 2004.

Evans, J. Martin. *Milton's Imperial Epic:* Paradise Lost *and the Discourse of Colonialism*. Ithaca: Cornell University Press, 1996.

Fallon, Robert T. *Milton in Government*. University Park: Pennsylvania State University Press, 1993.

Fallon, Stephen M. *Milton among the Philosophers: Poetry and Materialism in Seventeenth-Century England*. Ithaca: Cornell University Press, 1991.

Fenton, Mary C. *Milton's Places of Hope: Spiritual and Political Connections of Hope with Land*. Aldershot: Ashgate, 2006.

———. "Milton's View of Ireland." *Milton Studies* 44 (2005): 203–29.

Fish, Stanley. *How Milton Works*. Cambridge: Harvard University Press, 2001.

———. "Inaction and Silence: The Reader in *Paradise Regained*." In *Calm of Mind: Tercentenary Essays on* Paradise Regained *and* Samson Agonistes *in Honor of*

John S. Diekhoff, edited by J. A. Wittreich Jr., 24–47. Cleveland: Case Western Reserve University Press, 1971.

———. "Things and Actions Indifferent: The Temptation of Plot in *Paradise Regained*." *Milton Studies* 17 (1983): 163–86.

———. "Why Milton Matters; Or, Against Historicism." *Milton Studies* 44 (2005): 1–12.

Fixler, Michael. *Milton and the Kingdoms of God*. Evanston: Northwestern University Press, 1964.

Fizdale, Tay. "Irony in Marvell's 'Bermudas.' " *ELH* 42 (1975): 203–13.

Freud, Sigmund. "The Uncanny." In *The Standard Edition of the Complete Psychological Works of Sigmund Freud*. Translated by Alix Strachey. Edited by James Strachey, 17:219–52. London: Hogarth, 1955.

Friedman, Donald. "The Lady in the Garden: On the Literary Genetics of Milton's Eve." *Milton Studies* 35 (1997): 114–33.

Frye, Northrop. *Spiritus Mundi: Essays on Literature, Myth, and Society*. Bloomington: Indiana University Press, 1976.

Fuchs, Barbara. "Imperium Studies: Theorizing Early Modern Expansion." In *Postcolonial Moves: Medieval through Modern*, edited by Patricia Clare Ingham and Michelle R. Warren, 71–90. New York: Palgrave Macmillan, 2003.

Gellner, Ernest. *Nations and Nationalism*. Oxford: Blackwell, 1983.

Girard, René. *Violence and the Sacred*. Translated by Patrick Gregory. Baltimore: Johns Hopkins University Press, 1979.

Greenblatt, Stephen. *Marvelous Possessions: The Wonder of the New World*. Chicago: University of Chicago Press, 1991.

———. *Renaissance Self-Fashioning: From More to Shakespeare*. University of Chicago Press, 1980.

Greenfield, Liah. *Nationalism: Five Roads to Modernity*. Cambridge: Harvard University Press, 1992.

Gregerson, Linda. "Colonials Write the Nation: Spenser, Milton, and England on the Margins." In Rajan and Sauer, 169–90.

Gregory, Tobias. "The Political Messages of *Samson Agonistes*." *SEL* 50 (2010): 175–203.

Grossman, Marshall. "*Destabilizing Milton*." Review. *Modern Philology* 104 (2006): 263–68.

———. "The Genders of God and the Redemption of the Flesh in *Paradise Lost*." In *Milton and Gender*, edited by Catherine Gimelli Martin, 95–114. Cambridge: Cambridge University Press, 2004.

Guibbory, Achsah. *Christian Identity, Jews, and Israel in Seventeenth-Century England*. Oxford: Oxford University Press, 2010.

———. "England, Israel, and the Jews in Milton's Prose, 1649–1660." In Brooks, 13–34.

———. "Israel and English Protestant Nationalism: 'Fast Sermons' during the English Revolution." In Loewenstein and Stevens, 115–38.

Hadfield, Andrew, and Willy Maley. "Introduction: Irish Representations and English Alternatives." In *Representing Ireland: Literature and the Origins of Conflict, 1534–1660*, edited by Brendan Bradshaw, Andrew Hadfield, and Willy Maley, 1–23. Cambridge: Cambridge University Press, 1993.

Hall, Kim F. *Things of Darkness: Economies of Race and Gender in Early Modern England.* Ithaca: Cornell University Press, 1995.

Halpern, Richard. "Puritanism and Maenadism in *A Mask.*" In *Rewriting the Renaissance: The Discourses of Sexual Difference in Early Modern Europe*, edited by Margaret W. Ferguson, Maureen Quilligan, and Nancy J. Vickers, 88–105. Chicago: University of Chicago Press, 1986.

Hardin, Richard F. "Milton's Nimrod." *Milton Quarterly* 22.2 (1988): 38–44.

Helgerson, Richard. *Forms of Nationhood: The Elizabethan Writing of England.* Chicago: University of Chicago Press, 1992.

Herman, Peter C. *Destabilizing Milton:* Paradise Lost *and the Poetics of Incertitude.* New York: Palgrave Macmillan, 2005.

Hibbard, G. R. "The Country House Poem of the Seventeenth Century." *Journal of the Warburg and Courtauld Institutes* 19 (1956): 159–74.

Hill, Christopher. *The Experience of Defeat: Milton and Some Contemporaries.* London: Faber and Faber, 1984.

———. *Milton and the English Revolution.* New York: Viking, 1978.

———. *Puritanism and Revolution: Studies in Interpretation of the English Revolution of the Seventeenth Century.* New York: Schocken, 1964.

Hillier, Russell M. "Grotius's *Christus Patiens* and Milton's *Samson Agonistes.*" *Explicator* 65 (2006): 9–13.

Hiltner, Ken. *Milton and Ecology.* Cambridge: Cambridge University Press, 2003.

Himy, Armand. "*Paradise Lost* as a 'Tractatus Theologico-Politicus.'" In Armitage et al., 118–34.

Hirst, Derek, and Steve Zwicker. "High Summer at Nun Appleton, 1651: Andrew Marvell and Lord Fairfax's Occasions." *Historical Journal* 36 (1993): 247–69.

Hobsbawm, E. J. *Nations and Nationalism since 1780: Programme, Myth, Reality.* 2nd ed. Cambridge: Cambridge University Press, 1990.

Hobson, J. A. *Imperialism: A Study.* 4th ed. London: George Allen & Unwin, 1948.

Hull, Keith. "Rhyme and Disorder in *Samson Agonistes.*" *Milton Studies* 30 (1993): 163–81.

Hyman, Wendy Beth. "Seizing Flowers in Spenser's Bower and Garden." *English Literary Renaissance* 37 (May 2007): 193–214.

Jameson, Fredric. "Religion and Ideology: A Political Reading of *Paradise Lost.*" In *1642: Literature and Power in the Seventeenth Century*, edited by Francis Barker et al., 315–36. Colchester: University of Essex Press, 1981.

Jenkins, Hugh. *Feigned Commonwealths: The Country-House Poem and the Fashioning of the Ideal Community.* Pittsburgh: Duquesne University Press, 1998.

Johnson, Samuel, *The Rambler.* Vols. 3–4 of *The Yale Edition of the Works of Samuel Johnson.* Edited by W. J. Bate and Albrecht B. Strauss. New Haven: Yale University Press, 1969.

Johnstone, H. T. "Rhymes and Assonances in the *Aeneid.*" *Classical Review* 10 (1890): 9–13.

Kahn, Victoria. "Disappointed Nationalism: Milton in the Context of Seventeenth-Century Debates about the Nation-State." In Loewenstein and Stevens, 249–72.

Kendrick, Christopher. *Milton: A Study in Ideology and Form.* New York: Methuen, 1986.

Kerrigan, John. "Orrery's Ireland and the British Problem, 1641–1679." In *British Identities and English Renaissance Literature*, edited by David J. Baker and Willy Maley, 197–225. Cambridge: Cambridge University Press, 2002.

Kerrigan, William. "The Riddle of *Paradise Regained.*" In *Poetic Prophecy in Western Literature*, edited by Jan Wojcik and Raymond-Jean Fontain, 64–80. Rutherford, NJ: Fairleigh Dickinson University Press, 1984.

———. *The Sacred Complex: On the Psychogenesis of* Paradise Lost. Cambridge: Harvard University Press, 1983.

Kerrigan, William, and Gordon Braden. *The Idea of the Renaissance.* Baltimore: Johns Hopkins University Press, 1989.

Kilgour, Maggie. " 'Thy perfect image viewing': Poetic Creation and Ovid's Narcissus in *Paradise Lost.*" *Studies in Philology* 102 (2005): 307–39.

Knapp, Jeffrey. *An Empire Nowhere: England, America, and Literature from* Utopia *to* The Tempest. Berkeley: University of California Press, 1992.

Krause, F. Michael. *Milton's Samson and the Christian Tradition.* Princeton: Princeton University Press, 1949.

Kristeva, Julia. *Powers of Horror: An Essay on Abjection.* Translated by Leon S. Roudiez. New York: Columbia University Press, 1982.

———. "Stabat Mater." In *Tales of Love.* Translated by Leon S. Roudiez, 234–63. New York: Columbia University Press, 1987.

Krook, Anne K. "The Hermeneutics of Opposition in *Paradise Regained* and *Samson Agonistes.*" *SEL* 36 (1996): 129–47.

Labriola, Albert C. "Milton's Eve and the Cult of Elizabeth I." *Journal of English and Germanic Philology* 95 (1996): 38–51.

Lacan, Jacques. *The Four Fundamental Concepts of Psychoanalysis.* Translated by Alan Sheridan. Edited by Jacques-Alain Miller. New York: Norton, 1981.

Lamb, Mary Ellen. "Patronage and Class in Aemilia Lanyer's *Salve Deus Rex Judaeorum.*" In *Women, Writing, and the Reproduction of Culture in Tudor and Stuart Britain*, edited by Mary E. Burke et al., 38–57. Syracuse: Syracuse University Press, 2000.

Legouis, Pierre. *Andrew Marvell: Poet, Puritan, Patriot.* 2nd ed. Oxford: Oxford University Press, 1968.

Lewalski, Barbara K. *Milton's Brief Epic: The Genre, Meaning, and Art of* Paradise Regained. Providence: Brown University Press, 1966.

———. Paradise Lost *and the Rhetoric of Literary Forms.* Princeton: Princeton University Press, 1985.

———. "Re-writing Patriarchy and Patronage: Margaret Clifford, Anne Clifford, and Aemilia Lanyer." In *Patronage, Politics, and Literary Traditions in England, 1558–1658*, edited by Cedric C. Brown, 59–78. Detroit: Wayne State University Press, 1993.

———. *Writing Women in Jacobean England.* Cambridge: Harvard University Press, 1993.

Lewis, C. S. *A Preface to* Paradise Lost. London: Oxford University Press, 1942.

Lieb, Michael. *The Dialectics of Creation: Patterns of Birth and Regeneration in* Paradise Lost. Amherst: University of Massachusetts Press, 1970.

Lim, Walter S. H. *The Arts of Empire: The Poetics of Colonialism from Raleigh to Milton.* Newark: University of Delaware Press, 1998.

Loewenstein, David. *Milton and the Drama of History: Historical Vision, Iconoclasm, and the Literary Imagination*. Cambridge: Cambridge University Press, 1992.
——. *Representing Revolution in Milton and His Contemporaries*. Cambridge: Cambridge University Press, 2001.
Loewenstein, David, and Paul Stevens, eds. and intro. *Early Modern Nationalism and Milton's England*. Toronto: University of Toronto Press, 2008.
Lupton, Julia Reinhard. *Citizen-Saints: Shakespeare and Political Theology*. Chicago: University of Chicago Press, 2005.
MacCallum, H. R. "Milton and Figurative Interpretation of the Bible." *University of Toronto Quarterly* 31 (1962): 397–415.
Maley, Willy. "How Milton and Some Contemporaries Read Spenser's *View*." In *Representing Ireland: Literature and the Origins of Conflict, 1534–1660*, edited by Brendan Bradshaw, Andrew Hadfield, and Willy Maley, 191–208. Cambridge: Cambridge University Press, 1993.
——. *Nation, State and Empire in English Renaissance Literature: Shakespeare to Milton*. Houndsmills: Palgrave Macmillan, 2003.
Marcus, Leah. *The Politics of Mirth: Jonson, Herrick, Milton, Marvell, and the Defense of Old Holiday Pastimes*. Rpt. ed. Chicago: University of Chicago Press, 1989.
Markley, Robert. *The Far East and the English Imagination, 1600–1730*. Cambridge: Cambridge University Press, 2006.
Martin, Catherine Gimelli. "Dalila, Misogyny, and Milton's Christian Liberty of Divorce." In *Milton and Gender*, edited by Catherine Gimelli Martin, 53–74. Cambridge: Cambridge University Press, 2004.
——. "Fire, Ice, and Epic Entropy: The Physics and Metaphysics of Milton's Reformed Chaos." *Milton Studies* 35 (1997): 73–113.
Martz, Louis L. *Milton: Poet of Exile*. 2nd ed. New Haven: Yale University Press, 1986.
Matar, N. I. "Milton and the Idea of the Restoration of the Jews." *SEL* 27 (1987): 109–24.
McBride, Kari Boyd, and John C. Ulreich. "Answerable Styles: Biblical Poetics and Biblical Politics in the Poetry of Lanyer and Milton." *Journal of English and Germanic Philology* 100 (2001): 333–54.
McCabe, Richard. *Spenser's Monstrous Regiment: Elizabethan Ireland and the Poetics of Difference*. Oxford: Oxford University Press, 2002.
——. "Translated States: Spenser and Linguistic Colonialism." In *Edmund Spenser: Essays on Culture and Allegory*, edited by Jennifer Klein Morrison and Matthew Greenfield, 67–88. Aldershot: Ashgate, 2000.
McCauley, Lawrence H. "Milton's Missing Rhymes." *Style* 28 (1994): 242–59.
McClintock, Anne. *Imperial Leather: Race, Gender, and Sexuality in the Colonial Contest*. New York: Routledge, 1995.
McClung, William A. *The Country House in English Renaissance Poetry*. Berkeley: University of California Press, 1977.
McColley, Diane Kelsey. *Milton's Eve*. Urbana: University of Illinois Press, 1983.
——. *Poetry and Ecology in the Age of Milton and Marvell*. Aldershot: Ashgate, 2007.
McCoy, Richard C. *Alterations of State: Sacred Kingship in the English Reformation*. New York: Columbia University Press, 2002.
McEachern, Claire. *The Poetics of English Nationhood, 1590–1612*. Cambridge: Cambridge University Press, 1996.

McLeod, Bruce. *The Geography of Empire in English Literature, 1580–1745.* Cambridge: Cambridge University Press, 1999.

Miller, Leo. *John Milton and the Oldenburg Safeguard: New Light on Milton and His Friends in the Commonwealth from the Diaries and Letters of Hermann Mylius.* New York: Loewenthal Press, 1985.

———. *John Milton's Writings in the Anglo-Dutch Negotiations, 1651–1654.* Pittsburgh: Duquesne University Press, 1992.

Miller, Shannon. *Engendering the Fall: John Milton and Seventeenth-Century Women Writers.* Philadelphia: University of Pennsylvania Press, 2008.

Mohamed, Feisal G. "Confronting Religious Violence: Milton's *Samson Agonistes.*" *PMLA* 120 (2005): 327–40.

———. *Milton and the Post-secular Present: Ethics, Politics, and Terrorism.* Stanford: Stanford University Press, 2011.

Molesworth, Charles. "Property and Virtue: The Genre of the Country House Poem in the Seventeenth Century." *Genre* 1 (1968): 141–57.

Montrose, Louis Adrian. "The Work of Gender in the Discourse of Discovery." *Representations* 33 (1991): 1–41.

Morgan, David. *The Mongols.* 2nd ed. Malden, MA: Blackwell, 2007.

Mueller, Janel. "The Figure and the Ground: Samson as a Hero of London Nonconformity, 1662–1667." In *Milton and the Terms of Liberty,* edited by Graham Parry and Joad Raymond, 137–62. Cambridge: D. S. Brewer, 2002.

Nairn, Tom. *The Break-Up of Britain: Crisis and Neo-nationalism.* 2nd ed. London: Verso, 1981.

Ng, Su Fang. "Aemilia Lanyer and the Politics of Praise." *ELH* 67 (2000): 433–51.

———. *Literature and the Politics of Family in Seventeenth-Century England.* Cambridge: Cambridge University Press, 2007.

Nohrnberg, James. *Like unto Moses: The Constituting of an Interruption.* Bloomington: Indiana University Press, 1995.

———. "*Paradise Regained* by One Greater Man: Milton's Wisdom Epic as a 'Fable of Identity.' " In *Center and Labyrinth: Essays in Honor of Northrop Frye,* edited by Eleanor Cook, 83–114. Toronto: University of Toronto Press, 1985.

Norbrook, David. *Writing the English Republic: Poetry, Rhetoric and Politics, 1627–1660.* Cambridge: Cambridge University Press, 1998.

Nyquist, Mary. "The Genesis of Gendered Subjectivity in the Divorce Tracts and in *Paradise Lost.*" In *Re-membering Milton,* edited by Mary Nyquist and Margaret W. Ferguson, 165–93. New York: Methuen, 1988.

O'Brien, Robert Viking. "Cannibalism in Edmund Spenser's *Faerie Queene,* Ireland, and the Americas." In *Eating Their Words: Cannibalism and the Boundaries of Cultural Identity,* edited by Kristen Guest, 35–56. Albany: State University of New York Press, 2001.

Pagden, Anthony. *European Encounters with the New World.* New Haven: Yale University Press, 1993.

Palmer, Daryl W. *Writing Russia in the Age of Shakespeare.* Aldershot: Ashgate, 2004.

Palmer, Patricia. *Language and Conquest in Early Modern Ireland: English Renaissance Literature and Elizabethan Imperial Expansion.* Cambridge University Press, 2001.

Parker, William Riley. "The Date of *Samson Agonistes.*" *Philological Quarterly* 28 (1949): 145–66.

———. *Milton: A Biography.* 2 vols. Oxford: Clarendon, 1968–69.

———. *Milton's Debt to Greek Tragedy in* Samson Agonistes. Baltimore: Johns Hopkins University Press, 1937.

Patterson, Annabel. "*Bermudas* and *The Coronet*: Marvell's Protestant Poetics." *ELH* 44 (1977): 478–99.

———. *Milton's Words.* Oxford: Oxford University Press, 2009.

———. *Reading between the Lines.* Madison: University of Wisconsin Press, 1993.

Picciotto, Joanna. *Labors of Innocence in Early Modern England.* Cambridge: Harvard University Press, 2010.

Pocock, John Greville Agard. *The Ancient Constitution and the Feudal Law: A Study of English Historical Thought in the Seventeenth Century.* Rpt. ed. Cambridge: Cambridge University Press, 1987.

———. "British History: A Plea for a New Subject." *Journal of Modern History* 47 (1975): 601–28.

Purcell, J. M. "Rime in *Paradise Lost.*" *Modern Language Notes* 59 (1944): 171–72.

Quilligan, Maureen. "Freedom, Service and the Trade in Slaves: The Problem of Labor and *Paradise Lost.*" In *Subject and Object in Renaissance Culture,* edited by Margreta de Grazia, Maureen Quilligan, and Peter Stallybrass, 213–34. Cambridge: Cambridge University Press, 1996.

———. "On the Renaissance Epic: Spenser and Slavery." *South Atlantic Quarterly* 100 (2001): 14–39.

Quint, David. *Epic and Empire: Politics and Generic Form from Virgil to Milton.* Princeton: Princeton University Press, 1993.

Radzinowicz, Mary Ann. *Toward* Samson Agonistes: *The Growth of Milton's Mind.* Princeton: Princeton University Press, 1978.

Rajan, Balachandra. "Banyan Trees and Fig Leaves: Some Thoughts on Milton's India." In *Of Poetry and Politics: New Essays on Milton and His World,* edited by P. G. Stanwood, 213–28. Binghamton, NY: Medieval & Renaissance Texts & Studies, 1995.

———. "'To Which Is Added *Samson Agonistes*—.'" In *The Prison and the Pinnacle,* edited by Balachandra Rajan, 83–110. Toronto: University of Toronto Press, 1973.

Rajan, Balachandra, and Elizabeth Sauer, eds. *Milton and the Imperial Vision.* Pittsburgh: Duquesne University Press, 1999.

Rankin, Deana. *Between Spenser and Swift: English Writing in Seventeenth-Century Ireland.* Cambridge: Cambridge University Press, 2005.

Revard, Stella P. "Vergil's *Georgics* and *Paradise Lost:* Nature and Human Nature in a Landscape." In *Vergil at 2000: Commemorative Essays on the Poet and His Influence,* edited by John D. Bernard, 259–80. New York: AMS Press, 1986.

Rogers, John. "The Enclosure of Virginity: The Poetics of Sexual Abstinence in the English Revolution." In *Enclosure Acts: Sexuality, Property, and Culture in Early Modern England,* edited by Richard Burt and John Michael Archer, 229–50. Ithaca: Cornell University Press, 1994.

———. *The Matter of Revolution: Science, Poetry, and Politics in the Age of Milton.* Ithaca: Cornell University Press, 1996.

———. *"Paradise Regained* and the Memory of *Paradise Lost."* In *The Oxford Handbook of Milton*, edited by Nicholas McDowell and Nigel Smith, 589–612. Oxford: Oxford University Press, 2009.

———. "Transported Touch: The Fruit of Marriage in *Paradise Lost."* In *Milton and Gender,* edited by Catherine Gimelli Martin, 115–32. Cambridge: Cambridge University Press, 2004.

Rosenberg, D. M. "Milton's *Paradise Lost* and the Country Estate Poem." *Clio* 18 (1989): 123–34.

Rosenblatt, Jason. *Torah and Law in* Paradise Lost. Princeton: Princeton University Press, 1994.

Rumrich, John P. "Milton's Arianism: Why It Matters." In *Milton and Heresy,* edited by Stephen B. Dobranski and John P. Rumrich, 75–92. Cambridge: Cambridge University Press, 1998.

———. "Milton's *Theanthropos:* The Body of Christ in *Paradise Regained."* *Milton Studies* 42 (2003): 50–67.

———. *Milton Unbound: Controversy and Reinterpretation.* New York: Cambridge University Press, 1996.

Rushdy, Ashraf, H. A. *The Empty Garden: The Subject of Late Milton.* Pittsburgh: University of Pittsburgh Press, 1992.

Said, Edward. *Orientalism.* 25th anniversary ed. New York: Vintage, 1994.

Sauer, Elizabeth. *Barbarous Dissonance and Images of Voice in Milton's Epics.* Montreal: McGill-Queen's University Press, 1996.

———. "Milton's *Of True Religion,* Protestant Nationhood, and the Negotiation of Liberty." *Milton Quarterly* 40.1 (2006): 1–19.

———. "Toleration and Nationhood in the 1650s." In *Milton and Toleration,* edited by Sharon Achinstein and Elizabeth Sauer, 203–23. Oxford: Oxford University Press, 2007.

Saunders, J. J. *The History of the Mongol Conquests.* London: Routledge and Kegan Paul, 1971.

Schwartz, Louis. *Milton and Maternal Mortality.* Cambridge: Cambridge University Press, 2009.

Schwartz, Regina M. "From Shadowy Types to Shadowy Types: The Unendings of Paradise Lost." *Milton Studies* 24 (1988): 123–39.

———. *Remembering and Repeating: On Milton's Theology and Poetics.* 2nd ed. Chicago: University of Chicago Press, 1993.

———. *Sacramental Poetics at the Dawn of Secularism: When God Left the World.* Stanford: Stanford University Press, 2008.

———. "Through the Optic Glass: Voyeurism and *Paradise Lost."* In *Desire in the Renaissance: Psychoanalysis and Literature,* edited by Valeria Finucci and Regina Schwartz, 146–68. Princeton: Princeton University Press, 1994.

Schwarz, Kathryn. *Tough Love: Amazon Encounters in the English Renaissance.* Durham: Duke University Press, 2000.

Schwyzer, Philip. "Purity and Danger on the West Bank of the Severn: The Cultural Geography of *A Masque Presented at Ludlow Castle, 1634." Representations* 60 (1997): 22–48.

Shawcross, John T. *The Development of Milton's Mind: Law, Government, and Religion.* Pittsburgh: Duquesne University Press, 2008.

——. "The Genres of *Paradise Regain'd* and *Samson Agonistes:* The Wisdom of Their Joint Publication." *Milton Studies* 17 (1983): 225–48.

Shoulson, Jeffrey. *Milton and the Rabbis: Hebraism, Hellenism, and Christianity.* New York: Columbia University Press, 2001.

Smith, Nigel. *Is Milton Better Than Shakespeare?* Cambridge: Harvard University Press, 2008.

Stevens, Paul. "How Milton's Nationalism Works: Globalization and the Possibilities of Positive Nationalism." In Loewenstein and Stevens, 273–301.

——. "'Leviticus Thinking' and the Rhetoric of Early Modern Colonialism." *Criticism* 35 (1993): 441–61.

——. "Milton and the New World: Custom, Relativism, and the Discipline of Shame." In Rajan and Sauer, 90–111.

——. "Milton's Janus-Faced Nationalism: Soliloquy, Subject, and the Modern Nation State." *Journal of English and Germanic Philology* 100 (2001): 247–68.

——. "Milton's 'Renunciation' of Cromwell." *Modern Philology* 98 (2001): 363–92.

——. "*Paradise Lost* and the Colonial Imperative." *Milton Studies* 34 (1996): 3–22.

Strier, Richard. "Milton against Humility." In *Religion and Culture in Renaissance England,* edited by Claire McEachern and Debora Shuger, 258–86. Cambridge: Cambridge University Press, 2006.

——. "Milton's Fetters, or, Why Eden Is Better Than Heaven." *Milton Studies* 38 (2000): 169–97.

Swaim, Kathleen M. "Hercules, Antaeus, and Prometheus: A Study of the Climactic Epic Similes in *Paradise Regained. SEL* 18 (1978): 137–53.

Teskey, Gordon. *Delirious Milton: The Fate of the Poet in Modernity.* Cambridge: Harvard University Press, 2006

Trubowitz, Rachel J. "Body Politics in *Paradise Lost.*" *PMLA* 121 (2006): 388–404.

——. "'I was his nursling once': Nation, Lactation, and the Hebraic in *Samson Agonistes.*" In *Milton and Gender,* edited by Catherine Gimelli Martin, 167–83. Cambridge: Cambridge University Press, 2004.

Turner, James Grantham. *The Politics of Landscape: Rural Scenery and Society in English Poetry, 1630–1660.* Oxford: Basil Blackwell, 1979.

Ulreich, John C. "Substantially Express'd: Milton's Doctrine of the Incarnation," *Milton Studies* 39 (2001): 101–28.

——. "Typological Symbolism in Milton's Sonnet XXIII." *Milton Quarterly* 8.1 (1974): 7–10.

Vinge, Louise. *The Narcissus Theme in Western European Literature up to the Early Nineteenth Century.* Translated by Robert Dewsnap and Nigel Reeves. Lund: Gleerups, 1967.

Visconsi, Elliot. *Lines of Equity: Literature and the Origins of Law in Later Stuart England.* Ithaca: Cornell University Press, 2008.

Watkins, W. B. C. *An Anatomy of Milton's Verse.* Baton Rouge: Louisiana State University Press, 1955.

Wayne, Don E. *Penshurst: The Semiotics of Place and the Poetics of History.* Madison: University of Wisconsin Press, 1984.

Weiner, Gordon M. "Irish Jewry in the Seventeenth and Eighteenth Centuries." In *From Strangers to Citizens: The Integration of Immigrant Communities in Britain, Ireland, and Colonial America, 1550–1750,* edited by Randolph Vigne and Charles Littleton, 276–82. Sussex: Sussex Academic Press, 2002.

Wilding, Michael. "Milton's *A Masque Presented at Ludlow Castle, 1634:* Theatre and Politics on the Border." *Milton Quarterly* 21.4 (1987): 35–51.

Williams, Raymond. *The Country and the City.* New York: Oxford University Press, 1973.

Wills, Clair. "Language Politics, Narrative, Political Violence." *Oxford Literary Review* 13 (1991): 20–60.

Wilson, Kathleen. "Empire, Gender, and Modernity in the Eighteenth Century." In *Gender and Empire,* edited by Philippa Levine, 14–45. Oxford: Oxford University Press, 2004.

Wittreich, Joseph. *Feminist Milton.* Ithaca: Cornell University Press, 1987.

———. *"Image of that horror": History, Prophecy, and Apocalypse in* King Lear. San Marino, CA: Huntington Library, 1984.

———. *Interpreting* Samson Agonistes. Princeton: Princeton University Press, 1986.

———. *Shifting Contexts: Reinterpreting* Samson Agonistes. Pittsburgh: Duquesne University Press, 2002.

———. "Still Nearly Anonymous: *Christos Paschon.*" *Milton Quarterly* 36.3 (2002): 193–98.

Wood, Derek N. C. *"Exiled from Light": Divine Law, Morality, and Violence in* Samson Agonistes. Toronto: University of Toronto Press, 2002.

Woolrych, Austin. "Milton and Cromwell: 'A Short but Scandalous night of Interruption.'" In *Achievements of the Left Hand: Essays on the Prose of John Milton,* edited by Michael Lieb and John T. Shawcross, 185–219. Amherst: University of Massachusetts Press, 1974.

Wortham, Christopher. "'A happy rural seat': Milton's *Paradise Lost* and the English Country House Poem." *Parergon* 9 (1991): 137–50.

Yerushalmi, Yosef Hayim. *Zakhor: Jewish History and Jewish Memory.* Seattle: University of Washington Press, 1996.

INDEX